AMERICA'S
NORTHERN
HEARTLAND

John R. Borchert

AMERICA'S NORTHERN HEARTLAND

University of Minnesota Press
Minneapolis

The University of Minnesota Press
gratefully acknowledges publication assistance from the
Center for Urban and Regional Affairs of the
University of Minnesota.

Second printing, 1989

Published by the University of Minnesota Press.
2037 University Avenue Southeast, Minneapolis, MN
55414.
Published simultaneously in Canada
by Fitzhenry & Whiteside Limited, Markham.
Printed in the United States of America.
Designed by Gwen M. Willems.

Library of Congress Cataloging-in-Publication Data

Borchert, John R.
America's northern heartland.

Bibliography: p.
Includes index.
1. Northwestern States—Description and travel.
2. Northwestern States—Historical geography.
3. Northwestern States—Economic conditions. 4. Middle
West—Description and travel. 5. Middle West—Historical
geography. 6. Middle West—Economic conditions.
I. Title.
F597.B67 1987   977   86-4317
ISBN 0-8166-1498-9
ISBN 0-8166-1499-7 (pbk.)

Contents

FIGURES

TABLES

Preface

Not much more than a century ago the main wave of American pioneer settlement reached the northwestern Great Lakes and the Upper Mississippi Valley. By 1870 people had begun to create a region on that part of the unfolding map of the United States. Minneapolis-St. Paul had just passed Dubuque, Iowa, as the dominant urban center on the upper reaches of the great river. A few rail lines were beginning to reach out along isolated oxcart trails.

In the next half-century, from 1870 to 1920, immigrants took possession of the entire area from the Lake Superior district westward across the northern prairies and northern Great Plains to the Rockies—the part of the United States with the most extreme, continental climate and the location most remote from the coasts. They divided the land into more than 3 million parcels that ranged in size from 25-foot city lots to 20-square-mile ranches, from compact mining properties to vast forest holdings. By 1920 more than 5 million people lived in this Northern Heartland. The northern transcontinental rail corridor was established. A new network of railways and dirt or gravel roads spread across the region to link 3,000 cities, towns, and hamlets. The Twin Cities were the principal focus of the system, the heart of the Northwest Empire.

In the half-century beginning in the 1920s, people transformed the region in response to changes in technology and shifting national population patterns. The total population growth rate declined as net migration reversed from inflow to outflow. Meanwhile, farming became a highly capitalized heavy industry. Manufacturing, services, cities, income, and wealth grew at rates above the national average. The transportation and communication network was completely rebuilt, specialized, and modernized. The Twin Cities were still the main focus of the system. But some wholesale trade and services were decentralized to more than a dozen smaller metropolitan areas. At the same time, Twin Cities businesses had expanded much further into national and world markets. The share of the Twin Cities economy that depended on trade with the region had dropped from a little more than one-half to slightly over one-third. Yet there had been so much overall economic growth that the amount of business the metropolis carried on with the region, in constant dollars, was probably nearly triple what it had been in 1920.

Thus, there have been two main parts to this story of regional development: (1) a half-century of rapid immigration, population boom, and building of the basic settlement pattern; and (2) little more than half a century of slower population growth, net emigration, rapid economic growth, rebuilding, and dramatic population redistribution on the basic settlement framework. The region changed from an empire in a more segmented world to a neighborhood in a more integrated world. Though fully occupied, it remained one of the more thinly settled parts of the world's developed nations. A relatively few people are organized to use a very large amount of land. Warm communities and comfortable cities are woven into a varied fabric of natural landscapes and countrysides.

One theme runs through the century of development and transformation. That theme, in a word, is adaptation. People in the region have always been coping, monitoring, and adapting to global natural and human forces beyond their control, converting problems to opportunities. In the process of adaptation, a regional culture has emerged. It has had an unusual combination of vigorous individualism and close-knit communality, driving entrepreneurship and intense interdependence. To the extent that people in the region have coped and adapted successfully, they have controlled their individual and collective destinies. The same theme persists now into yet another round of adaptation to new conditions that are emerging in the 1980s.

I have tried to tell this story of regional development and transformation as an unfolding geography, relying heavily on the language of maps. Emphasis is on the evolving transportation network and the changing towns and cities at nodes in the network. The region's farms, forests, mines and waters form the background—the hinterlands—of the urban centers. From those centers people have organized and reorganized the region.

Time-series maps emphasize changing patterns of population in a setting of resources, places, and routes. In the brief period and the diverse region spanned by the maps, millions of lifetimes have been lived, each with its own ideas, emotions, hopes, and actions. Every place, every route, every change depicted on every map, every bit of narrative that interprets and connects the maps reflects the imprint of those lives upon the land.

Although this book is in one sense purely and simply the saga of a cast of people in a particular set of places, there is almost no attempt to detail either the lives of particular people or the internal layout of particular places. Libraries, bookstores, media, household attics, and personal recollections provide a deep reservoir and flowing stream of that kind of knowledge. In-stead, my purpose is to provide a framework in which to place and relate the pieces of information that almost bury anyone who reads and watches the avalanche of material about history, business, and public affairs that affect the region. The book attempts to put America's Northern Heartland into perspective for someone who moves here or matures here and wonders about the remarkable array of activities, fixed assets, and organizations. I also hope to provide a base for a growing body of detailed research on future changes in the structure and functions of the region.

My hope is to capture the reality, the spirit, and the dynamics of the region. Even to attempt to do that would have been impossible without the vast available store of literature and statistical and archival records. Most of the maps in the book are my original compilations. To interpret the maps I have drawn upon a selection of mainly historical and geographical compendia and a very small sampling of the wealth of local studies, biographical works, and media articles.

But beyond the published sources, hundreds of people in all walks of life, all across the region, have shared with me their experiences, observations, and perspectives. The patterns on the maps in this book portray in part the imprint of those people. Hence conversations with them have helped uniquely to interpret the maps. Footnotes identify only a few of those Upper Midwesterners to whom I am so deeply indebted.

I owe particular thanks to Gregory Chu,

director of the University of Minnesota Geography Department's Cartographic Laboratory, and his assistant, Carol Gersmehl, for their professional design and rendering of the maps; to Hee-Bang Choe, Philip Heywood, Sean Sullivan, Yeong-Ki Beck, and Don Pirius for cartographic drafting; to Kevin Anderson for his help in assembling statistical data and reference maps; to Judith Kordahl aand Margaret Rasmussen for word processing. Support from the University of Minnesota has been unfailing and comprehensive. Assistance from the University's Center for Urban and Regional Affairs and the First Bank System Foundation, for the First Banks, made possible the statistical research and cartographic production. I am indebted to many colleagues both within and beyond academia for stimulation and guidance, but especially to Thomas Anding, of the Center for Urban and Regional Affairs, for a quarter-century of lively exchange on the problems and character of the region, to Professor John Hudson, of Northwestern University, and Professor Warren Kress, of North Dakota State University, for valuable reviews of the original manuscript. Most of all, I must thank Jane Willson Borchert for patient, critical readings of the manuscript, enthusiastic accompaniment on thousands of miles of field trips, and my introduction to the Upper Midwest community nearly half a century ago.

Of course, omissions, faulty interpretations, and outright errors are my own responsibility.

AMERICA'S
NORTHERN
HEARTLAND

One-Tenth
of America's Land

To most Americans the Northern Heartland has long been the most mystifying part of their country. Spreading across the northern states, in the deep interior of North America, from Montana to Michigan's Upper Peninsula, from northern Iowa to the Canadian border, the region contains about one-tenth of the total land area of the 50 United States. It is as big as Texas and twice as empty (or half as crowded). In the western reaches the shopping trade area of Miles City, Montana, includes more land than the state of Connecticut; to the east the local trade area of Bemidji, Minnesota, is almost as large as New York's Adirondack Mountain region. Billboards on the edges of some small towns proclaim plenty of room to grow. They are always at least half-right; there is plenty of room. In many cases they are all right; there is also growth, some of it fast by any comparison, some of it remarkably steady by any comparison.

If you fly the scheduled airlines from Seattle-Tacoma to the Twin Cities, and on to Boston, more than one-third of the transcontinental trip crosses this region (Figure 1). Coming from Seattle you could mark the region's western boundary about where you see the Bear Paw Mountains rise a half-mile above the plains of north central Montana. There on a summer day a dark island of ponderosa pine forest stands above the sage- and grass-covered, deeply carved lower slopes; the whole mass overlooks the sea of strip-cropped wheat fields and rangeland that rolls northward into Saskatchewan. As you head eastward from the Twin Cities and leave the region, you could look far to the north of your route and imagine the boundary where the Porcupine Mountains rise 1,000 feet above Lake Superior. Rock ledges tower above Lake of the Clouds. The glacier-polished rocks and the clear lake are bright openings in the midst of a dense forest where 17 feet of snow fall in an average winter. The northern boundary of the region lies 250 miles north of the Twin Cities airport. There the Rainy River spills from border lakes that wash hundreds of miles of quiet, rocky Minnesota and Ontario shores. In contrast, on the region's southern edge, 150 miles south of the Twin Cities, the upper reach of Iowa's Skunk River winds southward between gently undulating, tile-drained corn fields.

From the Bear Paws to the Porcupines, from the Skunk to the Rainy, this region sprawls over one-third of a million square miles. What shall we call it? Perhaps the name used most widely and for the longest period in the region's short history is Northwest. This was the new Northwest, when the settlement frontier was advancing across the region from the 1850s to the 1910s. It was mostly distinct from the Old Northwest—the land east of the Mississippi and "northwest of the River Ohio," defined by the Northwest Ordinance of 1787. While the name Northwest was applied from the outside, it was also adopted by insiders in St. Paul, Minneapolis, and cities and towns from western Wisconsin to eastern Montana. With development of metropolitan centers at Seattle, Tacoma, and Portland, and emergence of the name Pacific Northwest, Northwest gradually dropped from vogue in this interior region. Meanwhile, Central Northwest was tried, then Upper Midwest and Northland. People from other parts of the United States often vaguely called it the Northern Plains. Those terms imply a unity to the region, which indeed it has. But they also mask its rich diversity. Because this book is in some ways a sequel to a regional study that

3

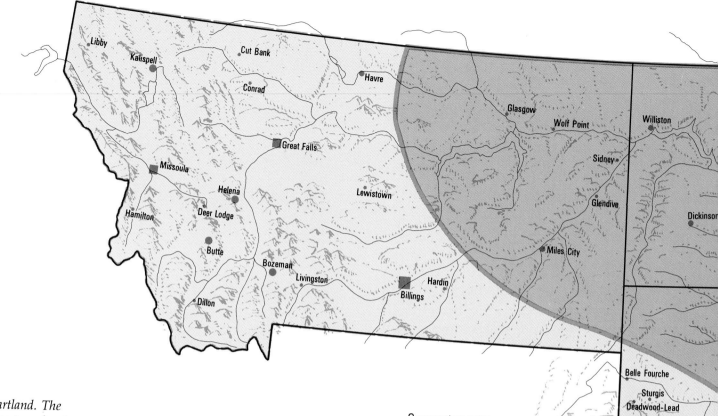

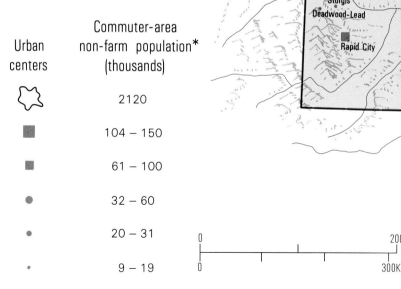

Figure 1. *America's Northern Heartland. The primary region of the Upper Midwest reaches from northern Iowa to the U.S.-Canadian border, from northern Wisconsin to eastern Montana. The Minneapolis Federal Reserve banking district and some transportation, wholesaling, and services extend the region's periphery across Montana and Michigan's Upper Peninsula. The spacing of cities on the map reflects the climatic gradients from the lush, productive Midwestern Corn Belt to the colder North and the drier West. The smooth, deep mantle of glacial deposits across much of the heart of the region contrasts with the rougher plains west and south of the Missouri, the glacier-scoured uplands surrounding Lake Superior, and the mountainous western margin.*

Urban centers

Commuter-area non-farm population*
(thousands)

2120

104 – 150

61 – 100

32 – 60

20 – 31

9 – 19

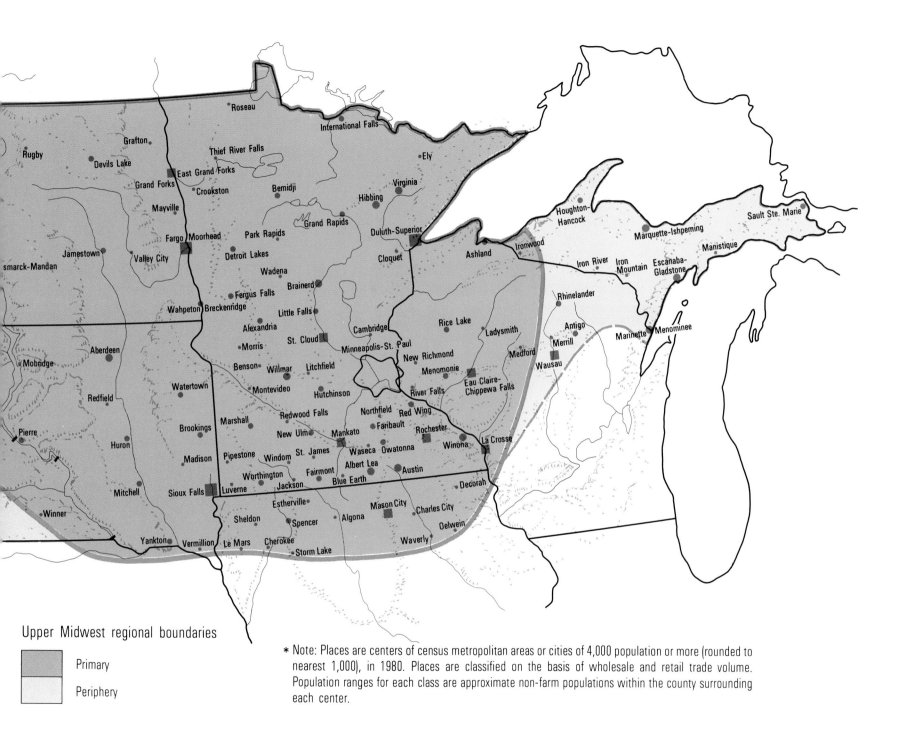

Rugby
Grafton
Devils Lake
Roseau
Thief River Falls
International Falls
Ely
East Grand Forks
Grand Forks
Crookston
Bemidji
Virginia
Mayville
Hibbing
Houghton-Hancock
Marquette-Ishpeming
Sault Ste. Marie
Grand Rapids
Fargo Moorhead
Park Rapids
Duluth-Superior
Jamestown
Valley City
Detroit Lakes
Cloquet
Ashland
Ironwood
Manistique
smarck-Mandan
Wadena
Iron River
Iron Mountain
Escanaba-Gladstone
Brainerd
Fergus Falls
Rhinelander
Wahpeton Breckenridge
Little Falls
Antigo
Marinette Menominee
Alexandria
Cambridge
Rice Lake
Merrill
Aberdeen
St. Cloud
Ladysmith
Mobridge
Morris
Minneapolis-St. Paul
Medford
Wausau
Benson
Willmar
Litchfield
New Richmond
Redfield
Watertown
Montevideo
Menomonie
Hutchinson
Eau Claire-Chippewa Falls
River Falls
Pierre
Redwood Falls
Northfield
Red Wing
Brookings
Marshall
Faribault
Huron
New Ulm
Mankato
Rochester
Madison
Pipestone
Windom St. James
Waseca Owatonna
Winona
La Crosse
Worthington
Fairmont
Albert Lea
Austin
Mitchell
Blue Earth
Sioux Falls
Luverne
Jackson
Decorah
Winner
Estherville
Mason City
Charles City
Sheldon
Spencer
Algona
Yankton
Vermillion
Le Mars
Cherokee
Waverly
Oelwein
Storm Lake

Upper Midwest regional boundaries

Primary

Periphery

* Note: Places are centers of census metropolitan areas or cities of 4,000 population or more (rounded to nearest 1,000), in 1980. Places are classified on the basis of wholesale and retail trade volume. Population ranges for each class are approximate non-farm populations within the county surrounding each center.

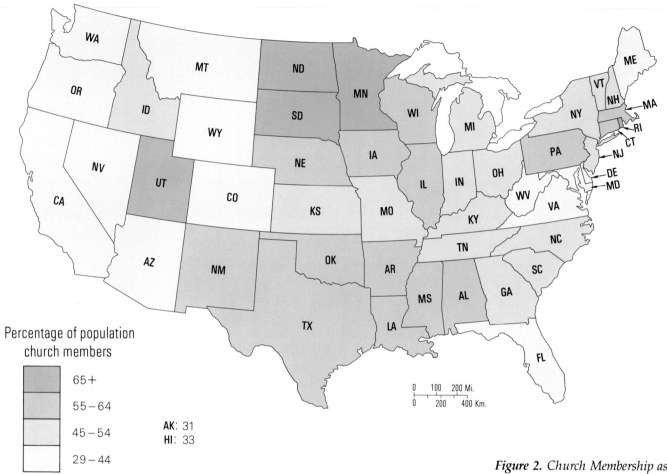

Percentage of population
church members

65+

55 – 64

45 – 54

29 – 44

AK: 31
HI: 33

Figure 2. Church Membership as a Percentage of Total U.S. Population, 1971. The Upper Midwest had one of the highest proportions of church membership in the United States, along with southeastern New England and the Mormon West. Source: note 2.

used the term *Upper Midwest* a quarter-century ago, I shall use the same term now.[1]

The Ties That Bind

To those who regularly travel the region, do business in it, and live in it, this is a big neighborhood, or an empire, or perhaps both. All over the far-flung area, familiar regional names mark chain and franchise stores, banks, and farm cooperatives. Familiar hymnals from familiar publishers are at hand in the church pews (Figure 2). (With southeastern New England and the Utah valleys, this ranks as one of the three most churched areas in the United States.) Familiar networks of friends and relatives, built on the migration patterns of several generations, bridge between the farms, the Twin Cities of Minneapolis and St. Paul, and the intermediate towns and hamlets. Familiar meetings and conventions come together most often at Minneapolis-St. Paul. And everybody shares the concealed satisfaction of surviving and even prospering in the world's most extreme climate (Figure 3). Hot winds, arctic gales, searing drought, dripping humidity, dust clouds, dense fogs, tropical downpours, tornadoes, chinooks, fence-high snowdrifts, breath-freezing stillness, baking sun—those tests of human adaptability occur in various combinations in every part of the world. But only in the Upper Midwest can you expect all of them in the course of any normal year.[2]

One measure of neighborhood is who talks to whom and how much. Telephone connections provide a measure of that kind of interaction, and the Upper Midwest is a buzzing hive of phone messages between places and people (Figure 4). The contacts have a geographic pattern. To be sure, there are calls from everyplace to every other place. But the calls from farm neighborhoods or hamlets go most frequently to the nearest shopping and service center. From shopping and service centers most frequent connections lead to the nearest larger centers of wholesale distribution, services, and shopping. And within the region, calls from all those places to a large metropolitan area flow predominantly to the Twin Cities. In a different way the professional sports radio networks outline the region (Figure 5). While the breadth and depth of their coverage has varied with success on the playing fields, the networks have persistently linked the localities in which there is enough loyalty to the regional teams to make the broadcasts commercially salable in the local markets.[3]

The Minneapolis–St. Paul metropolitan area is one of 30 high-order urban centers in the geographic structure of America's urban settlement (Figure 6). Those 30 centers are the home of nearly two-thirds of all the country's population. They are the locations of nearly all of the Federal Aviation Commission's major hub airports. They are the main concentration of corporate headquarters, professional services, arts, and professional sports. Those activities combine with their skylines to make the high-order cities the main symbols of metropolitan America.[4]

The primary region of the Upper Midwest is that part of the United States which is closer to the Twin Cities than it is to any other high-order metropolis. The pattern of phone messages reflects this fact. And what are the messages about? They undoubtedly reflect the sweep and diversity and historical evolution of the region. People are placing orders with wholesale distributors, transferring payments, arranging professional services, reserving seats for games or concerts or foreign tours, reserving hotel rooms for meetings, catching up on the affairs of migratory friends and relatives, and of course talking about the weather. Sometimes the same call serves several of those purposes. Thus the Upper Midwest is the primary trade and service area of the Twin Cities. The Twin Cities did not make the region. The region did not make the Twin Cities. The pattern just evolved in the complex process of settling the land of the United States.

Some strong linkages reach beyond this primary region of the Upper Midwest. The periphery of the region extends west into the Montana Rockies—to Glacier Park and Yellowstone, to the valleys of the Flathead and the Bitterroot. And it extends east across northern Wisconsin and Michigan's Upper Peninsula to the rapids of the St. Marys at Sault Ste. Marie. Phone traffic from smaller towns and cities in the periphery to the Twin Cities is less than the flow from those places to Seattle, Denver, Chicago, Milwaukee, or Detroit. Yet those smaller places in the periphery are more strongly linked to the Twin Cities than are other places of similar size outside the region.

The region's extended periphery largely reflects Twin Cities banking connections. With the creation of the Federal Reserve system in 1914, regional Federal Reserve banks were established at a dozen major cities. Minneapolis was one because it was the larger of the twins, and because the Twin Cities metropolitan area at that time was far larger than any other western or southern city except San Francisco and Los Angeles. The national map was divided into 12 Federal Reserve districts, each tributary to one of the system's banks. Then, as now, a territory existed in which correspondent ties between metropolitan and local banks clearly focused on the Twin Cities. The territory included Minnesota, North Da-

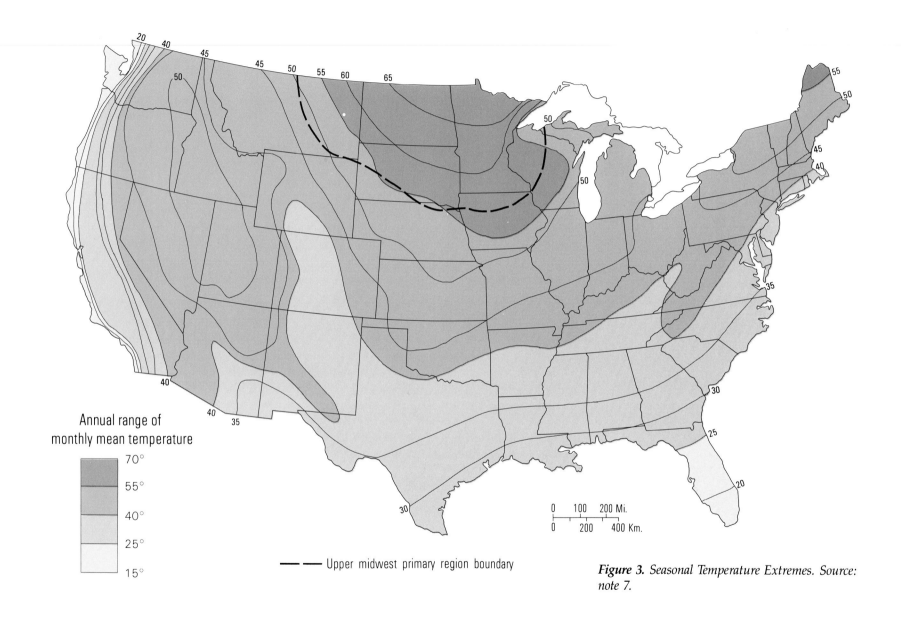

Annual range of
monthly mean temperature

70°
55°
40°
25°
15°

— — — Upper midwest primary region boundary

Figure 3. *Seasonal Temperature Extremes. Source: note 7.*

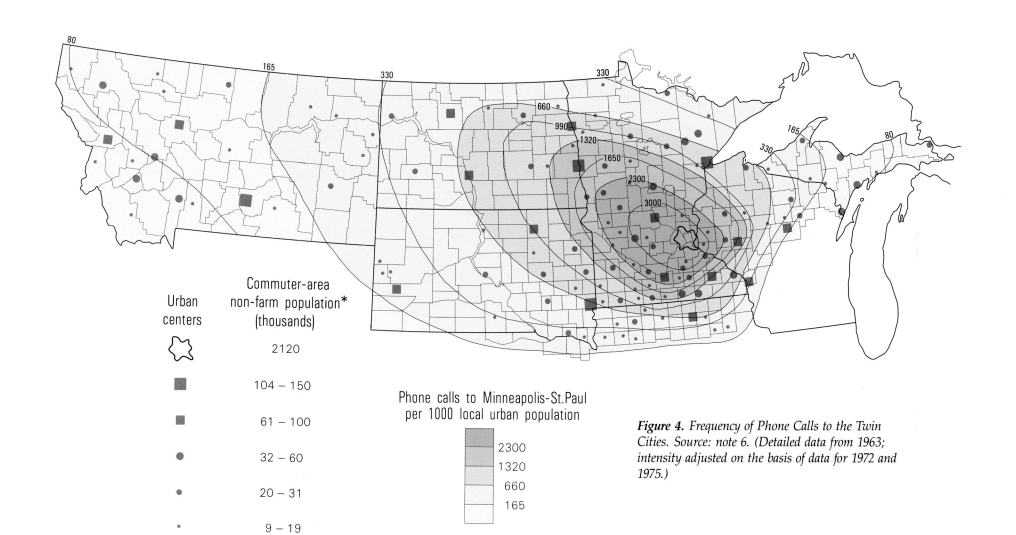

Urban
centers

Commuter-area
non-farm population*
(thousands)

2120

104 – 150

61 – 100

32 – 60

20 – 31

9 – 19

Phone calls to Minneapolis-St.Paul
per 1000 local urban population

2300

1320

660

165

Figure 4. Frequency of Phone Calls to the Twin
Cities. Source: note 6. (Detailed data from 1963;
intensity adjusted on the basis of data for 1972 and
1975.)

* See note with Figure 1.

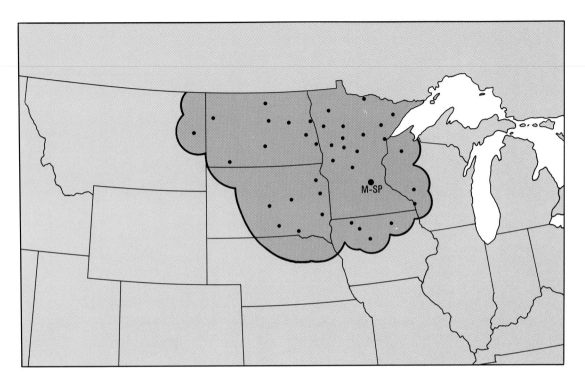

Figure 5. Professional Sports Radio Stations and Listening Area, 1983. The broadcast for Twin Cities professional baseball and football teams has coincided approximately with the Upper Midwest primary region. Source: Kaufman, note 3.

kota, much of Montana and South Dakota, and northwestern Wisconsin. Banking ties in much of that area reflected sheer proximity to the Twin Cities. In central and western Montana they reflected the legacy of business connections along the Twin Cities-based Northern Pacific and Great Northern railroads. There were important ties in nearby northern Iowa, too. But all of Iowa was foregone Chicago territory in this contest. Without part of Iowa, the population of the Twin Cities banking region was not quite enough to meet the minimum requirement; hence more of northern Wisconsin and the Upper Peninsula of Michigan were added. Metropolitan ties of those areas then, as now, ran mainly southward to Chicago, Milwaukee, or Detroit. But an important flow of commerce also moved east-west along the original Soo Line railroad, between

the Twin Cities, Sault Ste. Marie, and eastern Canada.[5]

Thus an Upper Midwest primary region reaches from the Bear Paws to the Porcupines and the Skunk to the Rainy. And a periphery extends west into the Montana Rockies and east to Sault Ste. Marie. The primary region and the periphery, together, are the banking region. Together they reflect the emergence of the Twin Cities regional metropolis and the rail, trade, and financial interests historically centered there.

Of course, the region is no monolith: it is a kaleidescope of ever-changing small communities and networks of people, who spend most of their time conducting local, day-to-day affairs. The overlay of regional connections, though always subtly guiding them in many ways, directly affects only a few people's daily schedules most of the time and most people's daily schedules rather seldom. The region's boundaries are no knife-edge; there are gradients. Strength and frequency of the binding internal ties decline gradually with increasing distance from the Twin Cities. Across western Montana the direction of dominant flows gradually shifts to Seattle. Across southwestern South Dakota and southern Montana the gradients shift toward Denver. Across western and northern Wisconsin they tilt sharply toward Chicago and Milwaukee.[6]

Climatic gradients occur as well. With the temperature extremes that accompany location in the continental interior, comes the reward of a predominance of bright days. Indeed from the Mississippi to the Rocky Mountain foothills the region is the sun belt of the Frost Belt. Westward across the Rockies the regimes of sunshine, cloud, and precipitation gradually swing toward the moderating influence of the Pacific. Winter cold also moderates and the growing season lengthens gradu-

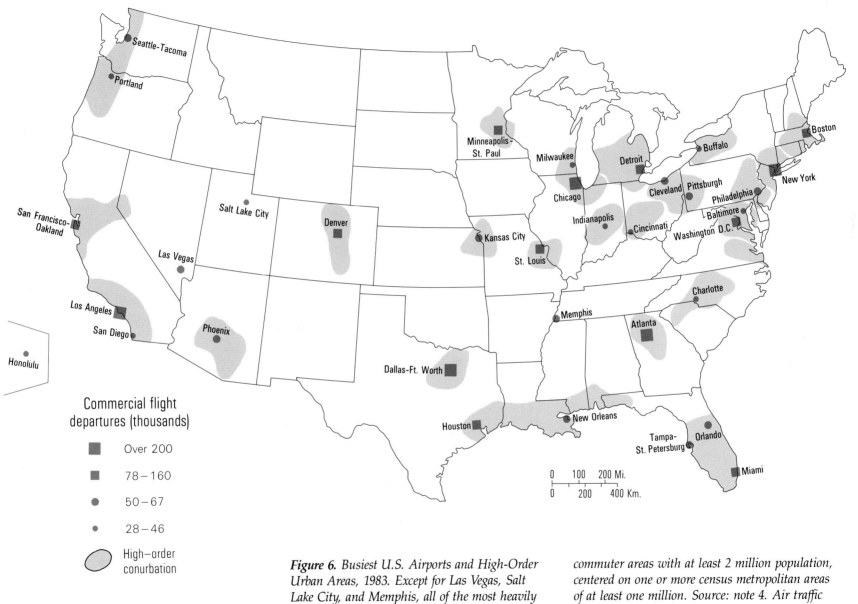

Figure 6. Busiest U.S. Airports and High-Order Urban Areas, 1983. Except for Las Vegas, Salt Lake City, and Memphis, all of the most heavily used air hubs are in high-order urban areas. The high-order urban areas, or conurbations, are daily commuter areas with at least 2 million population, centered on one or more census metropolitan areas of at least one million. Source: note 4. Air traffic data, 1983; population data, 1980.

Commercial flight departures (thousands)

■ Over 200

▪ 78 – 160

● 50 – 67

• 28 – 46

⬭ High-order conurbation

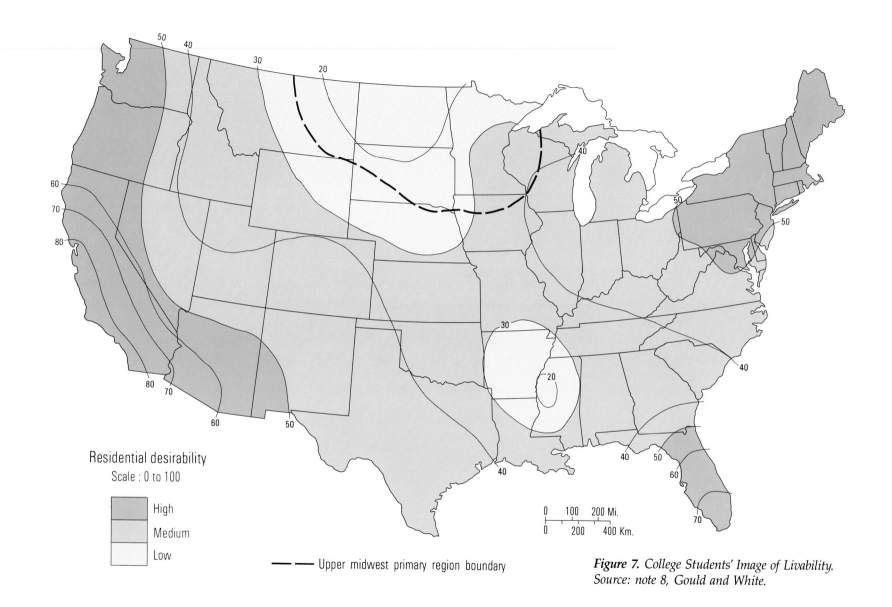

Residential desirability
Scale : 0 to 100

High

Medium

Low

— — — Upper midwest primary region boundary

Figure 7. College Students' Image of Livability.
Source: note 8, Gould and White.

ally toward the south. Eastward across the lake country the Atlantic regime of the northeastern United States and eastern Canada gradually takes over, and the yearly number of cloudy, snowy, or rainy days increases.

Perhaps the steepest gradient, in many ways, occurs at the United States–Canada boundary. To be sure, the border is open, friendly, easily crossed, and frequently crossed by many who live and work near it. Yet, to cross it and remain for long, you have to disentangle from one web of national history and geography and weave yourself into a different one. The two histories and geographies overlap and entwine in many ways all along the border. But they are recorded in separate sets of records—one set linked north and the other south, one set ultimately to Ottawa and the other to Washington. In the settlement and development of the Upper Midwest and the Canadian Prairies, many broad parallels and cross-linkages emerge. Yet the balance of binding ties today shifts very sharply to Toronto, Winnipeg, Calgary, and Edmonton at the Upper Midwest's northern boundary. For most Americans the mental map of climate ends there, too. Details of seasonal and daily variety dissolve into a uniform misconception or a blank. Canada's federal and provincial governments work hard at educating Upper Midwesterners about the warm, sunny summers north of the border. For it has been hard to get Midwestern Americans beyond the idea that central Canada is an icebox, from where the coldest weather comes.[7]

The External Image That Segregates

While internal ties bind the region, an awesome national mixture of disinterest and puzzlement has segregated it. You might guess that 95 percent of Americans view the region as uninhabitable, with a climate suitable only for testing batteries, motor oil, and pick up trucks. Most of the other 5 percent know better because they live here or they have lived here. Migration data make it clear that many would like to return, and many do. Business-executive surveys rate the Twin Cities at or near the top among large urban areas for quality of housing, neighborhoods, recreation, government, education, and culture. I have heard senior officials in Washington wax nostalgic over times they spent in "those remarkable communities" of Bismarck or Brookings, to name two. But those are the reactions of people who have lived in the place. And most have not.

The region is a blank on the mental maps of most Americans. For better or worse, no popular image or symbol takes shape. College students elsewhere do not spontaneously think of it as a place to live after they graduate (Figure 7). Families approaching retirement age do not hear of it as a place for enjoyment of their later years (Figure 8). In media stereotypes wheat ranchers are from Kansas, not North Dakota or Montana. Cattle ranchers are from Texas, never South Dakota. Carefully shirt-sleeved decision makers ponder printouts in the towers of New York, Chicago, perhaps Houston or San Francisco, not the Twin Cities. Outdoor recreation is pursued in the mountains, in the Southwest deserts, or on subtropical beaches, seldom in the Boundary Waters canoe country or on the quiet lakes of the North Woods. To be sure, over the years a jumble of names has shown through the mist—for instance, the Mayo Clinic, Burma Shave, Scotch Tape, Glass Wax, Sinclair Lewis, Lawrence Welk, Bronco Nagurski, Roy Wilkins, Mary Tyler Moore, Hubert Humphrey, and the characters of Lake Wobegon. But such emissaries appear to be as accidental and unusual as a chilly day in the Sunbelt. Frequently the national media quote someone who says "the Twin Cities are an excellent place to live." Thus Minneapolis-St. Paul become a vague, inexplicable anomaly amid the wastelands, glaciers, and boondocks. The personal and institutional emissaries and the peculiar reputation of the Twin Cities do as much to deepen the mystery as resolve it. As a New York cab driver said to me, "You got a ball club there. They got to have a place to play. So what does the place look like? Yankee Stadium and glaciers?" Momentary visions arise, but sooner or later the emptiness closes in again on that part of the national mental map that yawns between the Bear Paws and the Porcupines, the Skunk and the Rainy. At least so it seems sometimes from the heartland![8]

Varied Environments

In fact, 6 million people do live in the primary region of the Upper Midwest, 8 million in the banking region. They live in natural environments with vivid variations from one part of the region to another—environments which do, indeed, have a lot to do with glaciers (Figure 9). Those different environments not only offer the reality to fill the void that exists in so many imaginations, but also provide the stage on which the real story of the region's settlement has unfolded.[9]

THE FOREST ZONE

On the east and west the region is framed by two of the great wooded regions of the United States—the northern Great Lakes and the northern Rockies. The Great Lakes forest—the North Woods to 40 million Midwesterners who live and work to the south of it—shades the Upper Midwest east and north of a line from Lake of the Woods to the Dalles of the

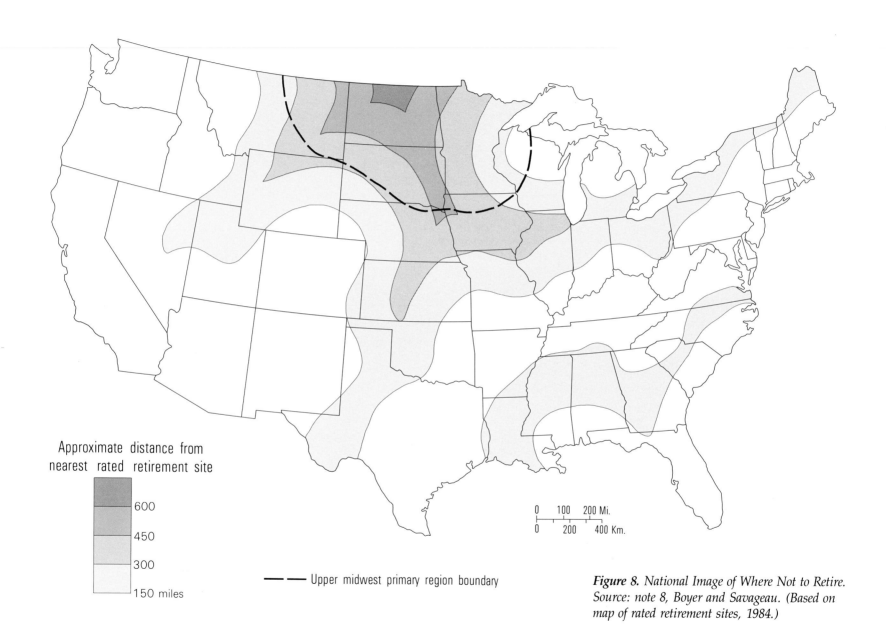

Approximate distance from
nearest rated retirement site

600

450

300

150 miles

— — Upper midwest primary region boundary

0   100   200 Mi.

0   200   400 Km.

Figure 8. National Image of Where Not to Retire.
Source: note 8, Boyer and Savageau. (Based on
map of rated retirement sites, 1984.)

FLATHEAD

BEARPAW
MTS.

BITTERROOT

BIG HOLE

GALLATIN
BEAVERHEAD

BIG HORN
MTS.

MISSOURI

A

COTEAU

B

BLACK
HILLS

PORCUPINE
MTS.

Figure 9. Upper Midwest Natural Environments.
Source: note 9.

Mountain Forest

Prairie, Broken Plains and Mountain Valleys

Glacial Moraine and Lakes, Pine and Mixed Forest } Northern Great Lakes Forest
Glacier-scoured Ridges, Pine and Mixed Forest

Moraine and Lakes, Mixed Prairie and Woodland } Eastern Transition Zone
Ridges and Valleys, Mixed Prairie and Woodland

Moraine, Prairie

Glacial Plains, Prairie } Cropland Corridor

A Red River Valley
B James River Plain

Cropland, partly improved pasture strewn with glacial boulders, and the ever-present forest backdrop, in the northern Wisconsin countryside between the Twin Cities and Wausau, are typical of the eastern part of the Upper Midwest. Photo by author.

St. Croix River, northeast of the Twin Cities, to north-central Wisconsin.

Today the forest is a crazy-quilt. Each patch is a grove dominated by one of many species—spruce, pines, balsam, tamarack, birch, aspen, oaks, maples, and other hardwoods. In the brief autumn patches of a brilliant variety of reds, browns, and golds flash among the evergreen, and for a week or two the quilt becomes a masterpiece. At that time, on a clear late afternoon, it is worth the price of a plane ticket to Duluth or Houghton just to see the quilt in aerial panorama.

Each patch has its story. In part the patches reflect the stages in the botanical succession as each particular piece of the forest recovers from its most recent cutting or burning, invades the derelict clearing of an abandoned farm, or grows in the neat rows of a new plantation. In part, also, the forest patches reflect the random pattern of sand, clay, gravel, boulders, and bog that make soil mapping on these glacial moraine deposits a cartographic nightmare. Disorderly heaps and terraces and saucers of glacial material form the land surface everywhere beneath the trees. But there are natural openings at the thousands of lakes and ponds and a few openings, too, where geologically ancient bedrock protrudes as bald hilltops through the glacial drift.

Water is in abundance. Dependable summer rain and winter snow supply the moisture. Cool summers reduce direct evaporation and the amount needed by growing vegetation. As a result the subsoil is moist. The lakes are full. Closely spaced, dependable streams meander and tumble from lake to bog as they head for Lake Superior, Lake Michigan, or the Mississippi.

In the northern part of the Great Lakes forest zone, the land rises in massive waves toward the great Canadian Shield. Made of some of the oldest, hardest, and most mineralized rock, the Shield forms the high ground of central and eastern Canada. There the continental glaciers of the ice age accumulated, and from there they spread chaos south to what is now the Ohio and the Missouri. The southern edge of the Shield is in the Upper Midwest, in the wilderness of the Boundary Waters Canoe Area and the Voyageurs National Park of northeastern Minnesota. As the elevation falls toward the south, only the higher ridges of hard rock protrude through the mantle of glacial deposits. Several of those ridges are the famous mineral ranges—the Mesabi and Vermilion of Minnesota; the Gogebic, straddling the Wisconsin-Michigan border; and the Copper, Menominee, and Marquette ranges of Upper Michigan.

The most impressive ridge is the great geologic fault scarp that forms the north shore of Lake Superior. Behind the clean pebble beaches and headlands, the country rises a thousand feet or more to the north horizon. Offshore a few miles the lake is nearly a thousand feet deep. Off the south shore another ridge, nearly submerged, rises faintly above the lake level to form the Apostle Islands. In summer the deep, cold lake, towering ridges, and rocky islands create anomalous narrow strips of maritime environment in the heart of the continent—always cool; with ample wind for sailing; sometimes fog-shrouded; with a long, mild growing season that is especially gentle for flowers of forest and garden. In deep winter the scene takes on the character of the wildest coast of Lapland—crashing waves amid driving snow with a southeast wind, grotesque giant ice curtains and stalactites, colorful pebble beaches encased for miles like souvenirs in a sheet of ice laid exquisitely by breaking waves, days when arctic sea smoke rises in whisps as far as the eye can see while

Ice-age glaciers scoured a deep trench for Lake of the Clouds and polished the hard, half-billion-year-old rocks that surround it. A mixed forest of pine and northern hardwoods mantles the rugged terrain of the Porcupine Mountains, in Michigan's Upper Peninsula. Photo by author.

Nearly 1,000 feet deep a few miles offshore from this point, midway between Duluth and the Canadian border, the open water of Lake Superior combines with a subzero arctic gale to create a unique, awesome midwinter scene. Photo by author.

the open lake steams beneath subzero air blowing from somewhere near the North Pole.

The other forest realm covers the western part of the region. As you move toward the west, it first appears in islands of ponderosa pine on the great isolated earth crustal domes called the Black Hills or the Big Horn, Bear Paw, Big Snowy, Belt, and Crazy mountains. Farther west the forest is nearly continuous in the corridor of crustal upheaval named the Rocky Mountains, from Yellowstone to Glacier Park and beyond. Most of the forest lies above the 4,000- to 5,000-foot contours, up to the timberline at 9,000 to 10,000 feet. In that range of altitude, both moisture and summer heat are adequate. Not only is the forest more dense and tall in the main ranges of the Rockies, but also it is more varied. West of the continental divide stands of douglas fir and lodgepole pine turn your thoughts toward the Pacific Northwest. Winter snow, spring and autumn rains are more reliable, thanks to more direct exposure to moisture from the Pacific.

The highest water yields in the region come from the mountain forests and the barren jagged peaks and snowfields above them. Most of the water pours out in torrents during the spring melt and spring rains. But some soaks in to saturate the forest litter and rocky slopes, then seeps out gradually during the warm season. All of it feeds the clear upper reaches and the muddier, lower main stems of famous tributaries of the Missouri and Columbia. Below the forest, grassy benchland slopes to the Great Plains on the east and into the broad valleys between the main ranges—especially the spectacular trenches of the Bitterroot and Flathead. In the classic western settlement pattern, cities, towns, and irrigated ranches lie in the wider valleys. Old mining towns and locations string along certain canyons. Logging roads and scenic highways lead to camps and cabins of exurbanites and to the edges of wilderness preserves in the mountain forests.

THE CROPLAND CORRIDOR

The wide plains between the two forests are the agricultural realm of the Upper Midwest. The heart of the agricultural country is in the prairie–glacial drift plains corridor. It trends southeast-northwest from northern Iowa to northern Montana. That corridor shares, with the rest of the North American Middle West and Great Plains and perhaps three or four regions on other continents, the world's finest upland soil resource for modern farming technology. The land was mostly treeless prairie at the time of white settlement; hence nature spared farm settlers the costly work of clearing it. The soils are formed on deep, fresh glacial deposits, generally high in soluble mineral plant food. Deep, dense roots from millennia of prairie grass growth made the soil initially high in organic matter and nitrogen. Though a few boulders remain, not yet decomposed from glacial times, the material is mostly a thick blanket of clay, loam, and silt.

But some important differences emerge within the corridor. South of roughly the latitude of the Otter Tail River in west-central Minnesota and the Sheyenne in southeastern North Dakota, the growing season is long enough for grain corn, and soybeans. Eastward from the wide, level valley of South Dakota's James River, the spring rains are ample and fairly dependable. Summer rains are fickle but adequate in most years. This warmest, best-watered part of the prairie-drift plains forms the Upper Midwest's part of the American Corn Belt and the richest part of the Upper Midwest agricultural base. Nature boosted the settlers there to a head start, and subsequent generations of farmers have parlayed their inheritance from the pioneers.

North of the Corn Belt, a sizable part of the cropland corridor is one of the most remarkable of legacies from the ice age, the Red River Valley. Of the great lakes ponded against the edge of the retreating glaciers in central Canada 10 millennia ago, the greatest was Lake Agassiz. The lake was named long after its demise, of course, for the Swiss-Bostonian naturalist Louis Agassiz. It covered a large part of what is now eastern North Dakota, northwestern Minnesota, and Manitoba. It rose to the height of a divide along the present Minnesota–South Dakota boundary and spilled over the divide, southeast down a mile-wide trench now occupied by the Minnesota River Valley. When the ice finally disappeared, the lake emptied northward through Hudson Bay to the sea. The vast lake floor, mostly clay and flat as a pancake, was then exposed to the sky and quickly covered with a carpet of prairie. And so it lay until large-scale white settlement began in the 1870s. Two brief, catastrophic events in the long history of the earth have created today's landscape there: the melting of the last ice sheets and the nineteenth-century spread of European people. From the air today you see a fantastic landscape of unbroken, flat, checkerboard fields. In summer the fields are square miles of wheat, square miles of potatoes, square miles of barley, square miles of oats or blue grass or sugar beets. The continuity and scale of the checkerboard overwhelms all but the larger urban centers in the landscape, while it sustains them as thriving nodes in the regional economy. Though smaller and less moisture-retentive, the plain along the James River through South Dakota is the second of these two major islands of flat land on the rolling prairie.

West of the Red and James valleys the climate is drier. Rains fail occasionally in spring, frequently in summer. The climatic break

comes near the meridian of 100 degrees west longitude. The Hundredth Meridian is the classic boundary of the semiarid West in much of our literature and official lore. Farmers near Lawrence Welk's hometown, southeast of Bismarck, live close to that meridian. They could show you prairie land shaped by the glaciers that is just as smooth as much of the Corn Belt. But their reliance on wheat and barley rather than corn reflects their lesser confidence in the moisture supply. As the glaciers pushed southwest into drier, warmer country, they thinned and stalled on long, high ridges that trend northwest-southeast on the plains. The longest and highest of those—the Missouri Coteau—still carries the name the French explorers gave it. Chaotic small hills, intervening shallow prairie potholes, and boulder fields pock the surface. Those are the features of glacial moraines, where the glacier's edge stood vacillating for hundreds of summers. The rate of ice advance equaled the rate of melting at the front; as a result the glacier just kept hauling in and dumping load after load of dirt and rock along the same line. Today the potholes fill to the brim in a wet spring. But during perhaps half of the summers in living memory, drought and evaporation have left many of these low areas as mere flat white beds of cracked alkaline mud. Nineteenth-century school geography maps used the label "Region of Salt Waters." That was the way the area looked to surveyors who saw it during the 1860s. But the larger, wetter potholes provide way stations for tens of thousands of waterfowl on the plains flyway between the Gulf of Mexico and their Canadian nesting grounds. North Dakota farmers on the Missouri Coteau could explain how they avoid potholes and the worst boulder fields, leaving those areas for grazing and waterfowl habitat.

West of the country around Havre and

Outbuildings make up a large livestock feeding operation in south-central Minnesota in the early 1980s. The black soil evolved beneath natural prairie grasses that mantled much of today's Upper Midwest cropland corridor before white settlement. Trees in the picture are all planted shelterbelts around the farmyards. Photo, Frederic Steinhauser.

In the drier wheat country west of the Hundredth Meridian, strips may be cropped in alternate years to conserve moisture on the gently rolling uplands. Where river valleys are incised into the plains, grass and sage sparsely mantle the sharp ridges, cedars pock the rocky ledges, and cottonwoods and box elder follow the narrow draws. This view is north from the breaks of the Yellowstone River in eastern Montana. Photo by author.

Great Falls, the prairie-glacial drift plains broaden and flatten again in an area Montanans call the Triangle, between the Missouri, the Rockies, and the Canadian border. This is the type locality of the famous warm chinook winds of midwinter. Rainfall and snowfall are a little more reliable than on the plains to the east. The Sun and Marias rivers, and numerous swift creeks, bring irrigation water from the neighboring mountains. With more moisture and milder winters, ranchers in the Triangle grow nearly half of Montana's wheat.

THE TRANSITION ZONES

A narrow transition zone separates the main cropland corridor from the Upper Great Lakes forest realm. The transition zone is widest and most unusual—for the Upper Midwest—southeast of the Twin Cities, through southwestern Wisconsin and northeastern Iowa. By chance the ice-age glaciers bypassed this area. As a result, splashing rain and streams have had more than a hundred million years to carve its surface into treelike networks of valleys and intervening ridges. The land is unglaciated and stream-dissected. The upland fields, on fertile but thin soil, command panoramic views across waves of high, rolling ridge tops and deep ravines. Clean limestone cliffs and intervening steep slopes of rock waste form the valley walls. Rich hardwood forests darken the north-facing bluffs and ravines, while cedars dot the otherwise open goat prairies on drier southwest-facing slopes. On the bottoms the rich floodplains and terraces support cropland, and the tributary rivers wind rather steeply toward the Mississippi. On the western, drier side of the transition zone, before agricultural settlement, prairies covered the ridgetops as well as the south-facing slopes. Scattered groves interrupted the tall grassland. But on the less

This southeastern Minnesota valley, west of LaCrosse, Wisconsin, lies in the stream-dissected, unglaciated part of the transition zone between the cropland corridor and the Upper Great Lakes forest. Steep, wooded valley walls separate the fertile, rolling ridgetops from the rich bottomlands several hundred feet below. Photo, Frederic Steinhauser.

Rough, lake-studded glacial moraine land in the Park Region of west-central Minnesota is typical of much of the Dairy Belt, on the northeastern margin of the Upper Midwest's cropland corridor. Photo by author.

drought-risky eastern edge of the zone, only scattered openings of prairie interrupted the dominant woodland. The lovely islands of prairie and grove inspired scores of place-names across the transition zone in the Upper Midwest.

In Minnesota, from the southernmost lake district at Albert Lea to the most northwesterly lake district around Detroit Lakes, the forest-to-prairie transition zone lies on the remarkably varied surface of the Upper Midwest's most extensive and roughest glacial moraines. From the tops of 100- or 200-foot knobs, early explorers could see for miles across a lush, rolling compage of hills, lakes, prairies, and woodlands. For good reason, they called it the Park Region. The name still fits the landscape, although the prairies are now pastures or fields. These transition areas are the historic heart of Upper Midwest dairy farming.

North of Detroit Lakes the big moraine loops eastward into the forest zone. But the forest-to-prairie transition zone continues northward across the international boundary, along strings of low, sandy beach ridges that once formed the shores of great Lake Agassiz. Groves of aspen and openings of prairie, at the time of white settlement, made the transition between wooded beach-ridges among vast bogs in the forest zone to the east and the flat prairies of the Red River Valley to the west.

Another, very much wider and very different transition zone spreads westward from the Missouri. South Dakotans call it West River country. North Dakotans call it the Slope and might tell you it's the section of the state with rattlesnakes. Summer tourists speeding from Chicago to the Black Hills get a feeling that this is where the West begins.

The general elevation begins to rise subtly from the Missouri toward the Black Hills, Big

Horns, and Rockies. Meanwhile, like the Upper Mississippi Valley below St. Paul, the trans-Missouri country was mostly beyond the reach of the ice-age glaciers and their smoothing veneer of drift. The face of the land reflects the work of the master rivers that flow from the mountains and Black Hills to the encircling Missouri. Their names are legendary in the West—the Yellowstone, Musselshell, Big Horn, Powder, and Tongue, the Little Missouri, Cheyenne, and White, and the smaller Knife, Heart, Moreau, Grand, and Bad. Except for the Yellowstone, these are slender streams, for they drain the driest part of the northern Great Plains. But without harassment by continental glaciation, there has been time for a quarter-million hundred-year storms to pound and erode their watersheds. The result is a series of deep, wide, rugged trenches radiating from the high country toward the Missouri, and along the Big Muddy. Valley walls are generally covered with prairie

A midwinter view looks southwestward across the wide Missouri in south-central South Dakota. The stream's crevassed ice cover separates the smooth veneer of glacial deposits, black prairie soil, and checkerboard of corn fields on the east side from West River ranching country. To many travelers, this is where the West begins. Photo by author.

and sagebrush. The surface is harsh but resembles velvet in shadowy panorama when the sun is low. In a few spectacular places, the soft, colorful, geologically young bedrock has washed easily and has seldom stabilized long enough for the plant cover to take hold. Those are the Badlands. The rivers are widely spaced, for it takes a lot of land to catch enough water to make a river in this dry country.

Gently rolling plateaus project toward the Missouri between the breaks of tributary valleys. With no glacial deposits to mask them, local buttes and pine-edged escarpments rise above the plateaus. They are landmarks on always distant skylines. To the early scouts they first intimated the mountains beyond the horizon to the west, and later they provided guideposts to wagon trains on the trackless prairie. Today you might get the local names for those features from ranchers, as you survey the five-square-mile expanse of each one's wheat fields or rangelands.

Global Forces — Natural and Human

The active powers of nature have created this varied stage for Upper Midwest settlement. The stage is the product of global flows of air, water, and the earth, itself. The global flow of air makes a dramatic and dynamic climate today (Figure 10). Daily television and newspaper maps tell that story. Two of the three most frequent positions of the atmosphere's west-to-east jet stream across North America converge from Alberta and Colorado to the Great Lakes. The low pressure centers that follow those routes swing their continuous procession of fronts, with accompanying temperature changes, cloud, and precipitation, across the Upper Midwest.

Those converging storms and jets draw air from three of the world's most contrasting sources across the region's forests, fields, lakes, and settlements. One source is the Canadian Arctic. Air from that source is cool in summer, frigid in winter, and always antiseptically clear, to let the northern lights, stars, and sun shine brighter. A second source is the Tropical Atlantic. Moist air streams from there westward across the Gulf of Mexico, north up the central lowlands, and into the passing lows and fronts. Storms lift it to form the mountainous thunderheads of summer and the leaden, layered clouds of winter. Then the storms wring from those clouds the downpours, blizzards, and drizzles that water the land. Those tropical maritime airstreams often reach the Upper Midwest at the surface east of the Hundredth Meridian in spring and summer, but west of the Hundredth Meridian only occasionally and mainly in the springtime. They seldom reach the region at the surface in winter but spread over it aloft to produce most of the winter's clouds and snow. The third source is the dry western plateau country, between the Rockies and Sierra-Cascades. That source is cool in winter, hot in summer, and always dry. Passing storms draw its dry air into the Upper Midwest frequently as far east as the Hundredth Meridian, less often into the eastern prairie region as far as Minnesota and Iowa. In winter continental incursions are the warm chinook winds of the High Plains and the less frequent thaws of the eastern areas. In summer they are the spells of hot winds which bring searing temperatures and, if they persist long enough, wilt sapling trees and turn fields to dust. Only over the high mountain country do these air masses give up some of their meager water content, from sheets of winter clouds and summer-afternoon thunderheads.[10]

Thus the global wind system today differentiates the region into a northeastern province of cool, moist summers and cold, snowy winters; a subhumid prairie province east of the Hundredth Meridian; a semiarid shortgrass prairie province west of the Hundredth Meridian; and the moist high country of the mountains and Black Hills. In the ice ages of the geologic near-past, a similar global wind system prevailed. But temperatures fell enough that in the cool, snowy northeastern province the snow accumulation in the longer winter became more than the sun and rain could melt during the shortened summer. For thousands of years the accumulation deepened, compacted, and began to spread. The spreading sheet stalled when it moved south of the major jet streams into realms of warmer or drier air, or both. Thus the same location in the global air flow that creates Upper Midwest weather patterns today created the glacial patterns that left their imprint on so much of the land in the ice age.

The global flow of water takes the moisture delivered from the ocean surface by the atmosphere and returns it to the oceans down the Missouri and Mississippi, the Columbia, the Red, and the Great Lakes (Figure 11). But in the interim, like the flow of air, the flow of water differentiates the Upper Midwest into contrasting realms. Rain water and snowmelt partly soak into the soil, partly run off directly to the nearest stream. The soak-in first nourishes the cover of crops, range, and forest. Whatever remains fills the ground water reserve and seeps through springs to the streams as indirect runoff. If none remains, then no springs or streams flow in the long periods between annual spring melts or infrequent severe summer storms. If there is not enough soak-in to support a forest, there is no forest. Thus the vegetation cover and the stream flow reflect the rainfall, snowmelt, and water budget of the region.

January

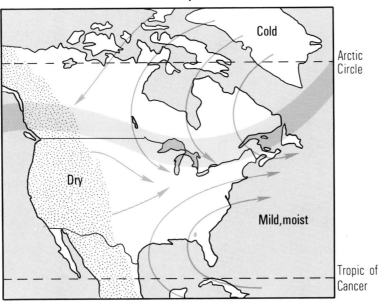

Cold

Arctic
Circle

Dry

Mild, moist

Tropic of
Cancer

July

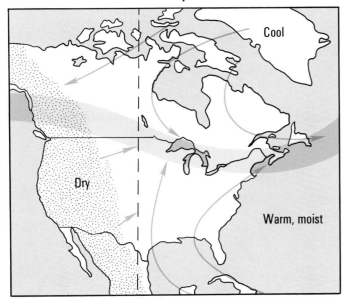

Cool

Dry

Warm, moist

100th Meridian

Average storm track/jet stream

Average wind

Western plateaus and mountains

Figure 10. The Upper Midwest's Position in the
Flow of Air across North America. Low pressure
centers that follow the northern paths of the atmosphere's jet stream swing their procession of
fronts across the Upper Midwest, with accompanying clouds, rain, and winter snow. They draw
air from three of the world's most contrasting
source regions. Source: note 10.

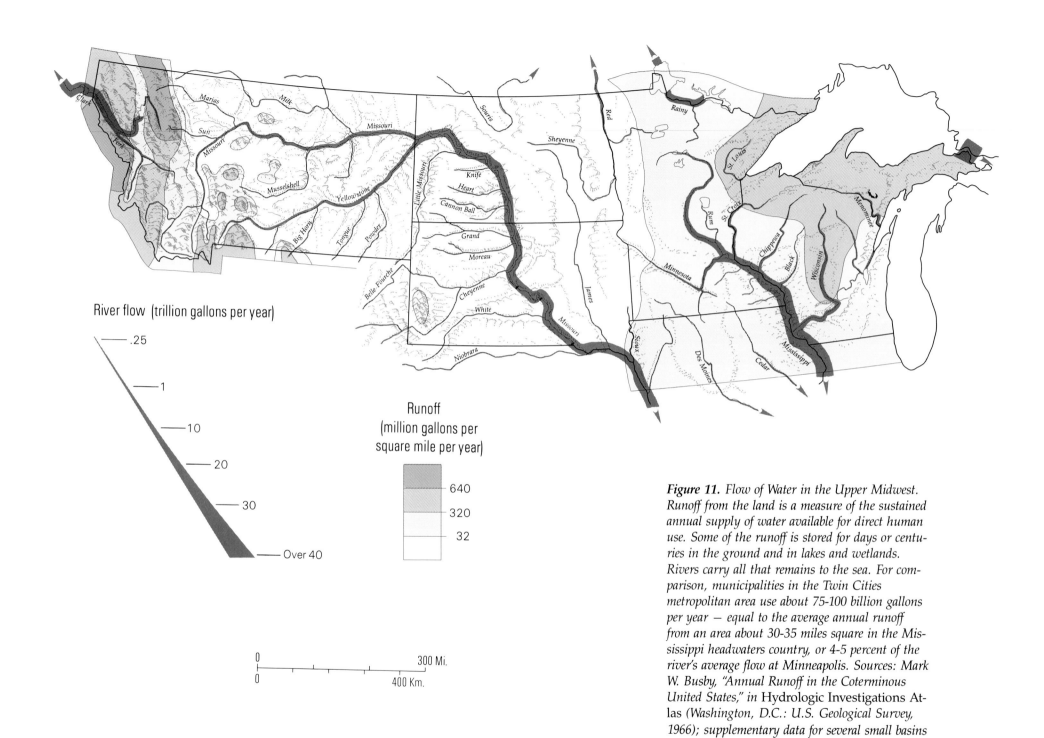

River flow (trillion gallons per year)

— .25
— 1
— 10
— 20
— 30
— Over 40

Runoff
(million gallons per
square mile per year)

640
320
32

0   300 Mi.
0   400 Km.

Figure 11. Flow of Water in the Upper Midwest.
Runoff from the land is a measure of the sustained
annual supply of water available for direct human
use. Some of the runoff is stored for days or centu-
ries in the ground and in lakes and wetlands.
Rivers carry all that remains to the sea. For com-
parison, municipalities in the Twin Cities
metropolitan area use about 75-100 billion gallons
per year — equal to the average annual runoff
from an area about 30-35 miles square in the Mis-
sissippi headwaters country, or 4-5 percent of the
river's average flow at Minneapolis. Sources: Mark
W. Busby, "Annual Runoff in the Coterminous
United States," in Hydrologic Investigations Atlas *(Washington, D.C.: U.S. Geological Survey,*
1966); supplementary data for several small basins
from USGS annual Water Resources Data.

In early spring the Baptism River pours 20,000 gallons of water per second, from a 1,000-square-mile drainage basin in northeastern Minnesota, over the escarpment along Lake Superior's north shore. Photo, David Borchert.

In late spring the Powder River brings a few hundred gallons of water per second from a 20,000-square-mile basin on the Great Plains. Pine-edged buttes rise above the dry grassland on the horizon in southeastern Montana. Photo by author.

In a dramatic expression of the conjuncture of global forces, the forested Rockies rise above the treeless plains on the region's western periphery in central Montana. Photo by author.

The cool, moist northeast and the western high mountains are also the realms of forests and lakes and the sources of large, dependable rivers. The subhumid, somewhat drought-riskier prairies east of the Hundredth Meridian are also the source of smaller rivers and a land of fewer lakes. The semiarid western plains were clothed in only a shortgrass prairie; today they support only more drought-resistant crops and send out only meager, widely spaced rivers.

Even the gradual flow and heaving of the earth's crust are reflected in the giant folds, faults, domes, and basins of the western mountains; in the massive subcontinent of ancient rock that forms the Canadian Shield; and in the mineral veins injected into fissures during eras of great crustal disturbance (Figure 12). Crustal shifts are also reflected in the broad basins, filled with miles-deep layers of sedimentary rock, which lie beneath the plains of Dakota and eastern Montana. Some of those rocks are oil- and coal-bearing and provide the large reserves of the Powder River, Knife River, and Williston basins.

People have set the stage and changed the scenes with comparable drama—and also through processes as inexorable and evolutionary as nature's. Suppose you were to talk with the people whom you inevitably would encounter if you were to go out to look at the different natural environments of the Upper Midwest. Loggers in the northern Wisconsin forest might talk about their forbears who were Chippewa Indians living in the region when white explorers, missionaries, traders, then loggers, townspeople, and farmers arrived. Taconite mill workers on the Mesabi Iron Range could tell you about their Finnish forbears who migrated to the Lake Superior district when the Czar was imposing a tighten-

Figure 12. *Upper Midwest Mineral Resources. The deposits reflect the history and location patterns of the gradual flow, heaving, and fracturing of the earth's crust through geologic time. Sources: James Turnbull,* Coal Fields of the United States *(Washington, D.C.: U.S. Geological Survey, 1960), sheet 1;* Oil and Gas Fields of the United States *(Penn-Well Publishing Company, 1982), note 9, Gerlach.*

ing tyranny on their homeland in the early 1900s. Farmers in the Iowa Corn Belt might tell you about their German grandparents; a Red River Valley family, their Norwegian and French Canadian backgrounds. One family on the Missouri Coteau in North Dakota could talk about the Russian-German settlement there in the 1890s, and another in the Montana ranching country might recall their great grandparents' stories of their trek from Missouri after the Civil War. An exurbanite couple in a Montana mountain cabin might discuss their real estate business in California and their parents' immigration from Italy to New York.[11]

The varied settlement map of the Upper Midwest reflects flows of people whose individual decisions have been motivated and constrained by massive migrations, social and political movements, conflicts, famines, and tyrannies in many corners of the world. At the same time, of course, their individual decisions and actions added up to these very same movements, migrations, and conflicts. The result has been a continuing avalanche of events with tumbling momentum and lives of their own. Meanwhile—within the world's established networks of settlement, transportation, and communication—streams of information,

inventions, goods, and capital constantly flow to and from the region and within it. Those flows continue to change the maps of the region's population, employment, income, and connections. The environment is dynamic. The region is a product of the convergence of global natural and human forces.

Little more than a century ago the Upper Midwest region was an embryo. Most of the land lay beyond the American frontier. In a century it became a prosperous, integral part of the world economy. The region today is a complex network of farms, small towns, cities, metropolitan areas, and connecting routes.

So, those who pose serious questions about the region seek to understand that remarkable transformation. What accounts for the Upper Midwest's location, shape, and look? What has been the anatomy of its initial development? Of its adaptation to dramatic national and worldwide changes? Why and how much has the region's identity persisted amid so much change?

One way to try to comprehend the process of change is through geographical snapshots of the region's settlement at different times. Three times are especially critical. Around 1870 American Indians sparsely occupied the land. The white invasions of the Upper Mid-

west on a large scale had just begun. The growth of the United States as a major steel producer and the steel rail era of transcontinental railroad building had just begun. By 1920 the occupation of the region by whites was essentially complete. The Northwest Empire had been created. The era of the automobile, airplane, cheap oil, and electronic communication was just emerging on a large scale. In the 1970s and 1980s, products of the era that began around 1920 are in place: industrialized agriculture, metropolitan settlements, highway-air-electronic networks. The empire has become in many ways a neighborhood in an increasingly unstable, intense, worldwide circulation system.[12]

In the 1980s we are now entering a stage of unprecedented growth of awareness of the worldwide system and its complexity.

Those three widely separated times frame two major epochs for understanding the Upper Midwest: an epoch of development and rapid population growth between 1870 and 1920, and an epoch of great adaptation and economic growth between 1920 and the 1980s. The two periods, in sequence, also provide some background for us to think about further change and adaptation in another period, beyond the 1980s.

CHAPTER 2

Dissolving
the Wilderness

THE 1870 MAP

In the quarter-century leading up to 1870, the United States census count for today's Upper Midwest banking region had risen from less than 2,000 to about 800,000 (Figure 13).[13] About three-quarters of that growth came from immigration, the remainder from natural increase of the burgeoning resident population. Perhaps two-thirds were foreign, the rest from the eastern United States. Of the foreign immigrants, three-quarters were German, Scandinavian, and Irish. Meanwhile, fewer than 100,000 Indians lived in the region— mainly on the land they had not yet ceded to the advancing whites.

The key to white settlement expansion was transportation. Settlers were enlarging the national economy, bringing new resources into the national system, creating new jobs and new wealth. But the new lands had to be tied to the developed Eastern core of the national economy. Improving the speed, capacity, and efficiency of the ties was a constant challenge.

The Primitive Transportation System

Natural waterways were the first links. Primitive wagon roads connected and extended the water routes. That primitive system was still important on the 1870 map. From St. Paul and Stillwater a fleet of side-wheel and stern-wheel riverboats, with their auxilliary barges, plied the Mississippi to the great St. Louis entrepôt. From there the historic system of the Western rivers led to New Orleans, Pittsburgh, and the Missouri River country. From the newly developing Upper Midwest the packets moved fur, grain, hides, and lumber downstream and returned with hardware, machinery, textiles, clothing, groceries, and whiskey, along with 1,000 or 2,000 immigrants each week of the navigation season. Upper tributaries of the Mississippi, from the Wisconsin on the east to Minnesota's Rum River on the west, floated the logs of spring drives from the edges of the northern forest, and the main stem carried football-field-sized rafts of logs and lumber to downstream mills and yards at Winona, Dubuque, Rock Island-

Davenport, Burlington, and all the way to St. Louis.

Completion of the first locks at Sault Ste. Marie in 1855 had extended the Great Lakes waterway northwest into Lake Superior. That provided a direct route to the East from the northern forests and mineral districts of the Canadian Shield—eventual waterway of the famous whaleback ore and grain carriers.

Most romantic yet cumbersome of the water arteries was the run from St. Louis to Fort Benton, Montana, or to its makeshift low-water outport 100 miles downstream at Cow Island—the alternate practical heads of navigation on the Missouri. The flat-bottom stern-wheelers were called the mountain boats at St. Louis. Fueled by wood cut on the floodplain or coal and lignite dug from the High Plains valley walls, targets of Indian potshots, the Missouri River packets provided a slender connecting thread across the genuinely wild West. Backbone of the St. Louis fur trade, they moved an estimated million hides and many tons of pure gold down from Fort Benton. They brought hundreds of immigrants as well

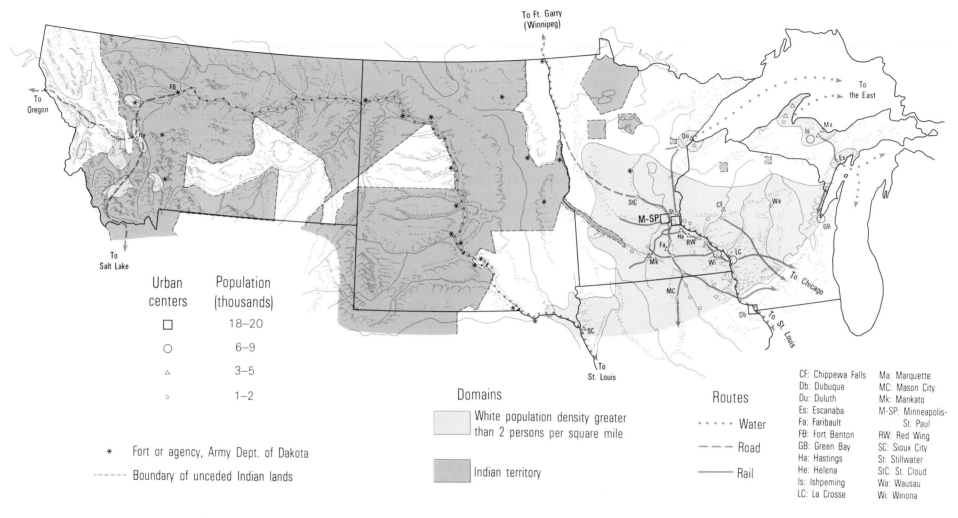

Urban
centers

Population
(thousands)

☐   18–20

○   6–9

△   3–5

○   1–2

*   Fort or agency, Army Dept. of Dakota

-----   Boundary of unceded Indian lands

Domains

White population density greater
than 2 persons per square mile

Indian territory

Routes

· · · · · Water

– – – Road

——— Rail

CF: Chippewa Falls
Db: Dubuque
Du: Duluth
Es: Escanaba
Fa: Faribault
FB: Fort Benton
GB: Green Bay
Ha: Hastings
He: Helena
Is: Ishpeming
LC: La Crosse

Ma: Marquette
MC: Mason City
Mk: Mankato
M-SP: Minneapolis-
     St. Paul
RW: Red Wing
SC: Sioux City
St: Stillwater
StC: St. Cloud
Wa: Wausau
Wi: Winona

Figure 13. The 1870 Map. The region was beginning to take shape. The Upper Mississippi Valley,
the Michigan mining districts, and the Montana
gold fields had been settled at densities higher

than the two-persons-per-square-mile figure used
by the Census Bureau to define the frontier. Half
the region had not yet been ceded by the Indians.
Sources: notes 15, 16, 17, 18, and 21.

as supplies of whiskey, guns, ammunition, hardware, drygoods, and groceries to the Montana gold camps, isolated army garrisons, Indian agencies, and trading posts. Boat captains estimated the distance at 3,000 river miles. The journey took seven weeks upstream, two and one-half down. A typical migrant family, traveling from the farm they sold in Missouri to settle in the Gallatin Valley of southwestern Montana, spent 40 days and nights on the boat from St. Joseph to Fort Benton. It is interesting to reflect that today no human habitation on earth is nearly as much as 40 days' travel time from St. Joseph, Missouri.[14]

Captain John Mullan's famous military wagon road twisted west from Fort Benton, across the Rockies, to the head of river packet navigation on the Columbia at Fort Walla Walla, Washington Territory. Completed in 1859, it provided a transcontinental river-wagon-river route from St. Louis to Portland and Astoria—for those few with the need, patience, and money.[15]

By 1870 the expanding railway net was undermining the packet boat business in the East and threatening it in the West. The first through railroad from the Twin Cities to both Chicago and the growing rail corridor across Iowa was already two years old. Two more direct connections to Chicago were imminent. The Milwaukee Road was building its short line between LaCrosse and St. Paul, and the Chicago and Northwestern had reached Eau Claire. Rail connections between Chicago and the Mississippi River had reached Rock Island and Galena in the 1840s, LaCrosse in the 1850s. They had already diverted much of the St. Louis traffic eastward to the Great Lakes and progressively shortened the route from St. Paul to the Atlantic Seaboard. Now, in the

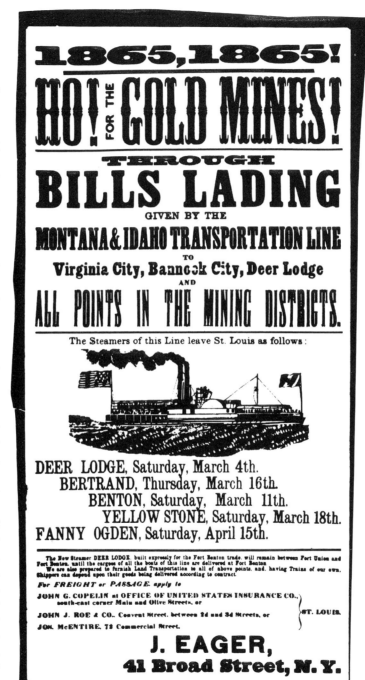

An 1865 handbill gave essential information to shippers and travelers headed from St. Louis across the empty Plains to the Montana gold fields. U.S. National Park Service.

1870s, dependence on the river packets was declining almost completely.

An alternative Eastern link had just opened. Philadelphia's Jay Cooke interests completed the Lake Superior and Mississippi railroad between St. Paul and Duluth in 1869. The embryonic "Zenith City of the Unsalted Seas" was the new land-water transfer point between the Northwest and the nation's economic core. At Carlton, where the line completed its climb from the Duluth waterfront over the St. Louis River gorge to the top of the escarpment and turned south toward St. Paul, Cooke had established a junction and finally begun to build the Northern Pacific. On the 1870 map the line reached 10 miles west on the projected 1,900-mile course to Seattle.[16]

On the agricultural frontier the St. Paul and Pacific had pushed its main line beyond Willmar and its branch line to St. Cloud. The St. Paul and Sioux City reached into the prairie beyond Mankato. From the river ports of Hastings and Winona, which some boosters viewed as competitive with St. Paul, two lines had pushed westward into the southern Minnesota farming country. Until this time rail building was bringing markedly improved transportation to areas where considerable settlement was already under way, and a network of local roads—albeit dirt—was already in place. Now, in the western Minnesota prairie, that sequence was beginning to reverse. The rails were catching up with the frontier and even getting ahead of it. Westward, county seat business districts, traditionally built around the courthouse square, were giving way to business districts lined up along the tracks and focused on the depot. The epoch of truly rail-led settlement was under way.

In addition to the Mullan road, a few other wagon routes still formed part of the arterial network. From the St. Paul and Pacific rail-

head at St. Cloud, the main stage and wagon road extended northwest to Georgetown, Minnesota, a few miles north of present-day Fargo-Moorhead, where it met the Red River steamer route to Winnipeg. On the other side of the territory, completion of the transcontinental railroad in 1869 had given a new importance to the "Mormon Express" route from Utah and the Oregon Trail to the Montana gold fields. Corinne, Utah, is a few miles east of the famous golden spike location at Promontory. The Bear River enters Great Salt Lake near Corinne, and Union Pacific engineers thought they foresaw an important future for the place as a transfer point to steamboats for Salt Lake City. Hence they selected it also as the railroad's transfer point for Montana. For more than a decade the Corinne route was the fastest to Montana from the East. Regular stages and hundreds of wagons served the gold fields. Celebrated New York and European artists, en route to San Francisco, stopped to perform at the Corinne opera house for travelers, mule skinners, bullwhackers, and prospectors. Today the opera house, depot, and most of the business district are gone. Across the tracks from the vacant opera house site, a farm supplies store of a giant Twin Cities–based agricultural cooperative provides a miniscule, less romantic tie with the Upper Midwest.[17]

These arterial routes appear on our small-scale maps of the region. Much has been written and dramatized about their role in advancing the frontier. But another part of the picture is usually missing. The arterials needed a dense supporting network of secondary roads if there was truly to be settlement of a region. The frontier is most often pictured as an open-air workplace of families clearing, burning, plowing, planting, building shelter for themselves and their animals, dealing with Indians

as well as with traders, bankers, and bill collectors. Yet it is at least as useful to think of the frontier as the edge of an expanding dense transportation network. As towns and farms were staked out, in accord with the land survey, the dirt roads advanced simultaneously. So think of the pioneer settlers also as road builders—digging, grading, bridging—coping with the need to get to town, on the one hand, and the need to get to the rural trade area, on the other hand.

Emerging System of Cities, Towns, and Trade Areas

As the frontier was advancing into the nascent Upper Midwest in 1870, nearly two-thirds of the region's population—about 520,000—lived on farms in the Upper Mississippi Valley. Those were pioneer general farms, producing partly for home consumption and partly for the market. Farmers were experimenting with a great variety of familiar European and American fruit, vegetable, and grain crops to see what would survive and yield in this strange climate. They were husbanding familiar European breeds of cattle, hogs, sheep, and poultry. And they were selling what they could ship to Chicago and the other large, more distant urban markets along the crude rail-river transportation system. The shipments were mainly grain, livestock, cheese, and sour-cream butter. Transportation costs were high, and net returns were low. Produce and fluid milk marketing was limited to nearby towns; and that market was still small, with low returns. In addition, these farmers still had much woodland to clear, countless boulders to move, fences and outbuildings to erect. A big share of the output from farm labor was used on the farm. Commercialization was only beginning. Only one-

In 1870 Minneapolis (population 13,000), in the upper photo, is viewed from the Winslow House in St. Anthony (population 5,000). The larger town sprawled over the plain between St. Anthony Falls and the rolling glacial moraine country rising two miles to the southwest. The Mississippi floated logs from the northern forest and powered the mills. A few miles downstream at St. Paul (population 20,000), the river broadened into the water transportation artery of the midcontinent. This port (lower photo), seen from Robert Street, was at that time the terminal for river freight mainly from LaCrosse and for rail freight from the cities at St. Anthony Falls and the frontier country just to the west. At the falls and head of navigation, the river nourished the growth of industry and commerce at the gateway between the distant cities of the East and the resources of the emerging Northwest. Upper photo, Minnesota Historical Society; lower photo, Illingworth, Minnesota Historical Society.

third of the region's population was needed in the towns to carry on commerce.

The most developed farmlands were in the hill country and the glacial moraines of the forest-prairie transition zone, through west-central Wisconsin and northeastern Iowa to central Minnesota, and into the prairie-drift plains across northern Iowa and southwestern Minnesota. America's Spring Wheat Belt was emerging there. The farms were still clustered and scattered, with large areas unclaimed or undeveloped. The fill-in process was quickening near the advancing rail lines, but it remained more gradual in the big spaces between them. On the northern fringe, in Wisconsin, several sizable clusters of farm settlement had developed around Wausau and Chippewa Falls. Those areas were north of the railroads. The soil was stony or sandy. The logging boom was providing winter work in the forest, a chance for additional work in the sawmills, and cutover land practically for the taking. German settlers dominated on that forest frontier, as they had earlier in so many areas across Wisconsin.

Wherever farming began, hamlets and small towns appeared at the same time. By 1870 at least 1,000 of these small nonfarm rural settlements existed, with a total population of about 100,000. At least one emerged at a crossroads in virtually every township. The common nucleus was a tavern, an ethnic church, a waterpowered grist mill, a creamery, a general store, and post office or railway stop.[18]

Thirty-seven larger towns and cities were home to the other 180,000 nonfarm people. The bigger towns distributed goods to the rural hamlets, consolidated the farm product shipments, ran the transportation arteries, and provided professional services as well as department stores and specialty stores for occasional shopping trips.

The largest of these higher-order places was not very large. Of 440,000 people in Minnesota, fewer than 40,000 lived in St. Paul and Minneapolis (including still politically separate St. Anthony). St. Paul and Minneapolis had passed Dubuque as the primary whole-sale-retail-service center of the Upper Mississippi Valley. St. Paul, at the practical head of steamboat navigation, with easy road access from the river to the uplands, was the main regional transportation and distribution center. Minneapolis, with the waterpower of St. Anthony Falls and the New England entrepreneurs attracted to it, was the booming industrial center.

One rank below the primary centers were two important cities in the 6,000–9,000 size class. Winona and LaCrosse were ports on the Mississippi. Both were sawmilling centers and grain collection and shipping points. For more than a decade LaCrosse had been the principal transshipping point in the rail-river corridor between Chicago-Milwaukee and St. Paul.

Another rank down the population order, six towns were medium-size shopping and service centers in the 3,000–5,000 class. Four were river towns, including Stillwater on the St. Croix, the region's second largest sawmilling center and log and lumber rafting point. Also in this class were Hastings and Red Wing, Minnesota. Tributary valleys allowed relatively easy access to the upland prairies at both of those places, and Red Wing's fireclay resource was exploited by an important pioneer crockery industry. Mankato was in the same size class. The Minnesota River served briefly as a steamboat route in the 1850s and 1860s, and Mankato grew at the big bend, where the waterway made its most southerly penetration of the prairies. Two of the six 3,000–5,000 cities were growing at waterpower sites. Faribault was the county seat in southern Min-

nesota's Cannon River Line of grain mills, and Chippewa Falls was the largest sawmill and grain mill center on the largest cataract on western Wisconsin's largest tributary of the Mississippi. Twenty towns were in the small shopping and service center class, with 1,000–2,000 population. Six of those were river towns on the Mississippi, and 14 were water-power sites.

Thus, in this emerging agricultural region every nonfarm settlement, from the largest city to the smallest hamlet, was growing at a strategic point in the developing circulation system. Country crossroads were the locations of the large number of small hamlets. Where natural terrain provided a special advantage—a navigable waterway and easy access to it, or the power of a rapid reach of river—the much smaller number of larger towns and cities had emerged. Each of those natural resources saved a critically large amount of capital that would otherwise have been needed to build a town. Furthermore, there was an emerging ordering of the settlements according to their population and their function in the system of production and exchange.

The leading edge of the Upper Mississippi Valley settlements marked the northwestern-most thrust of the contiguous American frontier in 1870. The northern forest section of the frontier stretched across the Upper Midwest from the shore of Green Bay to central Minnesota. The more dynamic western section ran southward from central Minnesota to extreme southeastern South Dakota.

Important outliers of settlement had grown along the Great Lakes shores, beyond the contiguous northern frontier. Eastern investors had developed the Copper Range on Michigan's Keweenaw peninsula and the nearby Marquette Iron Range, centered on

Ishpeming. The three largest towns on the Copper Range were strung together in a complex of mine derricks, smelters, docks, a few solid business blocks and substantial homes, and shanty districts with a total population of nearly 10,000. Ishpeming had boomed during the preceding decade, along with its neighboring mining town of Negaunee and its two busy ore and timber ports at Marquette and Escanaba. Meanwhile, at the newborn port of Duluth, in an array of shanties and waterfront storehouses, at the end of the new railroad, on one corner of St. Louis Bay, the 1870 census counted 3,100 inhabitants where only 14 families had lived a year earlier. Ishpeming, the largest of these urban islands in the wilderness, had surged into the 6,000–9,000 population class; five others, including Duluth, were in the 3,000–5,000 group.[19]

Far to the west, gold had been discovered in Montana in 1862. The first strike came at Bannack, on the mountainous edge of the Beaverhead Valley. Activity spread to notorious Virginia City in 1863 and Last Chance Gulch at Helena in 1864. Subsequent smaller strikes appeared as far east as the Judith Mountains, northeast of Lewistown. Much of the land had not yet been ceded by the Indians, but that hardly mattered. Each discovery brought a new wave of several thousand strangers to the locality. They came mostly from the East and Midwest—many choosing prospecting over soldiering during the Civil War. But also some Europeans and Chinese found their way north from the Union Pacific. Acres of shanties and one or two substantial buildings mushroomed in each camp. Meanwhile a smaller, less publicized group was arriving from every other part of the United States, with, again, a few from Europe. They came to ranch and to farm on the broad benches and along the potential irrigation

At a waterpower site in southeastern Minnesota's Zumbro River Valley, Rochester was a fast-growing center of pioneer farm trade in 1867, three years after the railroad had reached the city from the Mississippi waterway at Winona. St. Paul Daily News, *credit, Minnesota Historical Society.*

The 1870 census counted 3,100 people living in the raw, booming settlement at the end of the railroad in Duluth. W. H. Illingworth, photo, Minnesota Historical Society.

streams lower in the valleys. They settled in the Missouri headwaters along the Gallatin, Beaverhead, and Sun, and in the Columbia headwaters along the Bitterroot and the upper Clark Fork. They supplied the crowded gold camps, and some assembled considerable wealth in the process. By 1870 the rush had ended. Each boom had subsided quickly and usually left a residue of a few hundred people. They operated the successful mines and worked with the farmers and ranchers at the more rewarding, long-term job of building a stable economy and a few stable towns in these remote but extraordinarily beautiful valleys. Helena, with 4,000 people, had emerged as the territorial capital and largest city. In 1870 about 19,000 people lived in the western Montana country. On the eastern side of the Rocky Mountains, the frontier of that isolated cluster of Americans faced *east* across 900 miles of Indian lands toward the farming frontier in Minnesota and Iowa.[20]

Beyond the Frontiers

Between the agricultural frontier in Minnesota and the gold frontier in Montana lay one-quarter of a million square miles of land that was nearly empty, by the standards of the white settlers. Most of it was Indian territory. Only four large areas had been ceded through treaty by 1870. Two of the ceded areas, Minnesota and eastern Dakota, formed a logical western periphery of the established farming country. The other two, west of the Missouri, were isolated, desultory northerly projections from the vast cessions in Nebraska, Colorado, and Wyoming. Probably numbering about 50,000, the Indians lived in widely scattered, quasi-permanent villages and shifting bands.

The United States government had a very sparse and small presence. The army's Department of Dakota included Minnesota, the Dakota and Montana Territories—a suggestion of the banking region that would come half a century later. Commanded from upstairs headquarters over a downtown St. Paul storefront, the department had about 3,200 troops. They were deployed at Fort Snelling—the 50-year-old, original citadel at the head of the Mississippi waterway—and 20 remote outposts. The typical outpost had a stockade protecting a few cabins and huts in an area the size of a city block or smaller, separated from the nearest neighbor by 75 to 300 miles of roadless prairie. Three of the forts—Ripley, Abercrombie, and Ransom—had protected the oxcart routes to the Canadian Red River settlements. By 1870 the main route to Winnipeg bypassed Forts Ripley and Abercrombie, but not Pembina, North Dakota, or the mosquitoes, boulders, and gumbo of the Red River route. Three more forts flew the flag over the eastern Sioux lands along the Prairie Coteau near the present towns of Sisseton, South Dakota, and Lisbon and Devils Lake, North Dakota. The Missouri steamer route strung together 10 forts and Indian agencies from Fort Buford, near present-day Williston, North Dakota, to the New Ponca Agency, above Yankton, South Dakota. There was no base for 800 river miles or 400 land miles between Fort Buford and Fort Benton. On the Montana side of the Indian country, in addition to the company stationed at Fort Benton, other garrisons in Montana guarded the Sun River settlements and the gold fields to the south, the gold fields and ranches in the Belt Mountains east of Helena, and the Bozeman Pass at the eastern edge of the Gallatin Valley.

Connections were tenuous and slow. The eastern forts were supplied by wagon train from St. Paul. The others, though commanded from St. Paul, were supplied from Omaha and St. Louis by river steamers, and by connecting wagon trains beyond Fort Benton. Riverboats churned upstream at 60 miles per day, downstream at 150. Wagon trains might make 30 miles a day, sometimes as little as 10. Except perhaps for the Montana and Red River roads, wagons followed no more than ruts or tracks on the raw land. Surveys were sparse and discontinuous. Maps were crude and often doubtful.

The handful of troops were in the middle of a drama with a complex plot but neither a script nor a director. From one side came the shrill demands of promotional editors, speculators, traders, freighters, hunters, and demagogues, along with the inexorable westward press of settlers. On the other side, they faced the growing restlessness and long-festering social disorganization of the Indians. Tension remained in the aftermath of the Sioux uprisings that flared during the Civil War years. Everyone knew the stories of the bloody incidents between Sioux and white settlers at New Ulm and Spirit Lake, on the southern Minnesota and northern Iowa prairies. Now, more than ever, the tribes were contesting one another and the whites for possession of the buffalo range. The herds furnished food, clothing, and shelter for the Indians. But they also provided income in the barter with white traders for whiskey, guns, powder, and other goods. At the same time, the narrow zone of ceded land separating the farming frontier from the Indian domain was obviously unstable. It had shifted westward all the way from the Mississippi within living memory. Perceptive Indian leaders could sense a relentless squeeze as the farming frontier east of them closed like a vise against the gold and ranching

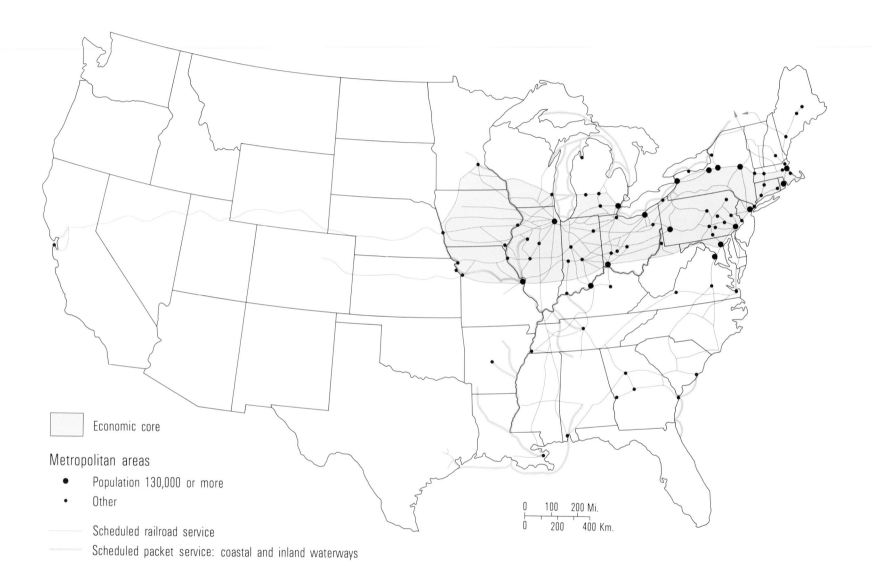

Economic core

Metropolitan areas

●　Population 130,000 or more

·　Other

——　Scheduled railroad service

——　Scheduled packet service: coastal and inland waterways

| 0 | 100 | 200 Mi. |
| 0 | 200 | 400 Km. |

Figure 14. *National Transportation System, 1869. National systems of commercial agricultural marketing, cities, and towns were in place along the transportation network. The American Manufacturing Belt and Corn Belt had taken their places on the world map and would form the core region of American economic geography for the next century. Source: 1868* Official Railway Guide, *modified to include the Union Pacific-Central Pacific line completed the following year.*

frontier west of them and the solid base of the Union Pacific corridor to the south.[21]

In contrast, beyond the northern frontier no significant military presence existed in 1870, nor did much tradition of it. The forest wilderness covered 50,000 square miles. Coniferous trees were dominant, especially the fabled white pines. Poorly drained in many places, sandy in some, rough and stony in the rest, short of hot and frost-free weather—the area offered little to reward crop farming. In fact, the advance of the farming frontier was already slowing to a crawl along the line from Green Bay to St. Cloud. But the wilderness held untapped resources for America's burgeoning heavy industries. The rich metallic ores and tall, straight pines were partly known, partly suspected, and almost totally unsurveyed and unmeasured. Big rivers could provide both the power to saw the logs and the waterways to float the product to the prairie markets. Perhaps 20,000 Indians and about 12,000 whites lived in the lands beyond the northern frontier in 1870. Indian domain had been reduced to seven reservations. Nine-tenths of the reservation land was in Minnesota, although about 60 percent of the Indian population was in Wisconsin and Michigan. Indians, whites, and mixed-bloods mingled in the long-standing trading and trapping business. Meanwhile, the invasion by agriculture was slow and spotty, logging was transient, and both had been thus far confined to the southern edge of the wilderness. Decisive armed conflicts over agricultural settlement had occurred much earlier and much farther south.[22]

Little organized transportation moved through the forest region from either the Great Lakes shores or the agricultural frontier. Mail was carried on foot between a few outposts on Lake Superior, a few towns on the agricultural frontier, and a few trading posts in the forest. An army road temporarily joined Bayfield—mainland port for the Apostle Islands—and the St. Croix Valley. A stage route anticipated the railroad that was soon to close the gap between Escanaba and Menominee-Marinette. And the new ore railroad cut through the narrow isthmus of wilderness between Escanaba and the Marquette Range. Otherwise, it seemed that Americans were largely bypassing the Lake Superior forest country in their westward drive toward the prairie grasslands. But it would not seem that way for long.[23]

A New Epoch

In a larger sense, a new epoch had dawned in the development of the American circulation and settlement system. Upper Midwest development was caught up in the larger drama. A national rail-waterway network was in place from the Atlantic Seaboard into Missouri and Iowa and north of the Ohio and Potomac rivers (Figure 14). In turn, a national commercial agricultural marketing system, and consequently a national system of cities and towns, were all in place along the transportation network. The American Manufacturing Belt and the Corn Belt had taken their positions on the world map. They would make up the core region of American economic geography for the next century.

The nation was ready to exploit and build upon the unique combination of fertile prairies and glacial plains in the Midwest, the gigantic reserves of high-grade coal in the Appalachians, the very large reserves of high-grade iron ore in the Lake Superior district, and the natural Great Lakes waterway to join those rich resource regions. Development had been stimulated by the Civil War. Now new metallurgical technologies were opening an era of cheap steel, changing the United States from a steel importer to a steel exporter. Accompanying revolutionary changes in the capacity and speed of the railroad freight system included heavier rail, heavier locomotives and cars, standard gauge, and improved coupling, blocking, braking. A standardized, integrated network, reaching to all the South and West, would emerge in the decade following 1870. The steel rail epoch of American development had begun.

The development of greatly expanded, more specialized agricultural regions and much larger-scale exploitation of Lake Superior ores and timber were imminent. A Northwest Empire was feasible.[24]

THE 1890 MAP

By 1890 the Northwest Empire was on the map (Figure 15). The Upper Midwest banking region was emerging. Within it the population had risen from 700,000 in 1870 to nearly 3 million. Of the 2.2 million increase, immigration accounted for 1.5 million, natural increase for 700,000. Immigrants were equally divided between foreign and United States sources. Sixty percent of the foreign immigrants came from German-language areas of Europe, 20 percent from Scandinavia, the remainder mostly from Ireland, Canada, and Bohemia. More than ever the key to change was transportation. Over the 20-year period, nearly 5 percent of the entire hot-rolled iron and steel production of the United States had been used to lay rail in the hinterland of the Twin Cities.[25]

The Spreading Rail Network

In the part of the region east of the Missouri the railway mileage had grown from about 1,000 to more than 10,000. The railroad map

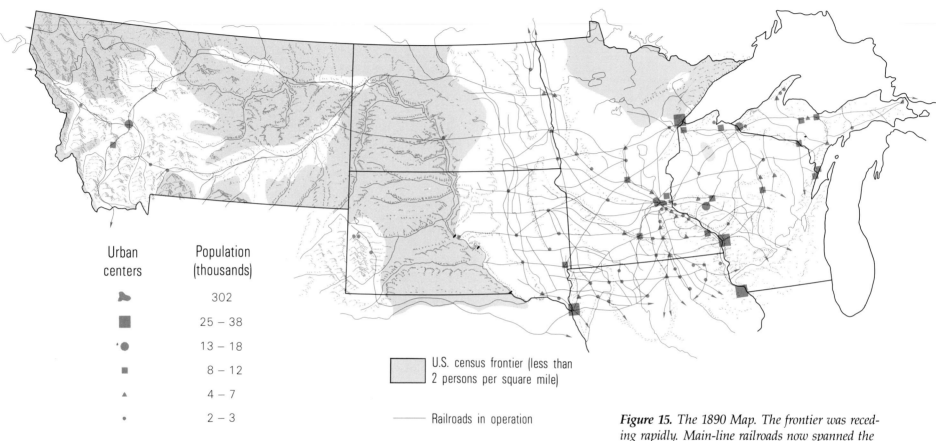

Urban
centers

Population
(thousands)

302

25 – 38

13 – 18

8 – 12

4 – 7

2 – 3

U.S. census frontier (less than
2 persons per square mile)

Railroads in operation

Figure 15. The 1890 Map. The frontier was receding rapidly. Main-line railroads now spanned the entire region, and the branch line network was developing as far west as the Missouri Coteau and north to Lake Superior. Commercial development and urbanization accompanied transportation improvements. The wilderness was beginning to dissolve. Source: note 26.

was shaped by three sets of main lines radiating from St. Paul-Minneapolis, Chicago, and Duluth-Superior. The Twin Cities–Chicago corridor now included six lines. Multiple competing lines formed another corridor from the Twin Cities southward to Des Moines, Omaha, and the midcontinent. Yet another bundle of lines swept west and northwest to Aberdeen, Fargo, the Red River Valley, and Winnipeg. The weakest corridor from the Twin Cities narrowed eastward to Green Bay and Upper Michigan.[26]

Two sets of lines radiating from Chicago and Milwaukee bypassed the Twin Cities on both the eastern and the southern margins of the Upper Midwest. The North Woods lines were extending the accelerating logging campaign into the northern forest all the way to Lake Superior, and they linked Chicago to the ports and mining districts of northern Wisconsin and the Upper Peninsula. The "prairie roads" ran west from Chicago-Milwaukee. They crossed the Iowa and southern Minnesota prairies through LaCrosse, Winona, Mankato, and Mason City to the James Valley in South Dakota. A third, looser radial web, focused on Duluth-Superior, also bypassed the Twin Cities on the north, west, and east. It linked directly with the Red and James valleys, Chicago-Milwaukee, and the Lake Superior mining districts.

Once the main lines were completed, fill-in by branch lines followed quickly. By 1890 the branch lines had already sprouted thickly from the trunks in northern Iowa and southern Minnesota, and they were beginning to sprout in South Dakota. The distance between trunk lines grew wider with increasing distance from the three major centers, like the widening spaces between spokes of a wheel from the hub toward the rim. The branch lines were essential to fill those voids, especially in

One of the last stern-wheelers on the upper Missouri takes on grain from North Dakota's Knife River settlements at the county landing in 1905. Shallow water and sandbars notwithstanding, the river still provided the cheapest way to move freight to the railroad at Bismarck. The storage shed and crude loading chute were minimal improvements; cargo was piled on the dirt bank. Though settled and farmed, this country was still very new. Photo, State Historical Society of North Dakota.

the farming areas, more distant from the Twin Cities and Chicago.

In the northern forest area several local specialized mining and logging networks were tied together by the regional trunk lines. Heavily used tracks connected the mines of five ranges with their lake ports; the Vermilion, Gogebic, and Menominee ranges had been opened since 1870 to join the older Copper and Marquette ranges. Meanwhile, extensive webs of temporary logging railroads kept shifting northward with the camps and crews of loggers.

To the west the northern transcontinentals had crossed the Great Plains and the Rockies. The Northern Pacific (NP) began its operation to Pacific tidewater in 1883. A brochure announced that the Pacific Express, "with Pullman and dining cars attached, leaves St. Paul at 8:00 P.M. every day in the week, running through to Portland without change of cars in 4 days." That was a reduction in travel time of about six weeks compared with the wagon and riverboat days. The railroad advertised land along its line, enough for "2,000,000 families, 10,000,000 souls," at $2.60 to $4.00 per acre. James J. Hill had gained control of the St. Paul and Pacific, extended it to the border near Pembina to connect with the Canadian line to Winnipeg, and built west from Grand Forks. In 1890, as his transcontinental line neared completion, his St. Paul, Minneapolis, and Manitoba system had just been renamed the Great Northern (GN).[27]

The NP and GN had begun to outline a new northern corridor across the western half of the United States. But at the same time other railroads were beginning to delineate the limits of that corridor. The 1890 map showed the first line to serve the Black Hills, and it led eastward to Omaha and Sioux City for connection directly to Chicago and the midcontinent.

In southwestern Montana a Union Pacific line had replaced the wagon and stage road to Utah with a direct rail connection from booming Butte to Salt Lake City, Los Angeles, and San Francisco. The Canadian Pacific had completed its line from Port Arthur-Fort William, on Lake Superior, to Vancouver. That would sharply define the northern edge of the GN-NP corridor along the international boundary.[28]

Dramatic changes in water and road transportation accompanied the explosion of railroad building. River packet traffic declined catastrophically. Slow boats on a few tortuous streams could not compete with the trains for passengers, express, mail, or general cargo. The upper Mississippi waterway had become obsolete except for the movement of logs and lumber. The upper Missouri was also going out of use. But it was being abandoned in discontinuous segments. Fort Benton lost part of its hinterland when the Northern Pacific reached western Montana in the early 1880s and was practically finished as a port when the Great Northern reached the area late in the same decade. Riverboat service from Bismarck 150 miles upstream to lignite diggings and Fort Berthold continued until after the turn of the century when the service was finally displaced by the last railway branch line construction and the beginnings of automobile transportation. Stern-wheelers had plied between Sioux City, Yankton, and Fort Pierre, connecting there with wagons and stages to the Black Hills, until rails reached Chamberlain and Pierre from Chicago in 1880.[29]

Great Lakes packet ships had the same competitive problem. But while the packet business declined, the fleet of specialized bulk carriers grew rapidly. Between 1870 and 1890 annual shipments through the Sault Ste. Marie canal rose from one-half million to 9 million tons. Iron ore accounted for half of the total, westbound coal and eastbound grain for most of the remainder. The quantum increase in Lake Superior grain shipments reflected the growth of long-haul movement by rail to Duluth-Superior. Never before had grain moved overland so far in such large quantity so cheaply. Coal was now moving in great quantity from the Appalachians through Lake Erie ports and the Lakehead for the boilers, blacksmith forges, and stoves of the Upper Midwest.

While these massive changes took place in the arterial transportation network, the supporting system of local roads was changing just as dramatically. More than 100,000 miles of rural dirt roads were added to the grid in the newly settled Minnesota and Dakota prairies, and several thousand more in the new settlements in Montana. More important, there was a great increase in the effectiveness of the dirt road secondary network because of the insertion of thousands of miles of railroad arterials. What had been a very primitive single-mode land transportation system, of wagon roads only, had become a much more sophisticated system of feeders and arterials. The dirt road in front of a farmhouse or country store looked the same as it always had, but it now led to a railroad only a few miles away. With 10 times the average daily speed and 50 times the capacity of a wagon, the train was a link to distant cities, ports, and markets.

Cities, Towns, and Hinterlands

With increasing intensity of transportation and exchange came a faster rate of urbanization. The region's nonfarm population rose 300 percent, or about 1.0 million, in 20 years, while the farm population rose only 150 percent, or about 1.2 million. Natural increase on the farms was nearly double that in the towns and cities. Thus the surplus farm population was already rising and spilling into the urban places. Of the 1.5 million net migration into the region between 1870 and 1890, half went to newly settled farms, and half filled new urban jobs and households created by the increase in transportation and trade. Total population of the hamlets, towns, and cities now numbered more than 1.2 million (Figure 16).

The urban settlement system had begun to grow not only bigger but also more complex. With more than a quarter-million new farms, spread over more than 100,000 square miles of newly opened land, there was a corresponding appearance of new rural hamlets and small towns. Nearly 2,000 more had joined the 1,000 already on the map in 1870. They sprouted at crossroads and rail stops in the prairie and forest-prairie transition zone. Meanwhile, scores of new logging towns had appeared in the northern forest. The total population of all the hamlets and small towns was more than 300,000.

Only 76 places in the entire region were classed as urban, with populations of 2,000 or more. But they accounted for nearly three-fourths of the nonfarm population and an equal share of the nonfarm growth. Among these larger places, there was a widening spread in size between the largest and the smallest, and an increasing variety in the functions they performed. The 1870 map showed four size classes; the 1890 map, six.

The Twin Cities had surged into a class by themselves, not only in the region but in the entire northern transcontinental corridor. The combined population had reached 300,000. Even Portland, Seattle, and Tacoma each numbered less than 50,000. The city growing around the falls had reached 165,000 in the 1890 census; the city growing around the

One of the last generation of whaleback freighters steams into Lake Superior from St. Louis Bay, Duluth-Superior, in 1920, past the predecessors of today's aerial lift bridge and break-water. One of the fleet of famous Great Lakes passenger liners is visible below the smoke plume, and a bit of central Duluth's impressive, turn-of-the-century facade of dockside warehouses projects above the freighter's bow. McKenzie, Duluth, MN, photo, Minnesota Historical Society.

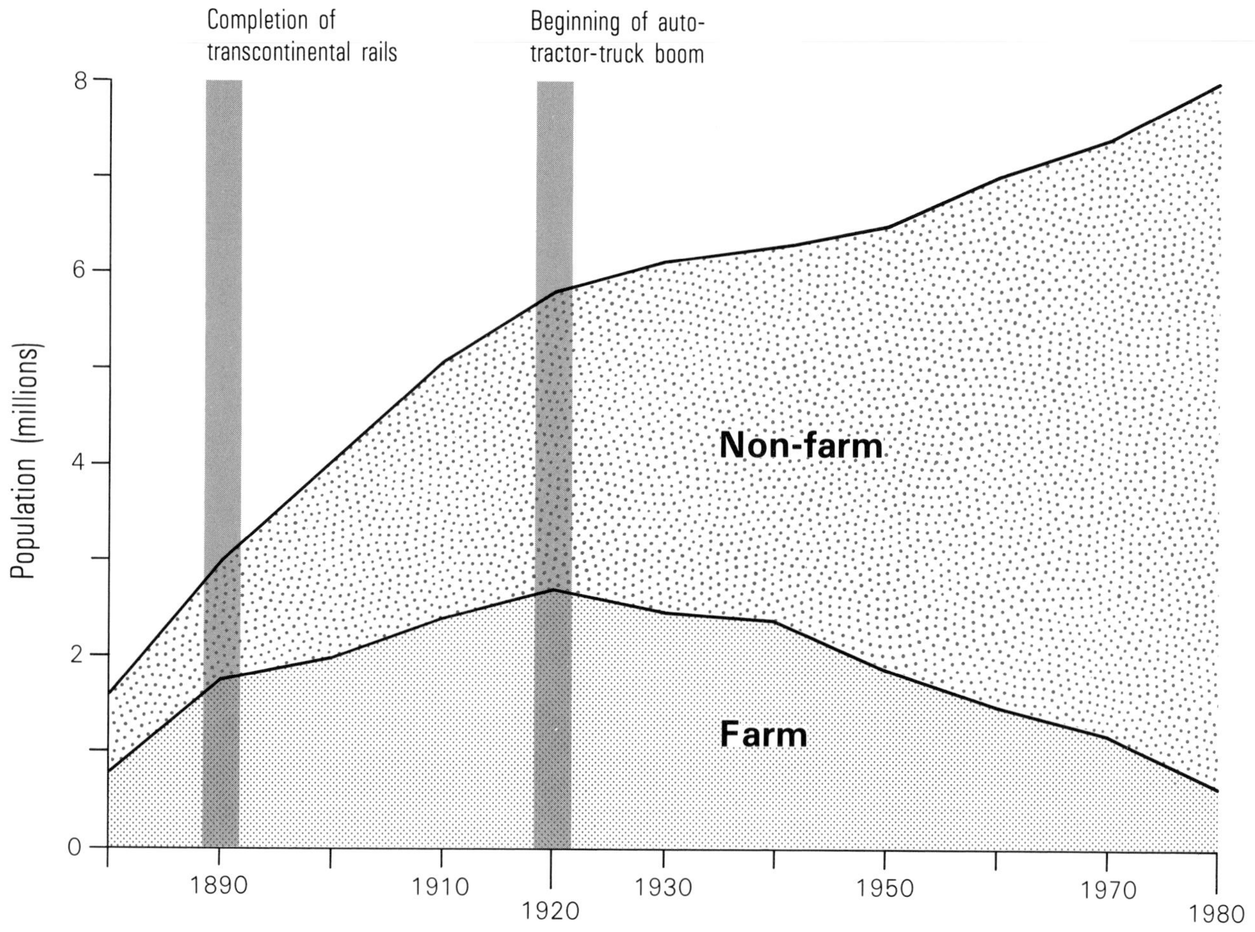

Completion of
transcontinental rails

Beginning of auto-
tractor-truck boom

8

6

Population (millions)

4

Non-farm

2

Farm

0

1890   1910   1930   1950   1970
                1920   1980

Figure 16. Changes in Farm and Nonfarm Populations, 1880-1980. The rate of urbanization increased sharply with the completion of the rail network and accompanying rapid commercialization of farming between 1890 and 1920. Then urban growth took on overwhelming proportions with the closing of the frontier and rapid increase in efficiency of mechanized farming after 1920. Source: note 17.

steamboat landing, 133,000. In the fall of that year, the two were raging at each other through press and public meetings over alleged frauds in the new head count. Each was concerned, from a different point of view, about the widening population gap since Minneapolis had pulled ahead of St. Paul in 1880. But such conflicts were hardly more than a diversion from the basic activity of the place. Immigrants arrived on the trains from Chicago at the rate of a few hundred to a few thousand per week. Many remained in the cities. More went through to the open farmlands in western Minnesota and beyond. From Pullman palace cars on the same trains came financiers, sales agents, and the families of St. Paul and Minneapolis elite returning from Eastern business and shopping trips. Railroading was entering its greatest boom period. Sawmilling was at its peak. Since 1885 Minneapolis had been the largest flour-milling center and primary wheat market in the country. Minneapolis-controlled lines of country elevators followed the rails to the Rockies and into Canada. Together with the big hardware and grocery wholesalers, chain bankers, and new brokerage firms, they were lacing together the region.

Below the Twin Cities level were two centers in the 25,000–38,000 size class. La-Crosse was a major center downstream on the Mississippi. Its growth had slowed. River traffic was moribund, and the agricultural hinterland was limited by the growth of new, competing centers farther west. In contrast, Duluth had been booming. A surge of Eastern capital had been pumped into the building of warehouses, grain elevators, sawmills, foundries, and business blocks. The notion was that something like another Chicago would grow at this new transcontinental transshipment point in the heart of the continent. The grain traffic was indeed materializing. The building boom, itself, provided strong support to the sawmills. Hardware wholesalers were managing to compete with Twin Cities firms in the western hinterlands. However, the weakening position of general cargo packet ships against rail competition through the Twin Cities was raising some doubt about the analogy to Chicago. So was the opening of the Canadian transcontinental railroad and a competing port at the Canadian Lakehead beside Thunder Bay. But that would be offset within two years by the opening of the fabulous Mesabi Iron Range.

Two cities in the same size class as Duluth lay just south of the region. Dubuque, like LaCrosse, had passed its heyday as a port on the upper Mississippi. But, across Iowa, Sioux City was booming. As a busy node in the prairie railroad lines from Chicago, it was competing with Omaha in the newly developed markets of the James Valley and the Black Hills.

Two cities in the region were in the 13,000–18,000 size class. One, Eau Claire, had become the principal industrial and railroad center at the rapids of the Chippewa in Wisconsin. The other, Helena, with the state capitol and a legacy of smelting and wholesale merchandising for the gold fields, was still the largest city in Montana. Sixteen large shopping and service centers were in the 8,000–12,000 population range. Their locations reflected the advantages of a natural resource concentration, or an early start, or both. Eight were iron-mining centers and Great Lakes ports shipping either ore or timber and receiving coal. Four more were at waterpower sites—Wausau, Chippewa Falls, St. Cloud, and Sioux Falls. St. Cloud had an additional early advantage as the railhead and staging

point on the Twin Cities–Winnipeg route. Sioux Falls, though laid out as a waterpower industrial town by Dubuque promoters in the 1850s, had the problem of unreliable flow of the Sioux River in the subhumid prairie climate. Then it had drawn only branch railroads and was growing in the shadow of Sioux City. Stillwater and Winona were continuing as thriving centers of sawmilling and timber transportation on the rivers. Winona had an added role as grain miller and shipper for the prairies to the west. And Mankato, from its early start in the days of Minnesota River steamboating, had consolidated its commercial position where the main Twin Cities–Sioux City rail line intersected one of the main Chicago–James Valley lines.

Fifty-four cities were medium and small shopping and service centers, in the 2,000–7,000 population range. They had not yet reached the size of the 22 select, larger cities; and most of them never would. But all had grown enough to stand out from the vast seedbed of hamlets and small towns scattered along the region's transportation arteries. Nearly all of these urban places were county seats, and that initial boost meant the presence of the land records, sheriff, jail, judges, and accompanying cadre of professional people and local press. But that was not always enough because most of the region's county seats were too small to be urban places.

Seven distinctly different factors, working singly or in many different combinations, had caused these 54 cities to move out from the crowd.

1. Cities prospered at the intersection of rail lines of two different regional grids: Twin Cities and Chicago or Twin Cities and Duluth. For commercial travelers and distributors, towns at those intersections had the advantage of direct access to different competing major wholesale centers. A few important examples from the large roster of places with that kind of location include Albert Lea, Mankato, Willmar, and Austin, Minnesota; Mason City and Sheldon, Iowa; and most of the centers in the James Valley.

2. A waterpower site provided an initial advantage, even if its practical value was giving way to steam or electricity by the 1890s. Examples include Cloquet and Fergus Falls, Minnesota; Rhinelander, Menomonie, and River Falls, Wisconsin; and the Cedar Valley towns in Iowa.

3. Selection of locations for state institutions boosted local basic employment and a resident professional community. Examples are the capitals at Pierre and Bismarck; the colleges at Vermillion, Brookings, and Rapid City, South Dakota, at Grand Forks and Fargo, North Dakota, and at River Falls and Menomonie, Wisconsin.

4. Important mineral deposits meant the powerful advantage of discovery and, of course, the hopeless disadvantage of depletion. But discovery stimulated the growth of many urban places. Examples in 1890 were already extremely varied. For instance, some of the Copper Range towns were declining while Butte's Anaconda mines and Lead's Homestake were booming.

5. Ports such as Manistique, Michigan, and Washburn, Wisconsin, served the booming logging industry in the northern forest region.

6. Development thrived in centers of large, tightly knit religious and ethnic communities such as the Norwegian concentration around Decorah, Iowa, and the German neighborhood of New Ulm, Minnesota.

7. Also significant in some communities'

Settlers hauling buffalo bones to the railroad siding through downtown Minot, North Dakota, 1883. Photo, State Historical Society of North Dakota.

growth was the experienced selection of a townsite with amenities of woods, water, and hills, and an initial thrust of capital and entrepreneurship, exemplified by Alexandria, Minnesota, and Watertown, South Dakota. Of all the factors, this one was perhaps the most important in the long run and the least tangible.

The same locational advantages, with different degrees of intensity and different chance combinations, accounted for the emergence of every urban center in the region. With urbanization under way, differential city growth and concentration of growth at larger cities were also under way. Boom, slowdown, decline, and instability had become part of the scene. Causes and effects of these variations in growth were already becoming complex, evolving, idiosyncratic. Each class of places, whether based on size or function, already contained many cities that were only temporarily in that class. Some cities were passing through a particular class on the way up, others on the way down—each for its own reasons. Meanwhile, the classes, themselves, were changing as the system was growing and changing. Many people were developing stakes in the security and future of these young cities. They included not only influential entrepreneurs and professionals but also small-home owners, clerks, and technicians. In even two short decades the complex causes and fickle results of growth had begun to unfold. The process was fascinating and frustrating to the boosters, leaders, and many others—not only in Minneapolis and St. Paul but also in the whole array of smaller urban centers.

Dissolving the Wilderness

The vast areas of northern forest wilderness and western Indian lands on the 1870 map were virtually dissolved 20 years later. The United States census defined the frontier as the line of two persons per square mile, average county density. In the northern forest zone, only far northeastern Minnesota still lay beyond that line in 1890. Elsewhere feverish logging and mining expansion had carried the frontier as far north as it could go in the United States. Even in the Minnesota Arrowhead Region a gold rush had come and gone, and iron mining had begun on the Vermilion Range.[30]

In the West railroad construction had led the prairie farming frontier out to the Souris and Missouri, though it had slowed down on the higher parts of the coteau east of Minot and Bismarck. Disagreement persisted among the Sioux over the status of the Black Hills. Nevertheless, white settlement already dominated the area. The separate frontiers of the western Montana valleys had merged and expanded. On the 1890 map, corridors of settlement bulged north past Great Falls to the Marias, east to the Judith Basin, the Musselshell, and far down the Yellowstone. A long corridor of white settlement followed the Great Northern High Line up the Missouri and the Milk between Williston and Havre.

The Indians were mostly subdued. Farms and ranches were beginning to operate around the Little Big Horn battlefield, the Bear Paws, and Slim Buttes, where soldiers, warriors, and Indian women and children had been killed in massacres in the 1870s. Within the vast areas of Indian land on the 1870 map, the tribes had mostly clustered around government agencies near the Turtle Mountains, Devils Lake, along the Missouri, north of the Big Horns, and on the Pine Ridge east of the Black Hills. On the Pine Ridge the last of the massacres occurred in 1890 at Wounded Knee. The division of lands was still not settled, but today's reservations were beginning to take shape.[31]

Meanwhile, on the same 1870 Indian lands, the buffalo were nearly extinct by 1890. In recent memory, herds of thousands had delayed riverboats on the Fort Benton runs and awed the adventurers on wagon trains from St. Paul to the gold fields. The herds had been slaughtered for robes and sport. But there was no practically accessible market for most of the meat. Virtually all of the carcasses had been left to rot and the bones to bleach. In the 1880s agents along the new transcontinental railroads had a market for the bones. Rendering plants back East reduced them to carbon black and fertilizer. The same industry had taken the bones from the central Great Plains during the construction of the Union Pacific and the Santa Fe, and it was turning to the north. The agents would buy the bones for cash or take them in trade for supplies. In response, settlers, Indians, and mixed-bloods alike fanned out on the prairie to gather the remains by the wagonload and haul them to the sidetracks. Millions of tons were shipped out on the Northern Pacific and Great Northern, mainly to St. Louis and down the Great Lakes to Detroit. By the early 1890s the supply was depleted. The cleanup of the northern Great Plains was finished.[32]

CHAPTER 3

Mature Settlement System

By 1920 railroad expansion had opened all the land the United States needed, and more (Figure 17). In the Upper Midwest what remained was clearly too dry or rough for any kind of agriculture except the most extensive grazing of sparse, natural grass range; or it was too infertile or wet or stony for all crops except trees. In the western part of the region, the population density line of two persons per square mile now enclosed only the driest parts of Montana—the Powder River and Little Missouri country, northwest of the Black Hills; the Jordan country, northwest of Miles City; and the Missouri River country from the Milk to the Bear Paws. On the north, the line enclosed only the Big Bog and the future Voyageurs National Park and Boundary Waters Canoe Area. Indeed, at the urging of Minnesotans, President Theodore Roosevelt had established the Superior National Forest in that area in 1909. In the mid-1880s Roosevelt had ranched where the then two-year-old Northern Pacific Railroad traversed the Little Missouri Badlands. He had occupied his cabin at Chimney Butte when the Census Bureau frontier line was drawn at the Missouri River. It was only a quarter-century later when he moved to conserve one of the last remaining empty parts of the region and the Census Bureau had discarded the term "frontier."[33]

The Mature Rail Network

Between 1890 and 1920 the Milwaukee Road and the Soo Line augmented the Great Northern and Northern Pacific in the northern transcontinental corridor. James J. Hill had consolidated control of not only the GN and NP but also the Burlington, with a main line between the Twin Cities and Chicago. In reaction, the Milwaukee Railroad had made its disastrously costly decision to build its own line to the Puget Sound. The engineers virtually laid a ruler on the map from the road's major junction at Aberdeen, on South Dakota's James River plain, to Miles City, Montana, on the Yellowstone. From there they built westward up the Yellowstone and over the dry upland to the Musselshell. They pieced together local lines in west-central Montana and paralleled the Northern Pacific from Three Forks nearly to Idaho.

Earlier, the Canadian Pacific (CP) had taken control of the road from Minneapolis to Sault Ste. Marie and of another Minneapolis rail-building venture which had crossed southern North Dakota to Bismarck. The systems were consolidated to form the Soo Line. The Soo engineers drew another straight line, avoiding the Missouri Coteau, from southeastern North Dakota to the CP's major division point at Moose Jaw, Saskatchewan. That completed the initial Canadian-controlled all-rail route between eastern and western Canada, through Minneapolis.

Meanwhile, lines of competing systems nibbled at the southern margins of the corridor. Two of the lines between Chicago and the James Valley had been pushed westward across the Missouri to the Black Hills. New routes had reached Billings from Denver and also from Chicago through Omaha.

Until about 1910, branch lines continued to fill the voids between the trunks. The established branch line network, in the fertile prairie-drift plains, from Iowa to the eastern Dakotas, became still more densely developed. Such growth made it possible to fill the remaining open land with farm settlement in those areas. West of the James and Red River valleys, the dense web of branches had been

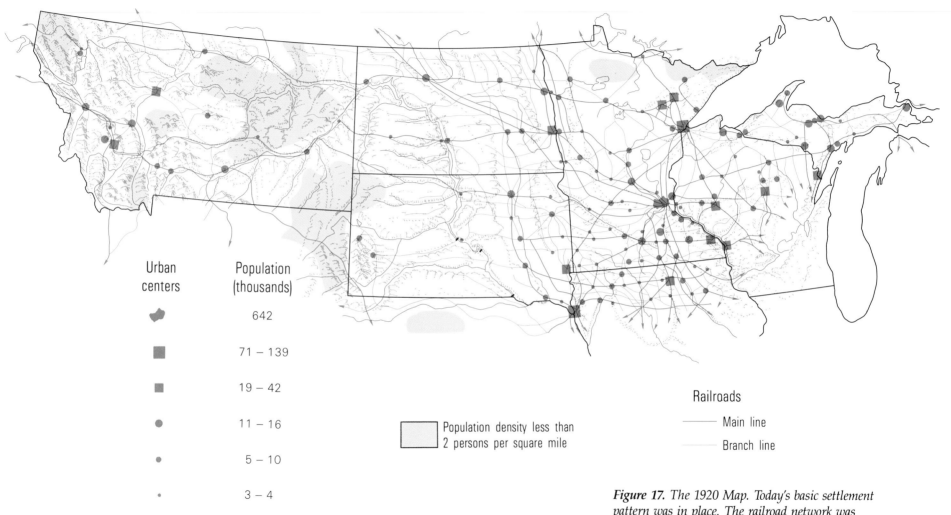

Urban
centers

Population
(thousands)

642

71 – 139

19 – 42

11 – 16

5 – 10

3 – 4

Population density less than
2 persons per square mile

Railroads

———— Main line

———— Branch line

Figure 17. The 1920 Map. Today's basic settlement
pattern was in place. The railroad network was
complete. Branch lines had reached and passed
their economic limits in the semiarid plains, and
the region's rail mileage was at its peak. Source:
Rand McNally Commercial Atlas (Chicago:
Rand McNally and Company, 1927).

extended beyond the Missouri and north to the Canadian border. A distinctive, needlessly dense lattice had developed across northern North Dakota. It was the legacy of James J. Hill's counterattack on the Soo Line's invasion of that part of his empire around the turn of the century.[34] In Montana, a few twentieth-century spurs pricked the edges of the country between the High Line and the international boundary, between the Yellowstone and the Missouri, and in the Triangle.

In northern Minnesota, lines from Duluth and the Twin Cities cut through the forest to cross the Rainy just east of International Falls and to join the Canadian transcontinental corridor. On the Mesabi Range, where no tracks and no mines existed in 1890, a dense network had spread in 1920. It moved more than 75 percent of America's iron-ore production, more than 30 percent of all the iron ore produced in the world. The Mesabi lines were steel rail symbols of the steel rail epoch in American development.

In fact, in 1920, transportation both in the region and in the whole country was almost totally dominated by the rail system. The system was nationwide. Its equipment and operations were standardized. It carried 76 percent of the total ton-miles of freight moved in the United States, compared with about 40 percent today. Other than the railroads, the most important arterial routes were on the Great Lakes. The practical, awesome fleet of bulk cargo ships carried iron ore, coal, grain, and a very limited amount of packgage freight. Their bulk cargo accounted for 13 percent of the country's total ton-miles, and half of it originated or terminated in the Upper Midwest. The rivers moved 5 percent of the total ton-miles. Their cargo was mostly coal, some oil. Almost all of it moved on the Ohio and lower Mississippi, virtually none in the Upper Mid-

Another town on the Great Plains was beginning at Hettinger, southwestern North Dakota, in 1908 — one of more than 2,000 places added to the map of the region between 1870 and 1920. The Milwaukee Road's new line west from Aberdeen, South Dakota, reached to the horizon. Families worked from tents or open-air camps to assemble their animals and load their meager goods into buckboards and box wagons for the trek to a parcel of land on the frontier. With virtually no social organization or physical structures, they faced the task of building everything. Photo, State Historical Society of North Dakota.

ABERDEEN THE METROPOLIS SEEN FROM THE WEST OVER THE TOPS OF 1200 OX CARS IN C M & ST, P FREIGHT YARDS COPYRIGHTED PHOTO BY N A BROTHERS

In 1915, seven years after the settlers were unloading at Hettinger, the Milwaukee Road yards at Aberdeen were clogged at harvesttime with trainloads of grain from the new farms to the west. Smoke poured into the autumn air from two dozen locomotives and the chimneys of the new metropolis of the James Valley. N. A. Brothers, photo, South Dakota State Historical Society.

west. Pipelines moved another 5 percent. But, again, virtually none of that movement was in the Upper Midwest. Wagons and a few trailblazing truckers hauled the remaining one percent—much of it to and from the railways—on the country roads and city streets.[35]

In the Upper Midwest the railroads collected the region's widely dispersed production of commodities. They hauled grain, livestock, cream, and eggs to central markets from thousands of elevators, cattle pens, and creameries on sidetracks in the agricultural areas. They moved trainloads of logs from forest sidings to lumber, pulp, and paper mills in the forest areas. They carried trainloads of iron ore to the docks on Lake Superior and at Escanaba and to the blast furnaces at Duluth. They moved ore concentrate to the smelters at Anaconda, Helena, and Great Falls. The railroads also transported nearly all the products of the region's industrial plants to the major urban markets of the Midwest and Northeast. Lumber, flour, and meat moved by the trainload. Butter, paper, and the output from the small but growing, diversified industries of machinery, clothing, and furniture moved out by the carload.

Meanwhile the railroads accounted for virtually the entire flow of goods into the Upper Midwest distribution system. Main lines from Chicago and Milwaukee brought goods from the American Manufacturing Belt to Upper Midwest warehouses and mail-order houses. Local dray lines delivered the goods to stores and homes. Railroads also brought the supply of bulk commodities to the towns and cities. The main items were building material and coal. Lumber came from the sawmills of the North Woods, the Rockies, and the Black Hills. Brick and tile came from Mason City and lower Midwest kilns. Cement came from Mason City's limestone quarries and mill or from the slag byproduct plant at Duluth's steel mill. High-quality Appalachian coal moved inland from the docks at Duluth-Superior, Green Bay, Ashland, and Escanaba. Some lignite came from local mines in North Dakota and soft coal from mines in Montana. The markets were mainly home furnaces or stoves and boilers in commercial buildings, factories, and creameries. Coal and lumber yards were ubiquitous. They lined the sidetracks in every town, beside the elevators, stock-loading pens, creameries, and freight sheds. The railroads not only held the region together and, for most purposes, linked it to the rest of the country, but also delivered all of the material to build and maintain the settlements.

By today's standards the system was simple, stable, hierarchical, and slow. Goods passed through many hands as they moved up or down the size-rank order of urban nodes in the network. Freight trains averaged 10 to 20 miles per hour; mail trains, 15 to 25. The fastest passenger runs in the Upper Midwest averaged less than 40. Wagons averaged 3 to 5 miles an hour. The system was labor-intensive: at every point were many people lifting, carrying, shoveling, pushing, shouting. But, obviously, it worked, in its way. In fact, for some reason, no doubt complex, this system delivered goods with a smaller percentage of wholesale overhead on retail sales than we pay today.

Completion of Population Growth and Expansion

The region's initial population boom persisted from 1890 to 1920. The total number in today's banking region grew from 3 million to 5.8 million. But trends were changing. Farm population grew 900,000, while nonfarm growth was 2 million. The farm population increase slowed as the frontier pushed onto marginal lands. Net migration off the farms was under way. One-third of a million shifted to town in the three decades. Meanwhile, improved railroad trunk lines and more branch lines encouraged more and faster commercial exchange, more production, more real income, more savings, more construction, more employment, and more urban people. The mix of immigrants and homegrown population was beginning to change noticeably. Net migration from outside the region dropped from 1.5 million between 1870 and 1890 to 900,000 between 1890 and 1920. At the same time, natural increase changed from 700,000 to 2 million. A growing share of the Americans originated in the Midwest, while more of the Europeans came from the Slavic-language countries and Italy (Figure 18).[36]

Thus, by 1920 the half-century of great immigration and population growth was coming to a close. While the transportation network had expanded and the frontier had dissolved, the number of people in the region had grown from 500,000 to nearly 6 million. Net migration accounted for half of the gain. But more movement actually took place than that number showed. Perhaps 4 million had come in, and a million had moved out. Most went on to the Pacific Northwest or joined the stream of more than one million Americans who moved to the Canadian Prairies. Some returned to their origins farther east. For perhaps a fourth of the immigrants the Upper Midwest was a revolving door.

The region's modern settlement framework was completed, too (Figure 19). Farms, ranches, logging, and mines provided the setting for cities, towns, rural hamlets, and a regional metropolis. Except for suburbs few places have been added since then, and surprisingly few have been subtracted. The broad, basic pattern of today's Upper Midwest was in place by 1920.

Rural development differed vividly from place to place. The main farming corridor had grown from western Wisconsin and northern Iowa to northern Montana. Within the corridor, two factors had produced a wide range of average farm size and density of farmsteads. One was the time of settlement. The smallest, most closely spaced farms were settled earliest. They were in the forest-to-prairie transition zone from western Wisconsin to northeastern Iowa and central Minnesota. Pioneers in those areas had, on the average, less free land, less capital, less machinery, and less mobility than those who came later and went farther west. Hence they started with smaller farms. A second factor was drought. In general, the farther west the settlement was, the greater the drought risk. Average yields were lower, and a farmer needed more land to make a living. But it is important to remember that, by historical chance, the drier lands were also settled later. By the time they were occupied, farmers had more opportunity to have the machinery needed to operate a large farm. As a result, average farm sizes were larger in the west, but later experience would show that they were still far from large enough to meet the demands of the evolving technology and economy.[37]

The famous bonanza farms of the Red River Valley were among the earliest large-scale, mechanized operations in the world. During the railroad's financial crisis in the 1870s, several Eastern investors had traded their Northern Pacific bonds for large tracts of the company's government land grant. They decided to break the prairie and establish farm units each of which would operate tens of thousands of acres. Each unit used a fleet of steam tractors, hundreds of horses, and scores

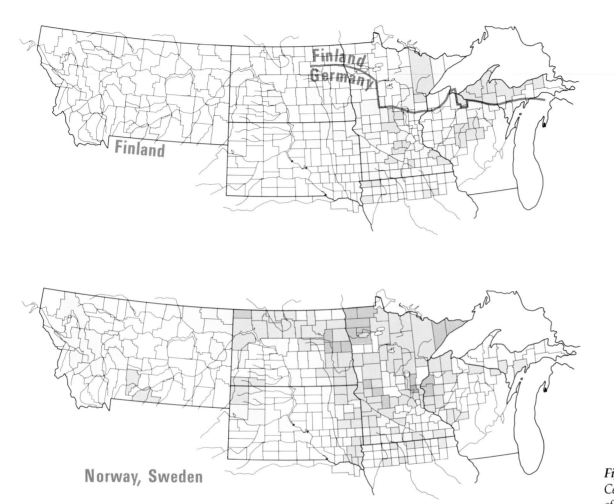

Percentage of
county population

30
20
10
5

Figure 18. National Origin of Foreign Born, 1910
Census. (2 pages) After 1890, increasing numbers
of immigrants from Italy and the Slavic-language
areas augmented the larger numbers who arrived
from northwestern Europe over a longer period of
time. Source: U.S. Census of Population, 1910.

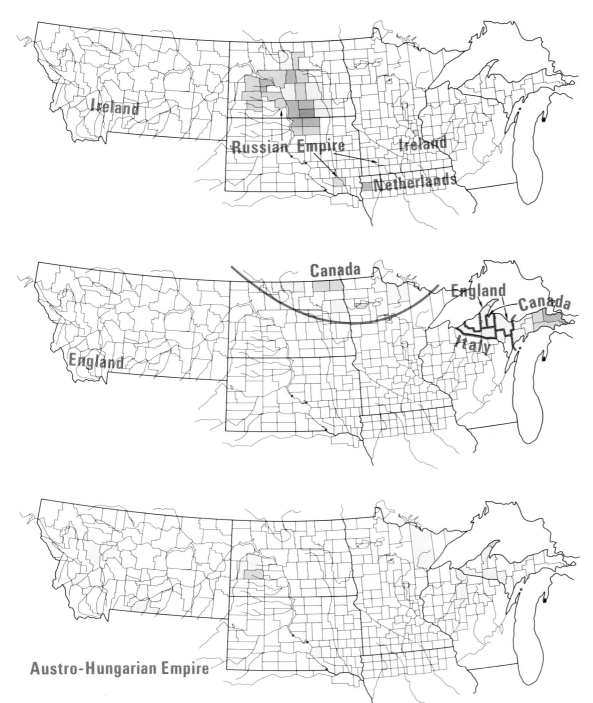

Figure 18, continued.

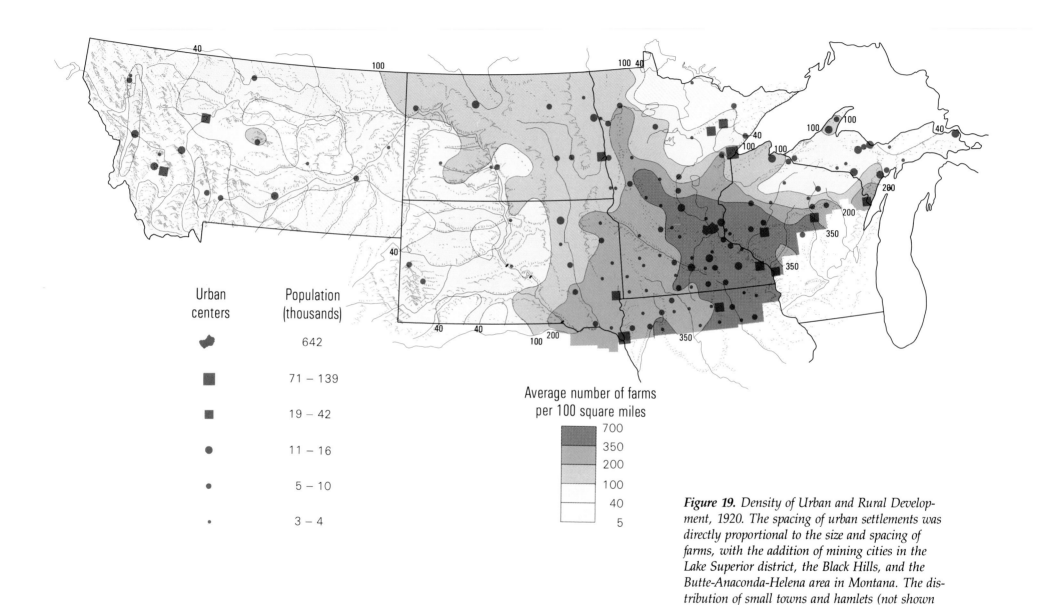

Urban
centers

Population
(thousands)

642

71 – 139

19 – 42

11 – 16

5 – 10

3 – 4

Average number of farms
per 100 square miles

700
350
200
100
40
5

Figure 19. Density of Urban and Rural Development, 1920. The spacing of urban settlements was directly proportional to the size and spacing of farms, with the addition of mining cities in the Lake Superior district, the Black Hills, and the Butte-Anaconda-Helena area in Montana. The distribution of small towns and hamlets (not shown on the map) also followed the pattern of farm size. Sources: U.S. Censuses of Population and Agriculture, 1920.

of plows and planting and harvesting machines. Some operating families supported experimental farms with vigorous programs of research and promotion. The bonanza operations peaked around the turn of the century. As the region developed, they were broken up and sold. As sales went on, average farm size in the area fell into line with neighboring parts of the region. But the episode gave a strong thrust and unique character to Fargo's early commercial, cultural, and civic growth.[38]

The landscapes of rural development also varied with climate and age. Most farmers in 1920 were still general farmers. That is, they grew grain and hay both for sale at the elevator and for feeding livestock on the farm. They raised stock for milk and meat, poultry for eggs and meat. But differences in the mix were notable. The smaller farms in the better-watered eastern areas kept more livestock and raised more corn and oats for both feed and cash. They had more milk and eggs to haul to the local creamery, more hogs to load on the cattle cars at the local rail siding. They were more diversified, their income more stable. Although most farms in the drier areas were also still general farms, they kept fewer livestock and grew more wheat for sale. Greater rainfall fluctuation made feed supplies and pasture less dependable: livestock feeding was more risky.

In the areas settled before 1890, an additional generation favored families in their building, earning, and saving. Farmhouses commonly had wings and porches added to the original basic rectangle. Bigger barns and more outbuildings reflected not only more livestock but also a longer history. Taller shade trees and bigger shelterbelts reflected both more rainfall and a longer history. In the newer areas, settled around 1900 or later, the farmsteads were typically in their first generation of

A dozen neighbors labored together at threshing time on this farmstead on the southern Minnesota prairie in 1917. The house with its additions, the shelterbelt, and the array of outbuildings represent a generation of work, saving, and investment. Corn had not yet replaced wheat and oats as the major grain crop; soybeans were unthinkable. Photo, Minnesota Historical Society.

A farm clearing followed the logging frontier near the Canadian border south of International Falls, Minnesota, in 1919. The pioneer family's home is partly hidden by the pile of stumps and tall weeds in the foreground. Photo, Minnesota Historical Society.

occupance. A basic frame house had replaced the original sod shanty, but only infrequently had time or money permitted the addition of a wing. Barns and outbuildings were fewer, vegetation much more sparse, surfaces dustier. Again, these things reflected not only the drier climate but also the shorter history. The irrigated strips along the Yellowstone and Milk were a distinctive combination of the younger west and the better-watered east. In the Western Montana Valleys, the rural landscapes were a unique four-way mix of newer and older, drier and better-watered. Because immigration was so recent, so large, and so geographically differentiated, ethnic variations were profound from one district to another. There were the unmistakably distinct country churches, stubborn differences in livestock and field practices, and varied details in the architecture of many houses and barns. Yet, those were mostly second-order variations on the overriding gradients of age and rainfall. Meanwhile, the universals were horses, wagons, dirt roads, privies, and windmills.

Outside the main farming corridor, no county averaged more than one farmstead in one or two square miles—in some counties only one in 20 square miles. In the western cattle country, the wide spacing reflected the very large size of the operating units and also the tracts of remaining public domain mixed among the private holdings. Most of the settlement was in the first generation of occupance. Low, rambling, frame or log houses were commonly set in sparsely wooded draws or coulees, next to a spring or stream, sheltered below the windswept plains. Corrals and sheds were nearby, with a bottomland patch of alfalfa as large as available water could irrigate. Mowed wild-hay land followed the winding bottoms wherever the soil remained moist through at least part of the summer.

In the forest country, the density of farmsteads was low, not because the farms units were large, but because so much of the land was not used for farming. In 1920 the forest in the mountain regions was mostly undisturbed except for the cleared slopes above the mining camps and along the routes of railroad construction. But the northern forests of Michigan, Wisconsin, and Minnesota were at the nadir of the notorious cutover stage of their history. Miles of stumps, slash, seedlings, brush, and burn surrounded remaining islands of virgin pine on the Indian reservations and other islands of bypassed hardwoods. Farm clearings, while clustered in only a few small districts, were more numerous and prominent than ever before—or since. Typically a small frame house or log cabin, with a small barn or a shed or two, stood between the dirt road and 20 or 30 acres of pastures and furrows plowed in ash-gray, acidic soil. Beyond that, windrows of smoldering stumps and heaps of boulders marked the zone of struggle between the farmer's commitment to crops and nature's commitment to forest. Farther in the background, a few cows might be visible among the stumps, or their bells might be audible through the brush. The deepest penetrations of the northern cutover followed the Lake Superior–Chicago and Twin Cities–Duluth rail lines, with lesser corridors along the train routes from the Twin Cities to Ashland, International Falls, and Lake of the Woods.

Altogether more than half a million farms and ranches spread across the region in 1920. In the forest-to-prairie transition zone, from western Wisconsin to central Minnesota, the northern Dairy Belt had emerged in the economic geography of the United States. The northern Corn Belt had taken shape on the prairie–glacial drift plains from northern Iowa to west-central Minnesota and the eastern base of the Missouri Coteau in South Dakota. And the American Hard Spring Wheat Belt was now established from the Red and James valleys across northern Montana.

The Mature System of Commercial Centers

More than 3,000 trade centers were seeded among the region's half-million farms, ranches, mines, and logging camps. The centers ranged in size from Minneapolis-St. Paul to the crossroads general stores and post offices. Nearly 3,000 were hamlets and small towns, with less than the 2,500-minimum population needed to be called an urban place by the census. Hundreds of them had only a few score inhabitants. Others, especially county seats, were larger. It was still the age of small towns. Their share of the total regional population rose from 17 percent in 1890 to 20 percent in 1920. Farm numbers had grown because remaining land had been occupied both at the frontier and in the older areas. Farm income had grown with increased trade and commercialization; but continued reliance on dirt roads, wagons, and buggies sustained the multitude of tightly constrained local farm trade areas. Sinclair Lewis's Gopher Prairie was in the heyday of its stability and functional importance.

While the wagon and buggy preserved and even strengthened the small towns, the mature rail net nourished the regional metropolis. Metropolitan Minneapolis and St. Paul had reached a population of nearly 670,000. Their share of Upper Midwest population rose from 7 percent to 11 percent. They accounted for 31 percent of the nonfarm growth in the entire region in the three decades before 1920. The Twin Cities were now one of the nation's 10 leading rail centers. They were the northwest anchor of the nation's primary rail corridor between the Middle Atlantic Seaboard and the Midwest. Minneapolis was still the world's leading flour-milling center. Trade marks of Pillsbury, Gold Medal, King Midas, and Occident did give the place a clear national image.[39]

A remarkable corridor of rail yards and diverse warehousing and manufacturing extended nearly 20 miles from the north edge of Minneapolis through the two downtowns to South St. Paul. The downtowns were home to banks, department stores, brokers, clinics, advertising agencies, and legal, architectural, and engineering firms that served the region. One of the nation's model streetcar systems radiated from the downtowns and extended the cities across 100 square miles of glacial moraine-and-lake terrain. The industrial-trackage belt held two-thirds of all the manufacturing jobs in the entire Upper Midwest. Of course, it contained the flour mills, terminal elevators, stockyards, packing plants, and railway yards and shops. But it was also a vast entrepreneurial seedbed. Small firms served the regional market for farm supplies and equipment, country stores, and the giant milling industry. They spawned a constant stream of ideas, new products, experiments, successes, expansions, moves, and failures. They were manufacturing in diverse fields for not only the regional but also the national market. They made household heating and plumbing equipment, some of the earliest commercial refrigerators and light bulbs, generators and motors; paint, pumps, steam tractors and threshers; garments and shoes; printing presses, books, magazines, office forms, calendars, playing cards; pioneer brands of mouthwash and shaving cream.

The Twin Cities were the focus of railway

Dominated by 12-story monuments to the railroads, newspaper, bank, medical services, and hospitality, an urban skyline had grown above the historic riverboat landing at St. Paul by 1915. C. P. Gibson, photo, Minnesota Historical Society.

Another downtown skyline had arisen in the steel rail era just west of the tall bank of flour mills and elevators at St. Anthony Falls. The major Minneapolis landmarks in 1910 were the city hall tower, the grain exchanges, banks, and insurance offices. Photo, Minnesota Historical Society.

freight, mail, express, and passenger traffic along the northern transcontinental corridor. They were also a powerful competitor of Chicago across northern Iowa and eastern South Dakota. That position was reflected in the strings of mail cars that rolled in and out of the St. Paul and Minneapolis terminals day and night (Figure 20). Beside mountains of mail bags were bundles of newspapers that brought a metropolitan version of the world to the region. Perhaps 400,000 papers each week moved out as a torrent on the main lines and finally trickled down scores of branch lines to distant county seats.[40]

The postal terminals were the equivalent of today's long-distance phone-switching centers. The mail trains played the role of today's telephone long-lines and satellites. Virtually all intercity business communication moved by mail. Long-distance phone ties were negligible by today's standards, and telegraphic messages were confirmed by mail. Capacity of the mail routes was a good indicator of the flow. The amount of space the Post Office Department leased on the trains reflected the amount of mail that had to be moved. And the amount of business mail was probably proportional to the total of all mail. In general, the more people who lived in a place, the more business they conducted.

On the map of mail volume, the flow of communication in the region resembled the gathering of waters in a river basin (Figure 21). You can feel the mail streams—the tiny branches, the bigger tributaries, the main arteries—swell as you trace them eastward across the prairies. The Northern Pacific stream widened at Dickinson and again at Fargo. Great Northern streams converged and widened at Havre, and the main stream east from there widened again at Minot. The two mail streams from Canada on the Soo Line wi-

A Great Northern train pulls alongside the station at Tagus, North Dakota, for a flag stop in 1910. Dogs bark, and travelers from varied walks of life prepare to board. With broom and shovel at rest, the coal and lumber wagon doubles as the local mail shuttle between the depot and the town's tiny post office. In the background, the open prairie reaches from the far edge of the station platform to the distant horizon. Photo, State Historical Society of North Dakota.

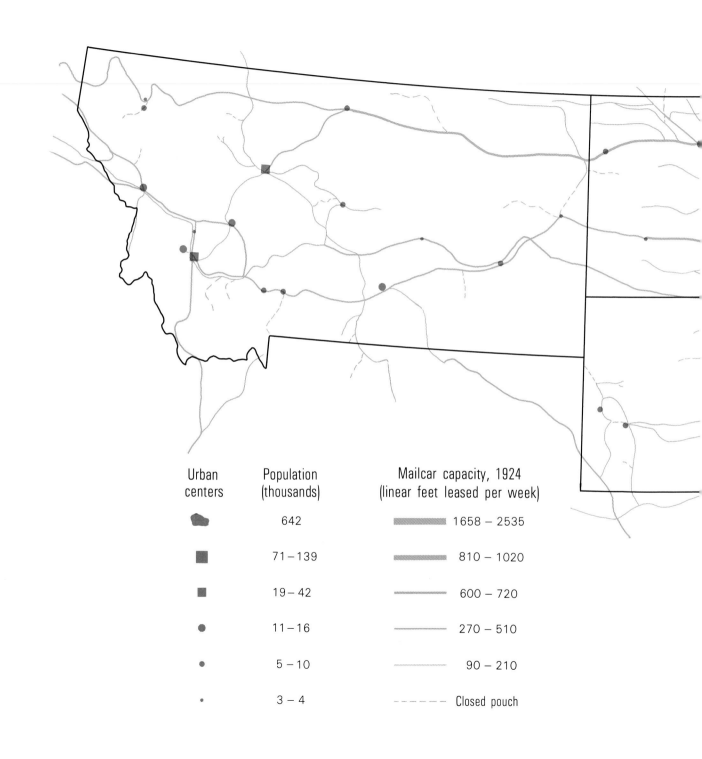

Urban
centers

Population
(thousands)

Mailcar capacity, 1924
(linear feet leased per week)

642

71 – 139

19 – 42

11 – 16

5 – 10

3 – 4

1658 – 2535

810 – 1020

600 – 720

270 – 510

90 – 210

Closed pouch

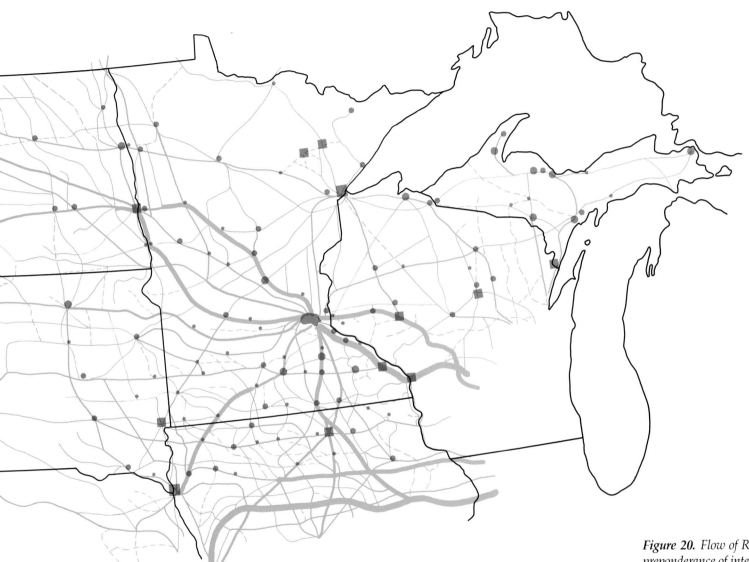

Figure 20. *Flow of Railway Mail, 1924. The great preponderance of intercity communication moved by railway mail. The Twin Cities were the main focus along the northern transcontinental corridor and a powerful competitor of Chicago across northern Iowa and eastern South Dakota. Source: note 40.*

Train service to and from Tagus and the rest of the region's 3,000 hamlets, towns, and cities was focused at the Twin Cities terminals. Largest was the St. Paul Union Depot. Downtown office buildings loom to the right of the cloud bank of smoke and steam on this early morning in 1925. St. Paul Daily News, *credit, Minnesota Historical Society.*

dened where branch lines joined them south of the border, at Kenmare and Thief River Falls, and widened again where the Vancouver and Winnipeg lines merged at Glenwood, Minnesota. And there were watersheds. In western Montana the main transcontinental streams widened westward toward Spokane, Portland, and Seattle-Tacoma. In Iowa and Wisconsin divides ran between the Twin Cities and Omaha or Chicago-Milwaukee.

However, there were two very important differences between the mail streams and a river system. First, the flow of mail was two-way: both from and to the tributary areas. The circulation system served an interacting community, not an assembly line. Second, the transportation divides were fuzzy, the watersheds overlapping. The probabilities and the averages favored the flow patterns and divides that appear on the map (Figure 21). At the same time, every place was to some extent independently connected to every place else. The system was open.

Within that open system, the flow of mail indicated that perhaps 55 percent of the Minneapolis–St. Paul basic economy depended on business with the rest of the region. The other 45 percent depended on business with the rest of the United States and the rest of the world. Of all the business done in the region, perhaps 60 percent represented exchange within the local communities. One-tenth was transacted with the Twin Cities, the remainder with a multitude of centers elsewhere in the country. The Twin Cities metropolis was indeed the region's largest city and largest commercial focus. Yet it was not the center of a regional command. It was competing in a pluralistic system of routes and nodes.

Outside the Twin Cities, the number of urban places had increased from 74 in 1890 to 128 in 1920. Most of the 54 newcomers were either county seats or railroad division points. In large part as a result of the increased number of places, the non–Twin Cities urban centers accounted for 46 percent of the total regional population growth. Their share of the region's population rose from 16 percent in 1890 to 22 percent in 1920. Meanwhile, the fortunes of each urban place continued to fluctuate.

Duluth and Superior had emerged as the second-ranking urban center in the region. The Zenith City and its Wisconsin partner were the world's greatest freshwater port. The harbor was the focus of rail routes to the Mesabi and the Twin Cities and of direct connections to the American and Canadian transcontinentals and to the Twin Cities–Chicago corridor. Sprawling facilities of national companies were loosely agglomerated among the marshes, scrub woods, and rock along 20 miles of harbor frontage. They included grain elevators; docks and storage for ore, coal, lumber, salt, and oil; the steel mill and two independent blast furnaces; rail shops and yards. A neighborhood of houses adjoined each separate industrial node. Outside the harbor, Duluth's upper-income residential spoke projected northeastward along the escarpment on the Lake Superior north shore. The downtown technical, professional, and small business corps lived on the slope of the escarpment; many of the city's sizable group of wealthy families occupied a line of mansions near the cliff at the water's edge. At the city's original point of development, next to the Northern Pacific terminal, impressive downtown and warehouse districts had grown. A highly efficient, nearly linear streetcar system linked the whole collection of settlements. The harbor was an exciting place— and a strange sight deep in the continental interior. The landscape expressed the quick fortunes, the sudden large-scale absentee in-

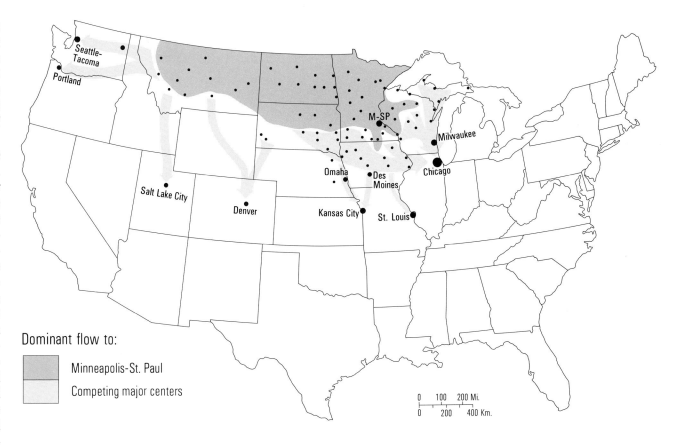

Figure 21. *Twin Cities Dominance of Railway Mail Flow, 1924. Within the darker shaded area, mailcar capacity to and from the Twin Cities exceeded that to competing cities shown. Source: note 40.*

Central Duluth at the end of the 1920s represented two generations of growth and building at the northwestern terminus of the Great Lakes waterway. The 1870 nucleus of settlement was located in the upper center of the picture, at the base of Minnesota Point. Hardware and grocery warehouses and freight sheds lined the slips which opened to St. Louis Bay (right). Predominantly white-collar residential areas spread northeastward between the Lake Superior north shore and the escarpment (top). Photo, St. Louis County Historical Society; Northeast Minnesota Historical Center.

vestments, and the hopes that had brought the port from one-fortieth to one-fourth the size of the Twin Cities in half a century.

Sioux City, Iowa, at the region's southern doorstep, was in the same size class as Duluth-Superior. Its direct rail connections with the James River plain and the Black Hills, coupled with its early river commerce, had made it the de facto metropolis of southern and central South Dakota. The growth period—not only rapid growth but much growth of any kind—was ending at both Duluth-Superior and Sioux City. But both city cores were already fine collections of railroad-era commercial architecture.

Thirteen urban areas were in the 19,000–42,000 population range. A mixed lot, they were smaller wholesale-retail-service centers than Duluth-Superior and Sioux City. Still they were the dominant centers of commerce for extensive parts of the region. The queen was Butte. A smoky collection of Victorian ostentation, warehouses, mines, mills, wealth, vice, and slums, the city sprawled over the "richest hill on earth." Since the opening of the copper mines in the 1880s, Butte had quickly become the metropolis of the northern Rockies, second in size only to Salt Lake City in the intermountain West. Upstarts such as Phoenix, Tucson, and Albuquerque paled by comparison.

In the size class with Butte, three other centers far across the region were creatures of the Lake Superior iron-mining industry. The cluster on the Marquette Range had grown slowly, although the balance had shifted from the mines to the faster-growing commercial center at the port. Meanwhile, on Minnesota's quarter-century-old Mesabi Range, the clusters centered on Hibbing and Virginia had just taken their turn as the fastest-growing urban areas in the Upper Midwest. Five cities with

their historical roots in logging, waterpower, and water transportation had become centers of diversified manufacturing and railroading as well as strong local trade and service centers. Two of the five—LaCrosse and Winona—had been adapting and diversifying for a long time, first because of the decline of river packet traffic, later because of the decline of lumber milling. Marinette-Menominee had boomed as a sawmill and lumber-shipping point for the Chicago market at the turn of the century. Log and lumber trade at Wausau and Eau Claire-Chippewa Falls had peaked even more recently.

Three more centers in the 19,000–42,000 size class had boomed since 1880 as strong centers for assembling and shipping farm commodities and distributing manufactured goods on the prairies. Fargo served the Red River Valley, and its wholesale trade reached across much of North Dakota. Sioux Falls competed with Sioux City in eastern South Dakota. Mason City served northern Iowa and augmented its trading income with a regionally important cement, brick, and tile industry based on the local bedrock. Far to the west, James J. Hill and Montana pioneer Paris Gibson had visualized the great falls of the Missouri as a powerful attraction for industry and commerce at the northern gateway to the Rockies. Hill's transcontinental line, at first, was routed to fit that expectation. The Anaconda Corporation located its copper refinery there. With railway shops, metallurgy, and Great Northern lines radiating to the four corners of Montana to carry its wholesale trade, Great Falls had passed Helena and climbed to second rank in the state.

Sixteen local trade centers had moved up to the 11,000–16,000 population class. Four in Minnesota had been well established for more than two generations. Mankato and St. Cloud

continued to exploit their positions at important intersections in the regional rail network. Mankato's farm trade had grown with the shift from wheat to corn and hogs in the southern Minnesota prairie. The shift had been spurred by the collapse of wheat prices following the Spanish-American War. St. Cloud was the center of one of America's most extraordinary rural concentrations of Roman Catholic German immigrants. As a result of relatively high birthrates and low out-migration rates, it was the center of an intensifying livestock-farming area and the focus for a large local labor and entrepreneurial force to help the growth of industry. Faribault was continuing its long process of diversification from waterpowered flour milling to other lines.

Rochester had already become a special place. The remarkable clinic of the local Doctors Mayo was bursting at the seams of its three-story building, preparing to build the first of its skyscrapers, filling the town's two surprisingly large hospitals, and supporting an exceptionally large cadre of professional and technical people. Through Pullman car service tied the town to Chicago, thence to the Eastern cities and Europe, and to Kansas City, thence to California, Latin America, and Asia.[41]

Meanwhile, the northern Michigan Copper Range towns were also more than two generations old. But their growth was slow. The mines were reaching more than two miles deep, into the hard rock, for lean ore. Corporate headquarters in the East were directing new investments to Latin America. It already seemed likely that the cultural community of the Finnish immigrant miners and the state college of mining technology would outlast the mines.

Other urban-economic outposts in the northern forest, in the same size class, were

Scenes in the commercial cores of St. Cloud and Fargo typify the changes during the steel rail era: St. Germain Street in St. Cloud about 1870 and 1920 (this page) and Broadway in Fargo, looking north across the Northern Pacific railway tracks in 1881 and the 1920s (at right). Photos: St. Cloud, 1870: N. J. Trenham, Alexandria, MN, photo, Minnesota Historical Society; St. Cloud, 1920: Guy's, photo, Minnesota Historical Society; Fargo, 1881: F. J. Haynes, photo, State Historical Society of North Dakota; Fargo, ca. 1920s: Archie L. Dewey, photo, State Historical Society of North Dakota.

The landscapes of Broadway in Rochester, Minnesota, about 1900 and 1920 reflected the quick and relentless onslaught of automobiles, as well as improvements in street surfacing and lighting. Photo, Minnesota Historical Society.

An instant landmark in the world of medicine in 1928, the new Mayo Clinic building towered above its three-story predecessor (left), Rochester's downtown retail area (right background), and the impressive new Kahler Hotel (far left). Photo, Minnesota Historical Society.

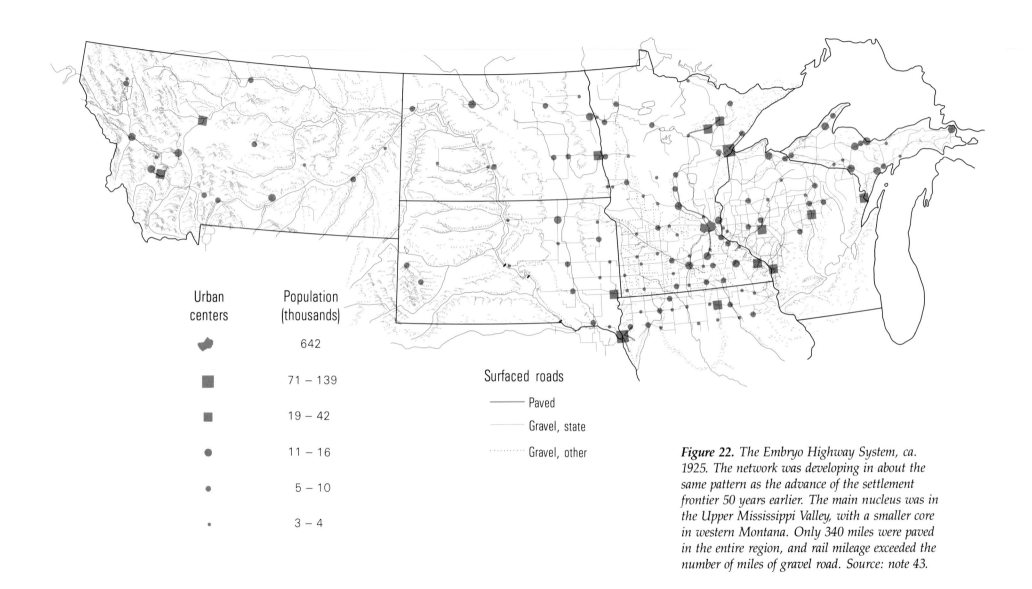

Urban
centers

Population
(thousands)

642

71 – 139

19 – 42

11 – 16

5 – 10

3 – 4

Surfaced roads

——— Paved

——— Gravel, state

·········· Gravel, other

Figure 22. *The Embryo Highway System, ca. 1925. The network was developing in about the same pattern as the advance of the settlement frontier 50 years earlier. The main nucleus was in the Upper Mississippi Valley, with a smaller core in western Montana. Only 340 miles were paved in the entire region, and rail mileage exceeded the number of miles of gravel road. Source: note 43.*

newer and growing faster: the mining and service centers at Iron Mountain and Ironwood, Michigan; the lumber, ore-shipping, and railroad centers at Ashland, Wisconsin, and Escanaba, Michigan; and the world-famous transportation service center at Sault Ste. Marie. A new family of fast-growing large shopping and service centers had emerged on the western farmlands. Grand Forks shared with Fargo the early momentum and rich farm trade of the Red River Valley. Spurred by exceptional rail accessibility and a strong railroad employment base, Minot's local business community had secured its leadership in distribution and services in northwestern North Dakota. Aberdeen had a similar position on the Milwaukee Railroad's new transcontinental line. At a major junction and division point, it emerged as the principal distribution center for the James River plain and as a market for grain and cattle from the newly opened country to the west. Elevators, stockyards, maintenance shops, and blocks of substantial multistoried warehouses lined the new transcontinental's swath of tracks through the flat city. At the center of the largest, oldest irrigated oasis on the Yellowstone, where the foothills of the Rockies touch the Great Plains, the thriving local trade center of Billings had also moved into the 11,000–16,000 size class. Rail lines now tied it to the cattle- and wheat-ranching country to the north and south. It had direct rail access to the East through Omaha and Kansas City. Along the Northern Pacific's main street of the Northwest, Billings was the first point west of the Twin Cities with a competing direct link to the south. Oil still lay untouched beneath the plains. But here was the location for the metropolis of Montana in a future epoch.

In the mountain valleys, Helena had slipped from its position as Montana's largest city. But, the state capitol, ore refining, and remnants of a once-thriving wholesale trade kept the place growing slowly, as they did in 1890. At the western edge of the banking region, Missoula was sheltered in the spectacular Flathead-Bitterroot trench, and its economy was stabilized by the state university campus. The city was growing modestly as a distribution center for the farming communities in the valleys and the lumber industry in the mountains.

In the lowest size classes, the number of urban places grew from 54 to 99 between 1890 and 1920. The most pervasive reasons were the maturation of the rail network and the accompanying increase in farm output, commerce, and industry. Aside from the forestry and mining areas, the spacing and size of the emergent urban places depended on the density and productivity of farms. The older, more fertile, better-watered areas had the thickest crop of urban-sized farm trade centers growing up from the vast seedbed of hamlets and small towns.

Some industries serving the local farm trade had begun to expand into the Midwestern and national markets. Most of those were based on agricultural raw materials—the flour and feed mill, brewery, slaughterhouse, cannery, or creamery. Other industries were not directly based on farm products. Yet they were also in the areas of older settlement and more intensive agriculture. There were two main reasons. First, the passage of more time encouraged and permitted local people to get something started: there had been at least two generations to accumulate capital, labor force, management, and entrepreneurial experience in the community. And almost all Upper Midwest service and manufacturing industries were started by people in their local communities. Second, those communities were closer to the Twin Cities and other large, diversified Midwestern market centers. Thus, for example, local insurance companies went to the national market from Owatonna and Watertown; a railway-maintenance equipment maker reached national and world markets from Fairmont; foundries and machine builders marketed from Albert Lea, Winona, Red Wing, LaCrosse, and Eau Claire. Besides industry, other special functions—colleges, railroad division points, capitals—were bringing new basic income from other parts of the region or nation to some of the emerging cities. Nevertheless, the overwhelming flavor of urban growth up to 1920, in places of all sizes and locations—was imparted by the resource-based industries, the railroads, and the length of historical legacy.

With the growth of industries and commerce, the population had become more than half nonfarm. Urbanization was well established and about to take off. Past were the bloodshed of New Ulm, Spirit Lake, Slim Buttes, and Wounded Knee; the brawls and brothels of Hayward, Deadwood, and Virginia City; the sod-hut hardships of Rolvag's *Giants in the Earth* and the crude cabins of *The Emigrants* of Moberg. Most Corn Belt and Dairy Belt towns were now two or three generations old. In the Great Plains and mountain valleys, the towns had lived at least one generation of their histories. Time and money had replaced the clapboard false fronts and rebuilt the downtowns with brick; paved streets and sidewalks; built waterworks; improved parks and squares; put up solid schools, monumental churches, lodge halls, and courthouses; developed streets of fine homes; grown shade trees. To be sure, the region was still badly underbuilt by Eastern standards. But there had been time to get organized and to begin to get a vision of how things could look and feel. In

Main Street, Sinclair Lewis could write believably in 1920 about Gopher Prairie and Zenith, where everything was patterned, ordered, established, hierarchical, predictable, boring. But, of course, the past—and the present—were prologue.[42]

The Embryo Highway Network

In 1920 the assembly-line outpouring of the American auto industry had just begun. So had the spectacular development of the nation's oil fields, refineries, oil companies, service stations, and garages. The good-roads movement had just begun, also. In 1920 there was not yet a set of road maps for the various Upper Midwest states that showed reliably and consistently the routes and types of surface. But by the mid-1920s highway departments were working in all the states, and maps were published.[43] What the maps showed is astonishing in today's environment. Almost no hard-surfaced roads ran between cities (Figure 22). There were 340 miles of paved roads in the entire Upper Midwest. Ninety percent of those were in the Twin Cities area, with the region's heaviest traffic, and in Duluth and the iron ranges, with the region's richest tax base. The gravel road network was less well developed than the railroad network, outside of parts of southern Minnesota and Wisconsin. Except for the five-mile paved stretch over the new Missouri River bridge, Bismarck—the capital city of North Dakota—was accessible only by dirt road. It was 100 miles from the end of the gravel at Jamestown. Surfaced roads from Minneapolis-St. Paul to Fargo, Sioux Falls, Sioux City, and Mason City were circuitous.

But, in a way, the map of surface roads was deceptive. There was that massive network of dirt secondary roads not shown on the map. Some were only unimproved ruts; most were graded with varying degrees of care or neglect. No one thought of the piece of road on the edge of the farmyard as a route to a distant metropolis or to everyplace in the nation, as we do today. But everyone knew its importance as a link to town and the railroad line, thence to the nation. Surfaced roads on the map were only a limited selection of threads from the dense fabric. The thin and ragged pattern of surfaced roads reflects the way people were organizing in the mid-1920s to get the system paved. Some states were ahead of others. Some trade centers were ahead of others. Some counties had more money; some had more vision and leadership. A select few had both.

Where there was no gravel, there was no reliable, all-weather alternative to rail transport. Nevertheless, the number of private automobiles and trucks was growing quickly. Fledgling trucking companies were hauling eggs, poultry, livestock, and farm supplies even on the unimproved rural roads. Where roads to town were not yet surfaced, irresistible pressure was mounting to "get the farmers out of the mud." Nearly everyone, at both ends of the road, backed the movement. Road builders were rapidly weaving a new transportation fabric. Of course, the auto and truck were only two applications of the internal combustion engine. In the spacious plains and great distances of the Upper Midwest, farm tractors, excavators, graders, and aircraft opened great new possibilities. Little Falls, Minnesota, native Charles Lindbergh would soon take his pilot training and begin planning his trans-Atlantic nonstop flight. Northwest Airways would soon fly the mail between Fargo, the Twin Cities, and Chicago. Radio broadcasting and rapidly improving telephone technology were tumbling onto the scene at the same time. Gopher Prairie, Zenith, and the Upper Midwest were heading from a period of development, rapid population growth, and maturation into a confrontation with momentous changes in the circulation system and with wrenching strains in the settlement system.

A Place in the National Pattern

The close of the Upper Midwest's epoch of development and rapid population growth was part of a much larger picture.[44] The spectacular spread of railroads across the Upper Midwest was part of the development of a national system between 1870 and 1920 (Figure 23). Several great regional corridors made up the system. The oldest and most densely developed corridor extended from the emerging megalopolis, between Boston and Washington, westward to Chicago, St. Louis, Kansas City, and Minneapolis-St. Paul. It embraced the American Manufacturing Belt and the Corn Belt—the nation's core economic region. With the surplus capital generated in the core, other corridors were extended south and west in the steel rail epoch. They reached to peninsular Florida, to the Gulf Coast between Pensacola and Houston, across the plains and mountains to the Pacific ports, and through the Pacific valleys from Seattle to San Diego. The corridors between Minneapolis-St. Paul and Chicago and between the Twin Cities and the midcontinent were part of the core. The northern transcontinental lines between the Twin Cities and Pacific Northwest were part of the western corridor.

The same epoch saw the rise of the great diversified industrial metropolis on the American scene. By 1920 there were 19 of them in the top three classes in the national urban size-ranking. They were the high-order

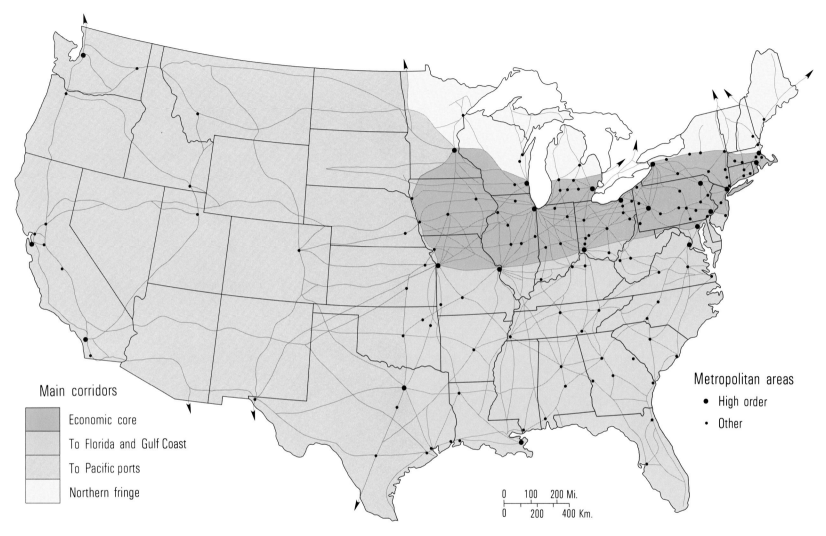

Main corridors

Economic core

To Florida and Gulf Coast

To Pacific ports

Northern fringe

Metropolitan areas

● High order

· Other

0   100   200 Mi.

0   200   400 Km.

Figure 23. National Rail System, 1920. Main
routes linked all of the high-order centers with one
another and extended to outlying resource regions
and international border crossings en route to
major cities of Canada and Mexico. *Source:* Rand
McNally Commercial Atlas *(Chicago:* Rand
McNally, 1927).

metropolitan centers of the country. New York, with 8.5 million, was at the pinnacle. Boston, Philadelphia, Pittsburgh, and Chicago each had populations over 1.5 million. Fourteen others, all larger than half a million, rounded out the high-order family, and as one of those, the Twin Cities had just joined the club. The 19 centers also fell into four different groups, each with distinctive regional, historical, and functional characteristics: the old port-industrial-commercial cities of the Northeast; the major industrial cities of the Great Lakes coal-iron-steel-heavy machinery complex; the commercial gateways on the western and southern edges of the economic core region; and the Pacific ports. The Twin Cities were one of the western and southern gateways, along with Baltimore-Washington, Cincinnati, St. Louis, and Kansas City.

The national steel rail system tapped natural resource regions in the South and West that had been poorly developed or untouched. It integrated them into a vastly expanded national economy. It laid the base for future high-order centers at critical southern and western locations—Atlanta, New Orleans, and the Carolina Piedmont; Seattle-Tacoma and Portland; Dallas-Ft. Worth, Houston, Denver, Salt Lake City, and Phoenix. The new national railroad network also created a system of regions. Each region was centered on the nearest high-order metropolis and defined by networks of trade, professional services, and banking. The Upper Midwest evolved as one of those regions.

The frontier was closed. A national circulation network and a national system of towns and cities were in place. But great lags and in-equities had affected regional development. Manufacturing was concentrated in the core region far in excess of that region's share of either the market or the resources of the nation. There were commensurate geographical inequities in income and related population characteristics—notably health, education, and construction. Now the complete national circulation system would permit accelerated, substantial regional shifts of capital and population. The new challenge was to use the network and further improve its speed, capacity, and efficiency. The time around 1920 opened not only a new epoch of auto and air transportation and electronic communication technology but also a new round of national internal change and reorganization.

CHAPTER **4**

Turbulence
and Continuity

People in the Upper Midwest adapted with remarkably little delay to the new epoch. They embraced the new transportation and communication technologies quickly and used them to create increased income, savings, and wealth. In the process they transformed the landscapes and the maps of the region once more. This time it was not a change from natural wilderness to settlement but a transformation of the settlement itself. The first half-century, 1870–1920, had been dominated by land expansion, immigration, and rapid population growth. Now the region turned to a new half-century dominated by land improvement, emigration, and economic growth.

The Transportation Explosion

During this new half-century highways became the ubiquitous, national, general-purpose carrier of people and goods. The swelling fleet of cars and trucks first replaced buggies and wagons in the short-haul business. Then they entered the long-haul market and captured the passenger traffic and much of the general cargo from the railroads. The number of buggies in the nation dropped from 30 million to virtually zero in 60 years, while the number of registered automobiles rose from 9 million to 120 million. At the same time, the number of horse-drawn wagons fell from 20 million to near zero, and the number of registered trucks rose from one million to 35 million. Between 1920 and 1980 the highway share of the nation's total ton-miles of freight grew from one percent to 24 percent. Highway passenger-miles grew from 39 percent to 85 percent.[45]

PAVING AND DECENTRALIZATION

Paving was the key, and many other improvements followed. Construction crews spun a 2-million-mile web of blacktop and concrete in the United States between 1920 and 1980. The total national road mileage outside cities increased only about 10 percent, but the surfaced mileage grew 550 percent. Maps show several Upper Midwest examples of this spectacular change (Figure 24). A 10-county area in northwestern Iowa had only 500 miles of surfaced roads, mostly gravel, as recently as 1928. By 1980 the same area had 2,000 miles of paved highways. Improvements were made everywhere in those counties, but the paved road network is 50 percent more dense on the glacial-drift plains than it is in the unglaciated hill country. Public investment in roads, like private investment in farm improvements, concentrated on the best land. Road improvements accompanied the gradual shift of agricultural productivity away from the areas near the Mississippi River, which had the advantage of an early start, to the upland prairie areas, which had the long-run advantage of level land and deeper soil. Across the state, in a 12-county area of northwestern Iowa, 2,300 miles of pavement in 1980 replaced about 40 miles of pavement and 560 miles of gravel in 1928.[46]

The change was even more striking in the areas of more recent settlement. In 15 northwestern Minnesota counties overlapping the Red River Valley, the Big Bog, and the moraine-and-lake country, more than 5,000 miles of pavement in 1980 replaced 500 miles of gravel in 1925. Roads had been improved at the same density in both the flat Red River Valley and the rough moraine-and-lake country. The improved roads reached large grain farms, small dairy farms, and recreational lake areas

79

Northwestern Iowa, 1928 Gravel roads

Northeastern Iowa, 1928 Gravel roads

Northwestern Iowa, 1980 Paved roads

Northeastern Iowa, 1980 Paved roads

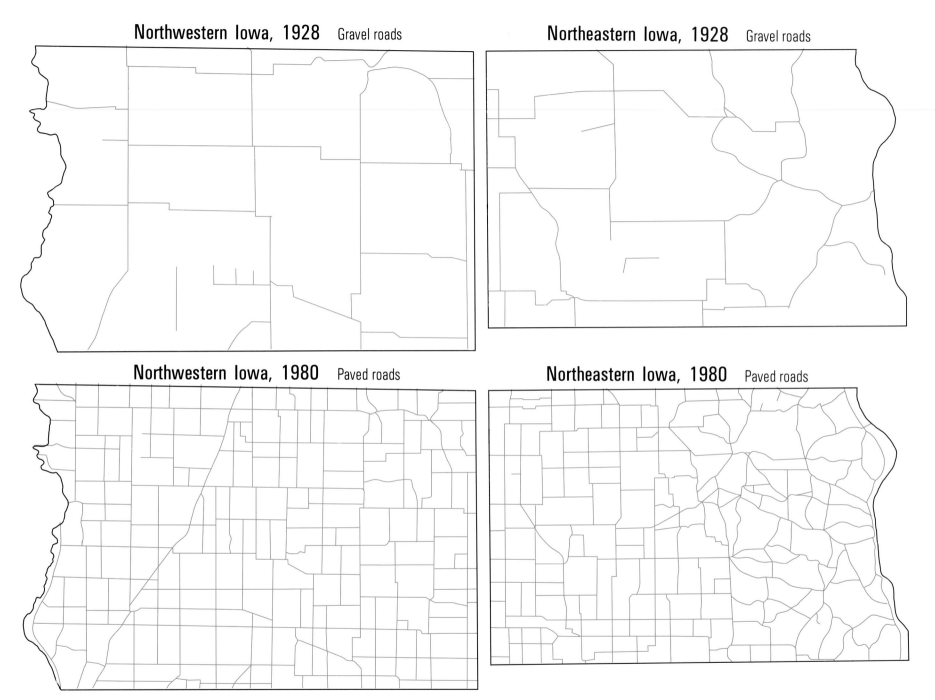

Figure 24. Transformation of State Highway Networks in the Auto Era. (4 pages)

Northwestern Minnesota, 1925

Gravel Roads

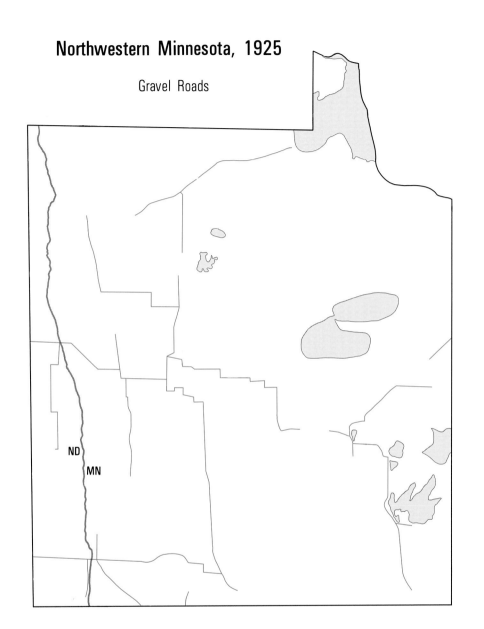

Northwestern Minnesota, 1980

Paved roads

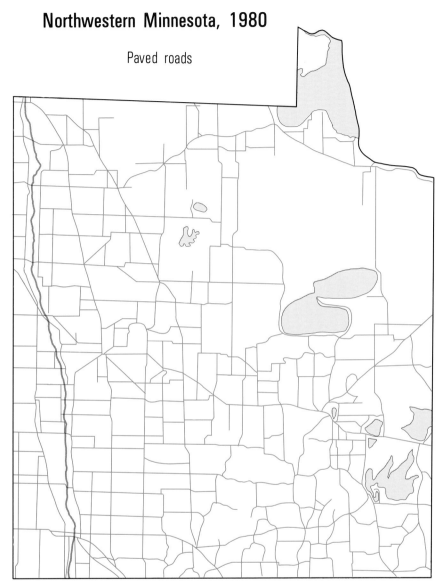

Figure 24, continued. The system grew from a few poorly connected segments of gravel road in the mid-1920s to a dense, integrated grid of pavement in 1980. Comparative mileage of mid-1920s gravel and 1980 pavement in the five different areas shown was 40 miles and 500 miles in north-western Iowa, 500 and 2,000 in northeastern Iowa, 500 and 5,000 in northwestern Minnesota, 300 and 1,500 in northwestern North Dakota and adjacent Montana, and 600 and 3,200 in northern South Dakota. Source: note 43.

Northwestern North Dakota, 1925   Gravel roads

Northwestern North Dakota, 1980   Paved roads

Figure 24, continued. Transformation of State
Highway Networks in the Auto Era.

Northern South Dakota, 1926   Gravel roads

Northern South Dakota, 1980   Paved roads

Figure 24, continued.

alike. Highways were less improved in the Indian reservations, but they crossed the Big Bog to join towns and farming districts on either side. In a vast area of northwestern North Dakota and adjacent Montana, about 1,500 miles of paved highway in 1980 contrasted with only 300 miles of gravel in 1923. And in a comparable area of northern South Dakota 3,200 miles of pavement had replaced about 600 miles of gravel. The investment there was heaviest east of the Missouri River, in the area of highest population density and agricultural productivity. Nevertheless, by east river standards, there was nearly twice as much pavement west of the river as population and land productivity would justify. The high level of west river improvements was possible because the formula for distributing highway tax money takes into account need as well as ability to pay. In part, highway funds serve to redistribute income from the more productive to the less productive areas. Unlike the railroad map, the road map in part reflects the role of the state as a community organization to share resources for the common benefit. Because the public built it, the highway network was a social and political as well as an economic enterprise.

Unlike the national rail network in yet another way, the new highway system was not hierarchical. As the road network improved, it became much less necessary to go through a few central junctions to ship or travel from one place to another. The railroad network was dominated by lines radiating from a few preeminent ports on the seacoast, the Great Lakes, and the Mississippi River system, and a few major interior centers such as Denver. In contrast, the highway system included not only many of those radial routes but also a dense grid developed along the township, range, and section lines. Most vehicles can move without interruption anywhere on the grid, as shown by a few Upper Midwest examples. The fastest route from Fargo to Sioux Falls in the railroad era went into the Twin Cities and back out to Sioux Falls—470 miles, two changes of train, two railroad companies. In the highway era there is a direct route—245 miles, no transfers. The fastest route from Devils Lake, North Dakota, to Bismarck in the railroad era went to Fargo, then to Bismarck—360 miles, one change of trains, two different railroad companies. In the highway era the route is direct—175 miles, no transfers. Under the old circumstances of travel, there was less tendency for business contacts to develop between Sioux Falls and Fargo or between Devils Lake and Bismarck. If someone wanted to transact business with both Fargo and Sioux Falls, a Twin Cities location was best. Or if a firm wanted to serve both Bismarck and Devils Lake, either a Fargo or a Twin Cities location had an advantage. To be sure, the established large populations at the major rail-era cities created a great deal of inertia for the transportation system. Nevertheless, the highways exerted a powerful pull toward decentralization.

Within urban areas the decentralizing effects of the auto and truck are well known: troubled downtowns; suburbanization of homes, shopping, and industry. But, in fact, highway transportation triggered a breakdown of hierarchical relationships by opening new lines of commerce and decentralization at every scale throughout the system. Getting out of the mud was a simple goal and perhaps one of the most widely held in American social history. But it took half a century and at least $40 billion (at 1980 levels) to attain the goal in the Upper Midwest alone. And along the way, the settlement pattern was shaken to its roots.

SPECIALIZATION AND ACCELERATION

In the same half-century the railroads were transformed from generalists to specialists. While total annual passenger-miles by all modes of travel increased nationally more than tenfold in 60 years, the railroads' share dropped from 48 percent to less than one percent. Freight ton-miles increased nearly fivefold in the same period. But the rail share decreased from 86 percent to 36 percent. The railroads virtually went out of the passenger business, and in freight they specialized increasingly in long hauls, large shipments, and bulk commodities. Average locomotive and freight car mileage per day tripled; specialized types of cars proliferated; efficiency in freight handling increased sharply with specialization.

Meanwhile, virtually all spending for maintenance and replacement of track was concentrated on selected main lines. In most years since the Great Depression of the 1930s, the new rail laid was not enough to replace even three percent of the first track mileage. At that rate the average track would have to last sixty to one hundred years. If half the system was being replaced even on an average 30-year cycle, the other half would never be replaced. From the record it is clear that at least since the early years of highway competition, no less than half the nation's railroad mileage has been in the process of creeping abandonment. The nadir of maintenance occurred in the 1950s. Since then capital improvement on many main lines has increased, and there has been more widespread acceptance of abandonment of both branch lines and duplicating long-haul main lines. Of the nation's 1920 rail mileage, 9 percent had been abandoned by 1950, another 17 percent by 1980. Those trends are reflected in the Upper Midwest. Many branch lines have disappeared. One of the

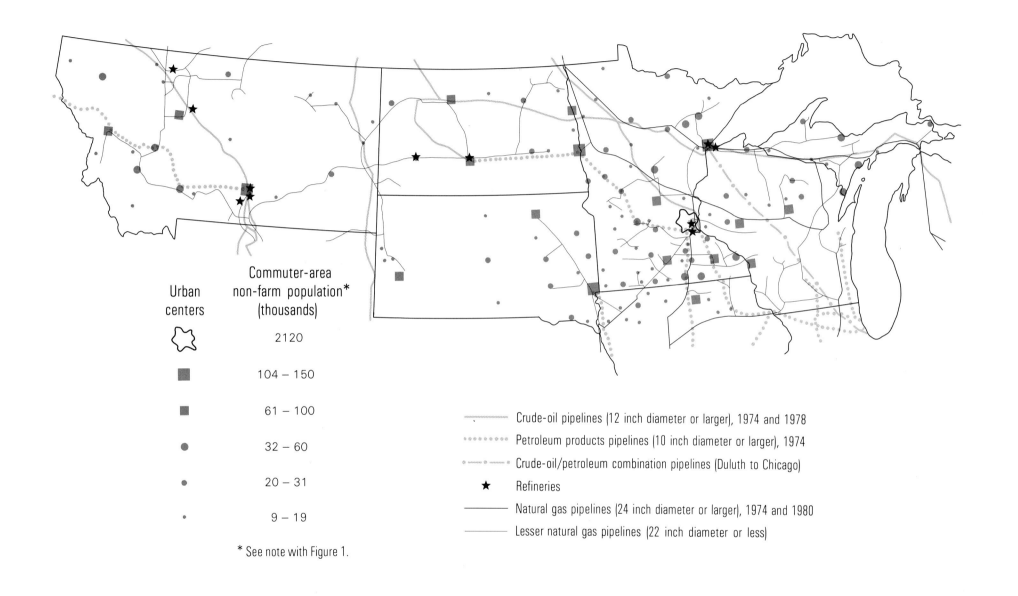

Urban
centers

Commuter-area
non-farm population*
(thousands)

2120

104 – 150

61 – 100

32 – 60

20 – 31

9 – 19

* See note with Figure 1.

∙∙∙∙∙∙∙∙∙∙ Crude-oil pipelines (12 inch diameter or larger), 1974 and 1978

∙∙∙∙∙∙∙∙∙∙ Petroleum products pipelines (10 inch diameter or larger), 1974

∙–∙–∙–∙ Crude-oil/petroleum combination pipelines (Duluth to Chicago)

★ Refineries

—— Natural gas pipelines (24 inch diameter or larger), 1974 and 1980

—— Lesser natural gas pipelines (22 inch diameter or less)

Figure 25. *Pipe Lines in the Upper Midwest, late 1970s. The network joined northern Great Plains oil and gas fields with Twin Cities and Eastern* *markets. It also tied the Twin Cities to oil and gas sources in Kansas, Oklahoma, and Texas. Source: note 47.*

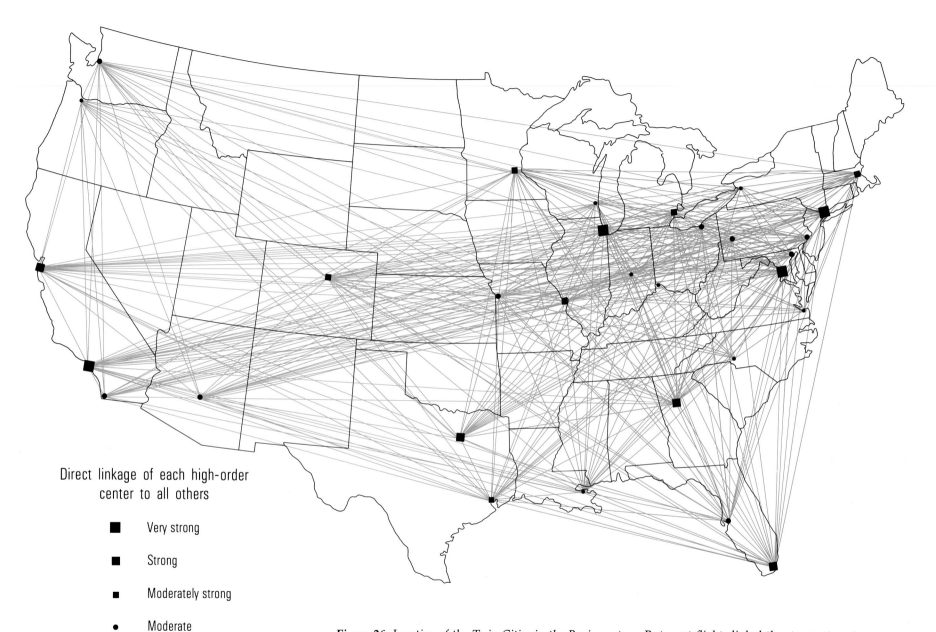

Direct linkage of each high-order
center to all others

■ Very strong

■ Strong

▪ Moderately strong

• Moderate

· Weak

Figure 26. Location of the Twin Cities in the Busiest U.S. Air Corridors, 1983. Almost every high-order metropolis was now linked directly with all others (2 pages) (above). The Twin Cities had become the regional gateway to a truly national sys-tem. But most flights linked the strongest centers (at right). While the air age opened new opportunities, it also reflected established patterns. Source: note 48.

Direct linkage of each high-order
center to all others

■ Very strong

■ Strong

■ Moderately strong

• Moderate

• Weak

Scheduled commercial flights per week

480 – 1058

240 – 430

120 – 230

Figure 26, continued.

multiple transcontinental main lines has been pulled up most of the way across Montana; another has been virtually abandoned between St. Cloud, Minnesota, and the Twin Cities. There are other cases; and miles of barely visible, rusting rails and rotting ties foreshadow more to come.[47]

Other, competing specialists have further divided the massive stream of intercity traffic. For the nation as a whole, pipelines account for 16 percent of the total ton-miles of freight; inland waterways, 14 percent; and air freight, less than one percent. Their combined shares exceed the trucking total and nearly equal the railway total. While automobiles account for 85 percent of the passenger-miles, airlines have taken 13 percent, leaving the remaining 2 percent to buses. On the Upper Midwest map, the pipeline pattern is somewhat reminiscent of the historic railroad pattern, with major east-west corridors passing through the Twin Cities and Twin Ports areas, another major corridor southward from the Twin Cities, independent connections south and west from Montana, and branch lines reaching out to the smaller cities (Figure 25). The lines join northern Great Plains oil, gas, and lignite fields with Twin Cities and Eastern markets, and they tie the Twin Cities to oil and gas sources in Kansas, Oklahoma, and Texas. Water transportation is confined to two historic routes—Lake Superior and the Mississippi River below the Twin Cities.

Air routes, in one way, are most analogous to the historic railroad pattern. The Twin Cities are the regional hub of an old-fashioned, radial, hierarchical system. The fastest scheduled routes from most smaller cities in the region to most others, or to most other high-order metropolitan areas nationwide, pass through Minneapolis-St. Paul. But, in another way, the air routes bear the least resemblance to historic patterns. In the railroad heyday, few people could even dream of today's direct links from the Twin Cities to every other high-order American metropolis and to the major world air hubs at London and Tokyo (Figure 26).[48]

The railroads, pipelines, waterways, and airways are not the only specialized carriers. More than 2 million miles of wire have been strung across the region to carry energy and messages. Electric power lines nationwide delivered the energy equivalent of 250 million tons of coal in 1980, compared with only 4 million tons in 1920. The Upper Midwest high-voltage transmission grid links the major urban and industrial markets and their neighboring coal-fired or nuclear generating stations, the complex of giant thermal-generating stations on the North Dakota lignite fields and Montana coal fields, and the large hydroelectric stations on the Missouri, the Columbia, and Manitoba's part of the Canadian Shield (Figure 27). Meanwhile, in 1981 for the nation as a whole long-distance inter-city phone calls exceeded the total number of first-class letters. Sixty years earlier the number of first-class letters was 30 times the number of long-distance calls. Long-distance traffic increased fiftyfold during that period, while the volume of first-class mail increased only fourfold. A proportionate shift occurred in the Upper Midwest.[49]

If specialization was one theme in the transportation explosion, another theme was acceleration. Average freight speeds tripled; average passenger speeds increased two- to threefold by land, sixteenfold by air. Instant communication became available to almost everyone at almost everyplace. As a result, the geographical service area reached out farther from every urban center, and more commerce was possible between the centers. A revolutionary increase occurred in the amount of business that could be done, and a sharp decrease took place in the number of places needed to do it. In that situation the railroad-era settlement pattern had suddenly become extremely unstable.

EMPIRE TO NEIGHBORHOOD: THE PERSISTENT REGION

Through this half-century of revolutionary change, the Upper Midwest regional circulation pattern persisted. A 1960 map of long-distance telephone traffic showed that the region of dominant flow to the Twin Cities still extended from the Bear Paws in Montana to the Porcupines in Michigan and from northern Iowa to the Canadian border (*See* Figure 4). Strong, though not dominant, ties reached out farther, to the eastern and western edges of the banking region. Fifteen years later another map of telephone traffic repeated the earlier pattern (Figure 28). It also showed the strong interaction that had developed between the Upper Midwest, Colorado, and the intermountain Southwest. An analysis of parcel post origins and destinations in 1965 produced a like pattern (Figure 29). In 1983 the region was confirmed yet again on a map of the Twin Cities share of airline flights originating at smaller cities in the Middle West and Great Plains (Figure 30). The area of Minneapolis–St. Paul air traffic dominance was almost identical with the area of railway mail dominance in 1924.[50]

Just as the railway mail flow had indicated the amount of business transacted between the Twin Cities, the region, and the rest of the world in 1924, so also the flow of long-distance phone calls probably reflected the same relations in 1975. The torrent of messages was still there and still growing. It was just moving on the phone lines instead of on racks of mail bags in the railway postal cars. The phone call pat-

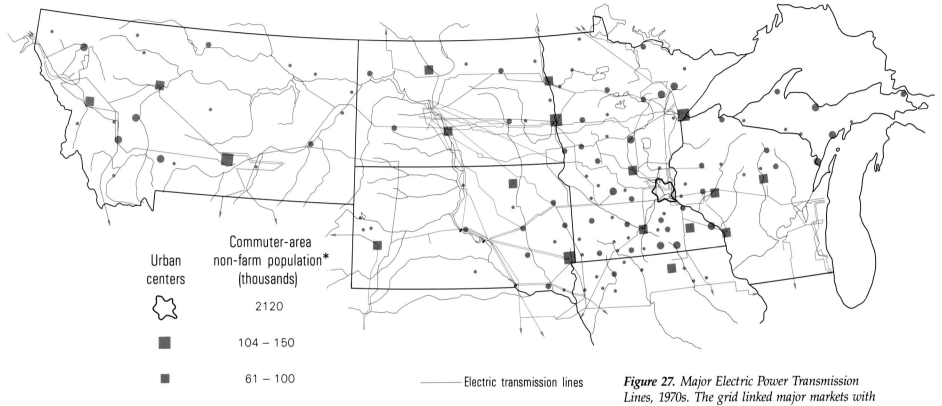

Urban
centers

Commuter-area
non-farm population*
(thousands)

2120

104 – 150

61 – 100

32 – 60

20 – 31

9 – 19

* See note with Figure 1.

——— Electric transmission lines

Figure 27. Major Electric Power Transmission
Lines, 1970s. The grid linked major markets with
neighboring coal-fired and nuclear generating stations and with resource-based power plants at major hydroelectric dams and the Northern Plains
coal and lignite fields. Source: note 47.

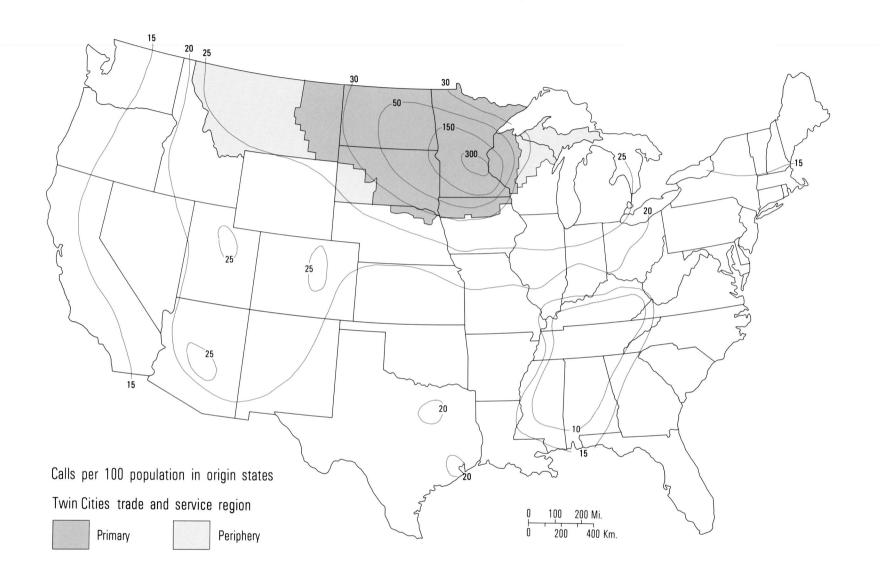

Calls per 100 population in origin states

Twin Cities trade and service region

Primary   Periphery

Figure 28. Phone Traffic: Twin Cities Focus, 1975.
The pattern reflected the outlines of the Upper
Midwest primary region and strong interregional
ties with Chicago, Detroit, and the Southwest.
Source: note 50.

tern indicated that perhaps 35 percent of the Minneapolis–St. Paul basic economy in 1975 depended on business with the rest of the region, compared with 55 percent a half-century earlier. The other 65 percent depended on business with the rest of the United States and the rest of the world, compared with 45 percent 50 years earlier. But that was only one way to look at the change. To be sure, the region's importance to the metropolis had declined in relative terms, but it grew in absolute terms. Between 1924 and 1975, Twin Cities personal income, in constant 1975 dollars, rose from about 3 billion to about 13 billion. Thus the region accounted for 55 percent of a $3-billion economy, or about 1.7 billion, in 1924; and it accounted for 35 percent of a $13-billon economy, or about 4.6 billion, in 1975.[51]

From the 1940s into the 1970s, the metropolis grew faster than the remainder of the Upper Midwest. It did so in part by increasing its interaction with the rest of the region. Of all the business done in the rest of the region in 1975, it appears that about 13 percent was transacted with the Twin Cities, compared with 10 percent 50 years earlier. That change probably reflected increased trade with Iowa and northwestern Wisconsin which more than offset a somewhat weaker link with Montana and western South Dakota.[52]

Although the regional pattern persisted, it did so in a shrunken and more interactive world. That meant more competition. The region's hub airport provided a good vantage point from which to consider what happened. In 1983, Twin Cities International was one of 35 major airports in the United States. Together those 35 hubs handled more than one-third of the country's scheduled airline departures and more than two-thirds of all travelers. The Twin Cities were one among 29 high-order metropolitan complexes that together con-

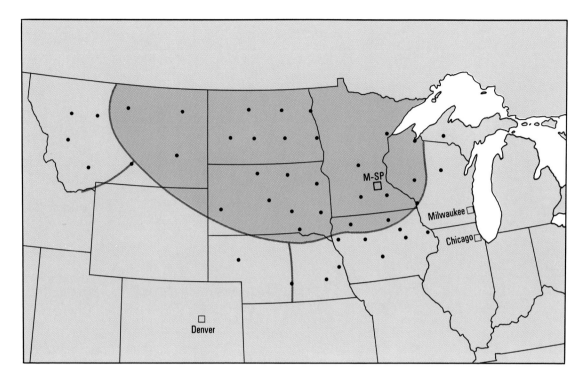

Figure 29. Parcel Post: Twin Cities Focus, 1965. The map outlines, for the cities shown, the region of dominant parcel post flow to the Twin Cities and competing high-order urban areas at Chicago-Milwaukee, Denver, and Seattle-Portland. Source: note 50, Post Office Department.

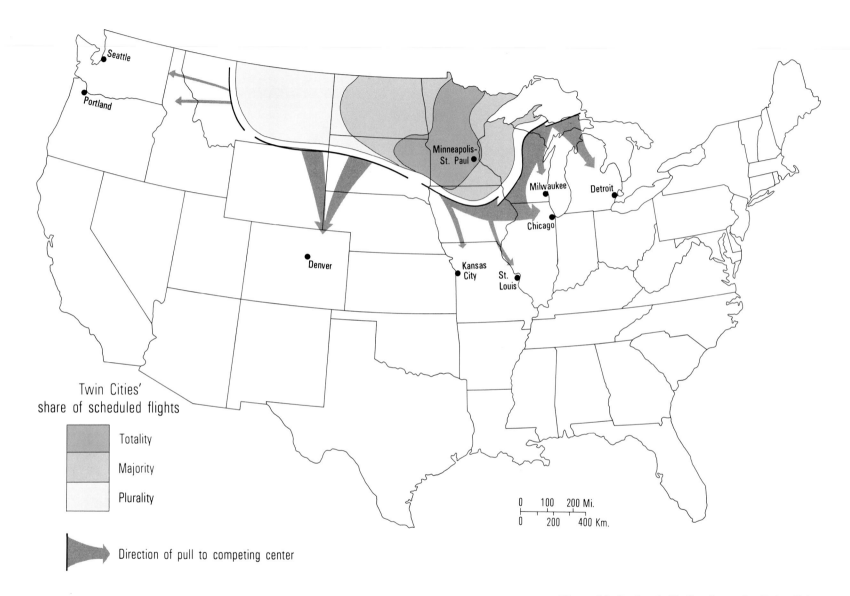

Twin Cities'
share of scheduled flights

Totality

Majority

Plurality

Direction of pull to competing center

Figure 30. Regional Air Service to the Twin Cities Hub, 1983. The area of dominance is almost identical with the Minneapolis-St. Paul area of railway mail dominance in 1924. Source: note 48.

Seattle
Portland
Minneapolis-St. Paul
Milwaukee
Detroit
Chicago
Denver
Kansas City
St. Louis

0   100   200 Mi.
0   200   400 Km.

tained nearly two-thirds of the nation's people and transacted more than two-thirds of its business. Likewise, the region the Twin Cities hub airport served was one of 29 metropolis-centered regions which, together, encompassed the entire national competitive economy. The Upper Midwest's regional air hub was a crossroads in a dense network of routes that covered the map of the United States. Although air service was concentrated in an East Coast–California corridor, to a remarkable degree the routes connected each of the high-order metropolitan centers directly with all of the others and symbolized fast, intense, unending transfers of knowledge, talent, and capital among those centers and regions. Every place could feel quickly the shocks of new products, organizational arrangements, and investments at other places in the network. Thus the result of the transportation explosion was not only more competition but also more instability—more turbulence in the complex forces that kept changing the fortunes of each metropolis and region.

And, of course, the network was really worldwide. Three American hub airports—New York, Miami, and Los Angeles—were among the world's top-ranking international air transportation centers. Two hundred thirty non-stop or one-stop flights every week linked the Twin Cities to those international gateways in 1983. A dozen other American metropolitan centers had a significant number of direct flights to overseas and Canadian centers. The Twin Cities were one of that group, in a modest way. And they were directly linked to the other international hubs by more than 1,000 flights each week. The major air hubs on the world map were also the main centers of international business transactions, whether private or public. Those transactions added further to the relentless change that

pulsated through the transportation and communication network. They had further complicated the competitive, unstable environment of the Upper Midwest.

In 1920 the region was still an empire in a world that was much less accessible and more segmented. By 1980 it had become a kind of neighborhood, or community, in a world that was much more interactive and seemingly even more uncertain. People and institutions in the region have adapted to those environmental changes. Individually and collectively, they have made decisions and taken actions that maintained some of their legacies yet dramatically transformed the landscape. Much of the adaptation was reflected in the changing maps of population.

The Shift in National Migration Patterns

By 1980 the total population of the Upper Midwest reached nearly 8 million. One-third of the total lived within 100 miles of the Twin Cities metropolitan airport, and two-thirds lived east of the James River Valley and west of the upper Wisconsin.

But the long-term trends had changed. A slowdown in overall growth had accompanied a dramatic shift in large-scale migration. Between 1870 and 1920, population streamed into the region. Net immigration was 3 million, and the total population increase was 5 million. In the auto era the flow was reversed. Between 1920 and 1980, net emigration was 1.25 million, while the total increase dropped to 2.2 million—less than half the rate in the railroad era.

INCREASING HOMOGENEITY, EMERGING MINORITIES

As a result of the migraiton patterns, the population became much more homogene-

ous. By 1980 almost 98 percent were American-born. More than 70 percent were born in the Upper Midwest. Another 11 percent were born on the West Coast, and many of those were returning to the homeland of their Upper Midwest parents. European-born population dropped from one million in 1920 to 100,000 in 1980. Most of that much smaller number were the last of the early twentieth-century immigrants who were still alive. European-born made up only about one percent of the population in most counties. The figure was 3 or 4 percent in areas of sharp population decline—where large numbers of young people had departed and elderly survivors made up a significant part of the population—and in western and northern counties that were in the last wave of pre–World War I settlement. Small but significant European migration continued only in growing urban centers of international business employment or universities. Thus virtually the entire population of the region was now not only white but also English-speaking.[53]

Within that relatively homogeneous mass several small groups emerged as visible minorities. The growing Asian-born population had become nearly two-thirds as large as the small European-born component by 1980—a reflection of the nation's changing world orientation (Figure 31). About half of the region's Asians were refugees from the Vietnam War. Many of the other half, like the small continuing stream from Europe, were attracted by the universities and international business employment. The remainder of the foreign-born were virtually all Canadians. While about one-fifth of the Canadian-born lived in the Twin Cities, most were in towns and cities within 200 miles of the international boundary.

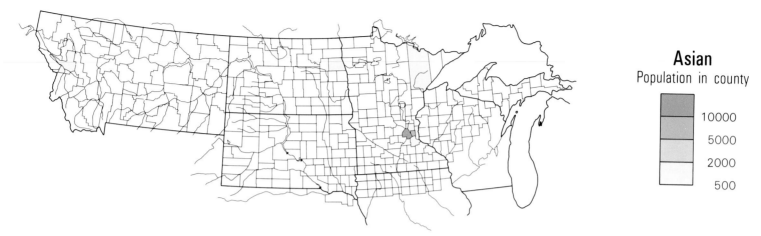

Figure 31. *Asian-Born Population, 1980. Refugees from the Vietnam War were living mainly in the Twin Cities. Others were attracted by several state universities and international business firms.*
Source: U.S. Census of Population, *1980.*

As another result of the migration shift, Indian population in 1980 outnumbered European-born whites for the first time since before the Civil War. The census count of 157,000, though still fraught with uncertainty, was probably the most accurate ever taken. Reported growth was nearly 50 percent in the decade from 1970 to 1980. About two-thirds of the increase could be accounted for only by immigration from other parts of the United States or by improved counting—probably the latter. Nearly two-thirds of the total lived in counties with reservations (Figure 32). Most of the others were about equally divided between the Twin Cities and a group of six smaller metropolitan areas including Great Falls, Billings, Rapid City, Bismarck-Mandan, Sioux Falls, and Duluth-Superior. Thus there has been relatively little mobility since the tribes were pinned to their reservations at the close of the rail-building era. What mobility there

was consisted mainly of oscillation between the reservations and a few urban ghettos. With the high growth rate, Indians had become a majority of the population in several western counties and significant minorities in seven metropolitan areas. In fact, all the net growth of Great Falls in the 1970s was accounted for by the increase in Indian population.

Meanwhile, immigrant minorities of 62,000 Blacks and 62,000 Hispanics lived in the region in 1980. Their combined numbers equaled nearly 80 percent of the Indian population and exceeded the number of European-born (Figure 33). Ninety-one percent of the Black population lived in the region's metropolitan counties—80 percent in the Twin Cities alone, and most of the others at major military air bases in six smaller urban areas. The Hispanic population had the same geographic pattern, but there were additional clusters in smaller urban labor markets—some

in the Western Montana Valleys and some in the sugar beet areas of the Red River Valley and canning vegetable areas of the Corn Belt, where many had come initially to labor in the fields. The Black civilian immigrants have come mainly from Midwestern and Eastern cities, while most of the Hispanic civilians moved north from the irrigated vegetable- and fruit-growing lands of south Texas and intermediate valleys of the mid-continent.

The persistence of the segregated, comparatively immobile Indian communities in the auto era is just one reminder that problems were created, and problems left unresolved, in the spectacular transformation of the region since 1870. At the same time, the immigrant Black, Hispanic, and Asian groups are only a very small example of the vast auto-era increase in the nation's population mobility. The urbanization of both the Indians and the immigrant minorities was especially symbolic.

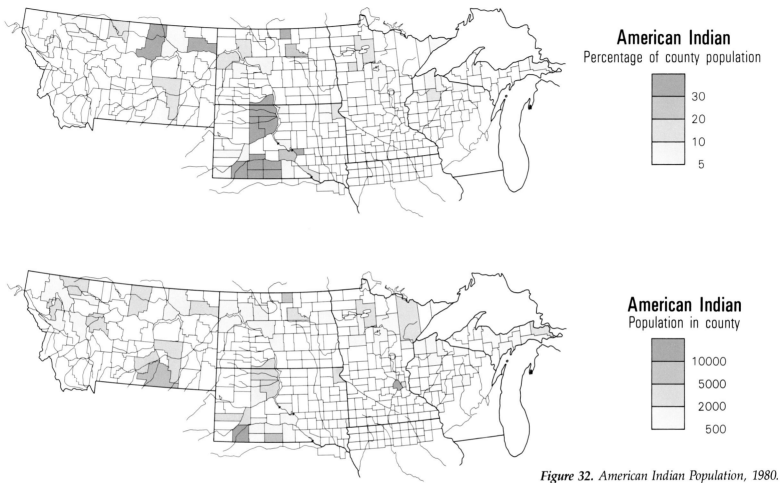

American Indian
Percentage of county population

30
20
10
5

American Indian
Population in county

10000
5000
2000
500

*Figure 32. American Indian Population, 1980.
American Indians outnumbered European-born in
the region for the first time since 1860. They accounted for a high percentage of the population in
counties near the larger reservations (top map).
But about one-third of the region's total number
were minorities in the Twin Cities and six smaller
metropolitan areas (bottom map). Source: U.S.
Census of Population, 1980.*

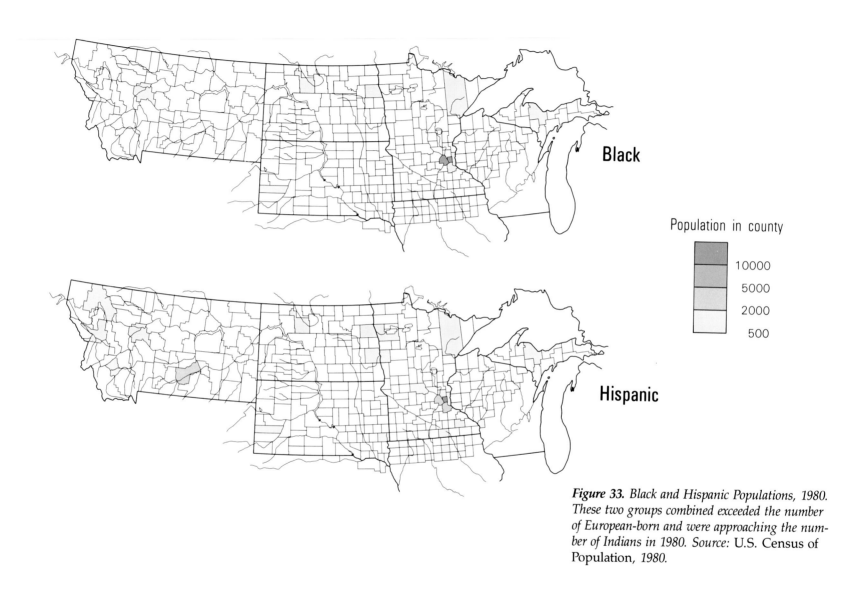

Black

Hispanic

Population in county

10000
5000
2000
500

Figure 33. Black and Hispanic Populations, 1980. These two groups combined exceeded the number of European-born and were approaching the number of Indians in 1980. Source: U.S. Census of Population, 1980.

After 1920 the Upper Midwest was no longer an open land frontier for a massive immigrant stream. That frontier was closed. But the accelerated world circulation system opened new horizons and opportunities. Internal migration was redistributing the American population along new lines of urban development in every part of the country.[54]

TURBULENCE AND CONTINUITY

The Upper Midwest's slower growth and net out-migration since 1920 could imply that the population became more stable. But that has not been so. The gross numbers have hidden a complex, turbulent process. Like any region, the Upper Midwest has always been something of a revolving door. The people moving in and out have embraced every age, income, and occupation group. They arrive and depart in search of work, security, stability, education, or experience. The distinctive thing about Upper Midwest migration in this era has been the reduced number of people arriving and the higher proportion of people leaving. In the 1960s and 1970s, nearly 60 percent of all movers were under age 30; two-thirds of those were under 25. Overall employment growth in the region has been enough to absorb only about two-thirds of the natural increase in that age range. The other third has eventually sought jobs elsewhere. In recent years, another 10 percent of the people who have moved have been 65 years old or more. The retirement age group has become much more able to head for the Sun Belt since the advent of pension and annuity programs on a large scale in the 1920s and 1930s. The remaining one-third of the movers were in the least mobile, 30 to 65 age range. In that bracket migration to and from the region has been about in balance, but normal changes in health, employment opportunities, and family circumstances have kept part of the population in motion at all times.

There is a great deal of trial-and-error in the migration process. In recorded Upper Midwest experience, the total number of moves in and out has been at least 4 or 5 times and as much as 30 times the net migration over an average five-year period. Thus the net shifts have been the result of relatively small imbalances in a constant, large stream of movers. In the four full states, total moves in and out per decade have averaged 20 percent to 40 percent of state total population. Births and deaths have added further to the turnover. In a way the history of each place is a demographic stream flowing through time—a turbulent mixing zone of continuous, simultaneous inflows and outflows. For example, the Minnesota population grew 1.1 million between 1950 and 1980. But more than 6.1 million moved in, moved out, were born, or died (Figure 34). North Dakota net growth during the same period was only 34,000—a seemingly static population. But 1.4 million people were born, died, or otherwise arrived or departed! Little wonder that the thirtieth anniversary high school reunion finds itself gathered in a city of strangers.[55]

Yet a current of continuity runs down the middle of the demographic stream. Somehow, amid all the coming and going, a significant number of people develop the memories, understanding, and commitment necessary to hold places together. How does that spirit develop? And how does it keep alive, in touch with the environment, sensitive to change, yet also sensitive to history? Lifelong individual efforts help. But ultimately it depends upon an ongoing process of community formation and re-formation. Both natives and newcomers are inducted continuously, and people of all ages and backgrounds teach and learn from one another. Statistically the states look like little more than big transient camps. But the current of continuity—the spirit of community—makes them much more than either statistics or camps.

CORRIDORS OF MOVEMENT

Net outflow has exceeded net inflow in every state in the region since the 1920s, and in the Dakotas since the 1910s. The first detailed study of the process covered the period from 1955 to 1960. At that time, four corridors accounted for 85 percent of the moves to and from other parts of the United States. The net flow was out of the region in all four corridors. The busiest migration routes led west and southwest to the Pacific Coast, Denver, Arizona, and New Mexico. That corridor carried 36 percent of all the migration to and from the Upper Midwest. Almost as important, with 35 percent of the migrants, was the corridor to Milwaukee and Chicago, and eastward through other major metropolitan employment centers to Boston, New York, and Washington. A third corridor, with 10 percent of the migrants, ran southward to St. Louis and Kansas City, and on to New Orleans, Dallas, and south Texas. Another 7 percent of all migrants moved between the Upper Midwest and the Southeast. The remaining 12 percent of domestic moves were between states of the region and neighboring Iowa and Nebraska.[56]

The different streams varied somewhat in their population characteristics. Both the southern and western corridors carried people in every age, occupation, and income group. A high proportion of the streams to and from the East were professionals, technicians, salespersons, or managers in large national business organizations and the federal government. Retirees and military made up the greater part of the southeastern flow. Meanwhile, foreign

Minnesota

North Dakota

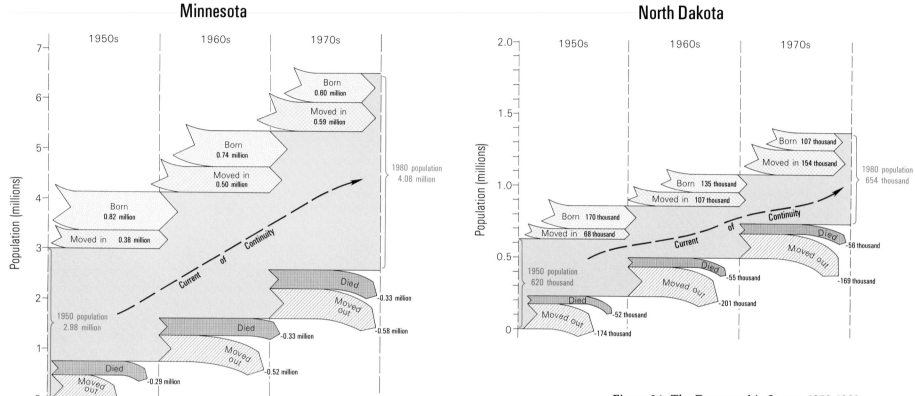

Figure 34. *The Demographic Stream 1950-1980. While Minnesota's population grew a little more than one million, more than 6 million arrived or departed by way of the moving van, stork, or hearse. North Dakota's population grew only 34,000, but more than 1.4 million were born, died, or moved in or out. A small current of community continuity runs through the turbulent stream. Source: note 55.*

1975 to 1980

To state   From state

40   Thousand
30   migrants
20
10
0

Trend: late 50 s to late 70 s

Continued net to state

Continued net from state

Reversal toward state

Reversal from state

Figure 35. Changing Migration to and from Upper Midwest States 1950s-1970s. Major features are the long-standing net movement from the region to the Intermountain and Pacific West, the growing net movement to the South, and the reversal of long-standing trends resulting in a net movement from the Northeast and Lower Midwest to Minnesota and a net movement from California to the Montana Rockies. Sources: notes 55, 58; U.S. Census of Population, 1980.

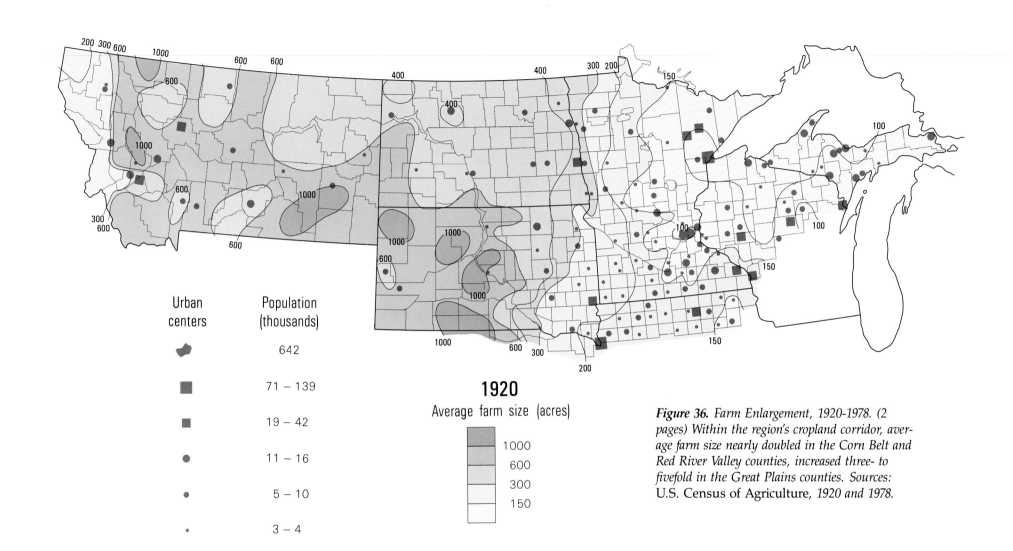

Urban centers	Population (thousands)
642
71 – 139
19 – 42
11 – 16
5 – 10
3 – 4

1920

Average farm size (acres)

1000
600
300
150

Figure 36. Farm Enlargement, 1920-1978. (2 pages) Within the region's cropland corridor, average farm size nearly doubled in the Corn Belt and Red River Valley counties, increased three- to fivefold in the Great Plains counties. Sources: U.S. Census of Agriculture, 1920 and 1978.

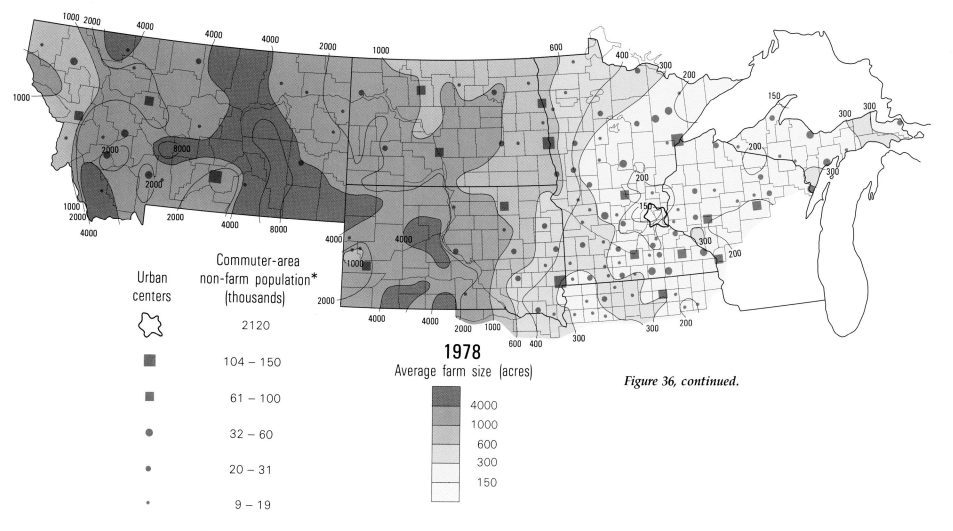

Urban
centers

Commuter-area
non-farm population*
(thousands)

2120

104 – 150

61 – 100

32 – 60

20 – 31

9 – 19

* See note with Figure 1.

1978

Average farm size (acres)

4000
1000
600
300
150

Figure 36, continued.

Table 1. Changes in Migration into and out of Minnesota and North Dakota, 1950s–1970s (In Thousands)[a]

Area	1955–60				1975–80			
	In	Out	Total	Net to MN–ND	In	Out	Total	Net to MN–ND
Iowa-Nebraska	24	36	60	−12	29	29	58	0
Illinois-Michigan	27	40	67	−13	39	25	64	+14
E. Mfg. Belt	29	31	60	−2	43	25	68	+18
Southeast	16	18	34	−2	37	45	82	−8
Missouri-Kansas	10	12	22	−2	12	13	25	−1
West South-Central	11	12	23	−1	18	33	51	−15
Mountain	11	20	31	−9	30	66	96	−36
Pacific Coast	26	74	100	−48	39	65	104	−26
Total	154	243	397	−89	247	301	548	−54

Sources: See notes 55, 57.

[a] The count includes those people who, at the time of the 1960 and 1980 censuses, lived in a different state than the one in which they had lived five years earlier. An unknown number of those people had made more than one move during the period. Hence actual mobility was probably even greater than the table indicates.

Table 2. Changes in Migration into and out of Montana, 1950s–1970s (In Thousands)[a]

Area	1955–60				1975–80			
	In	Out	Total	Net to Montana	In	Out	Total	Net to Montana
E. North Central	6	7	13	−1	10	5	15	+5
Northeast	3	3	6	0	7	3	10	+4
Southeast	4	3	7	+1	8	7	15	+1
Pacific NW	13	20	33	−7	15	25	40	−10
Other Mtn.	16	17	33	−1	25	32	57	−7
California	8	12	20	−4	16	11	27	+5
W. South Central	3	3	6	0	5	6	11	−1
W. North Central	16	11	27	+5	21	15	36	+6
Total	69	76	145	−7	107	104	211	+3

Sources: See notes 55, 57.

[a] The count includes those people who, at the time of the 1960 and 1980 censuses, lived in a different state than the one in which they had lived five years earlier. An unknown number of those people had made more than one move during the period. Hence actual mobility was probably even greater than the table indicates.

migration—not only military but also business and professional people and students—equaled 10 percent of domestic migration, notwithstanding the region's deep interior location.

Migration today is still concentrated in those same corridors. But some changes in volume and direction have occurred (Figure 35). The flow to and from Chicago and the East has increased slightly. But the direction of net movement has reversed sharply. A weak outflow from the region has changed to a strong inflow (Tables 1–2). Meanwhile, migration to and from the Southeast has more than doubled. The increase probably reflects not only more retirees to Florida but also more business-related moves to both Florida and the cities of the Georgia and Carolina Piedmont. Migration between the Upper Midwest, Colorado, and the Southwest has grown threefold. Net out-migration in that corridor is four times the 1950s level. In contrast, the volume of flow to and from California has stabilized, and the out-migration to California is down nearly one-half.[57]

Thus, during this era of adaptation, the Upper Midwest changed from primarily a destination for immigrants to an entrepôt in the national shift toward the West and South. The region takes in people from the East and sends people out in somewhat larger numbers to the West and South. The addition to the outflowing stream comes from the region's own wellspring of human energy and talent. The production of emigrants has come from farms, small towns, and urban centers of all sizes. There has been some tendency for a chain of movement up the hierarchy from farms and small towns to nearby urban places, then with increasing experience and contacts, to larger, more distant places. In any chain of moves, no matter how complex the pattern, there must be some places where the chain starts—where people keep leaving and few or none return. In the Upper Midwest those places have been farms and rural hamlets, and for many years the dominant larger, more distant place was the Twin Cities.[58]

The Shift from Farm to City

The region's farm population dropped from 2.7 million in 1920 to under 700,000 in 1980. The events were complicated, with no simple line of causation. But if one element could be singled out, many observers would point to the farm tractor. More power and speed in the fields opened the way to bigger farms, more production for sale or livestock feed, and more dollars earned per farm—but eventually 80 percent fewer people needed to do the farm work (Figure 36–37). To be sure, mechanical improvements were not new. Harvesting machinery and cumbersome steam tractors, for example, had been in use for decades. But the surge in efficiency and mobility of tractive power brought revolutionary changes in the size and variety of other field machinery. That, in turn, brought a surge of growth in both earning power and capital requirements. Higher capitalization meant more land for each farmer, and also opened the way for greatly increased use of scientifically developed seed and a multitude of specialized chemicals. Much has been said about the impact of the automobile on the rural scene. But never forget the tractor.

THE DECISION TO LEAVE OR TO STAY

During this massive reduction of farm labor force, the largest group of off-farm migrants has left at the age of high-school graduation. Some have moved to a nearby urban center, in recent decades most often to one large enough to have a wide range of business and government jobs and a trade school or two. Others have gone directly to distant centers, virtually always in a channel provided by relatives, college enrollment, or military enlistment. At a little older age level, many young farmers have taken jobs in neighboring towns and reduced their farming operations to part-time by selling off livestock or renting part of their land (Figure 38). They have thus contributed to the statistics that show both large farms and small farms increasing in number. Eventually some might quit farming altogether, sell their land, perhaps their houses. For still older farmers, who waited or were caught by circumstances at age 40 to 60, the shift has been hardest. Some have taken menial work in towns. Many have held on. With limited capital and low returns, they have helped to pull down average family income to the comparatively low levels that persist in rural areas. Those past 60 years old have eventually retired—on their farmsteads or in a nearby town, perhaps to sojourn in south Texas during midwinter. In each case, the statistical end result is a decline in the number of farm people and farm operators.

Then there are the survivors. Some have been farm youth who remained; others left for education or nonfarm experience and later returned. Both groups have taken over the fewer, bigger, and more complex units and gradually enlarged them further. There has been a constant renewal process, with an extra surge of new vitality at the end of World War II, when many young men returned from military service and took over from aging parents who had been holding on since the late 1930s. In the 1970s, a segment of the children of those World War II veterans began to take over in turn. By that time the capital requirements had grown still larger. The newest generation found itself in a stormy sea of unstable prices, high costs, and further heavy borrowing. In that generation, even some of the young, energetic, self-selected survivors faced the possibility of having to quit in the 1980s.

Like mechanization, the shift off the farm did not begin with the automobile and tractor era. The wave of net migration out of farming followed the settlement frontier westward across the region, with a 15- to 20-year lag. It set in during the 1880s in the southeastern counties and finally reached the Montana High Line in the 1920s. It was a natural development. As the frontier closed and families matured, the supply of surplus labor grew and the number of new farming opportunities declined. But the rate of change in this era has no precedent.[59]

THE URBANIZATION OF FARM WORK

While farm population declined 2.1 million, nonfarm numbers grew 4.2 million. In the region's main agricultural corridor from western Wisconsin to northern Montana, the same forces stimulated both changes. Increased capitalization and productivity raised real farm income per square mile two- to three-fold (Figure 39). Those square miles of farm land were also square miles of trade territory, nourishing the economies of urban centers. Of course, the remaining farm families developed substantially higher consumption levels than their forebears—in clothing, food, transportation, household goods, and entertainment. But that increase was not enough to compensate on Main Street for the greatly reduced number of farm households.

Beyond that change, however, increased income and commercialization meant that many tasks which had been family work on the old general farm became specialized and transferred to town. Oats production for

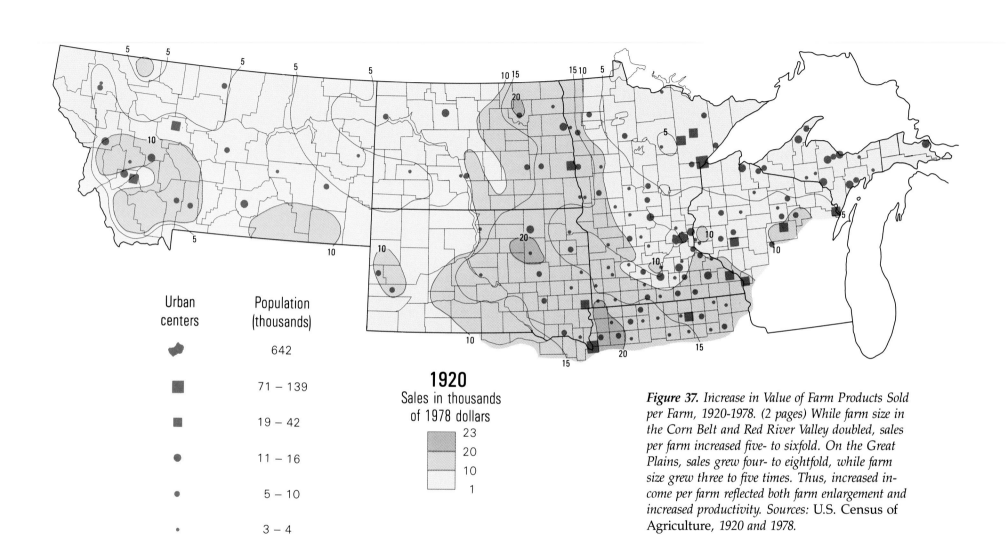

Urban
centers

Population
(thousands)

	642
	71 – 139
	19 – 42
	11 – 16
	5 – 10
	3 – 4

1920

Sales in thousands
of 1978 dollars

23
20
10
1

Figure 37. Increase in Value of Farm Products Sold per Farm, 1920-1978. (2 pages) While farm size in the Corn Belt and Red River Valley doubled, sales per farm increased five- to sixfold. On the Great Plains, sales grew four- to eightfold, while farm size grew three to five times. Thus, increased income per farm reflected both farm enlargement and increased productivity. Sources: U.S. Census of Agriculture, 1920 and 1978.

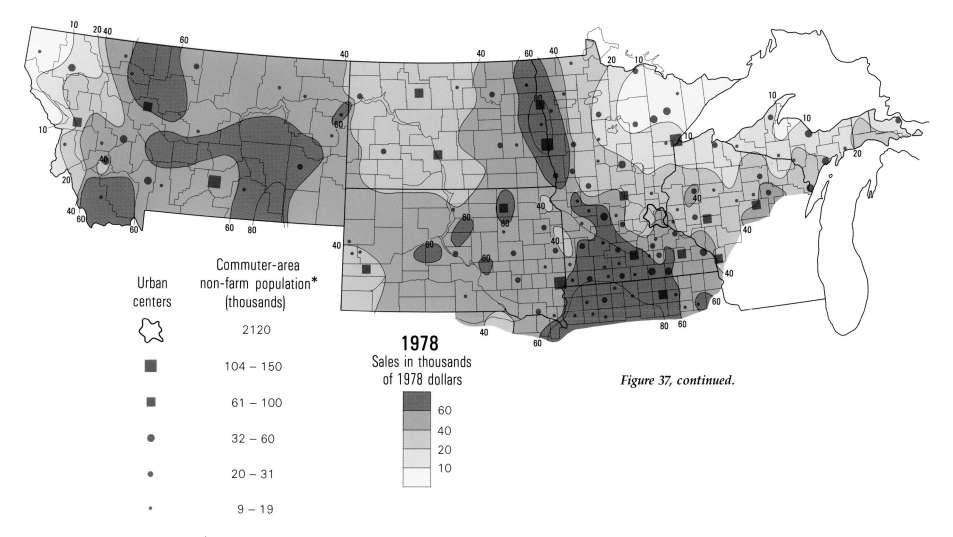

Urban
centers

Commuter-area
non-farm population*
(thousands)

2120

104 – 150

61 – 100

32 – 60

20 – 31

9 – 19

1978
Sales in thousands
of 1978 dollars

60
40
20
10

Figure 37, continued.

* See note with Figure 1.

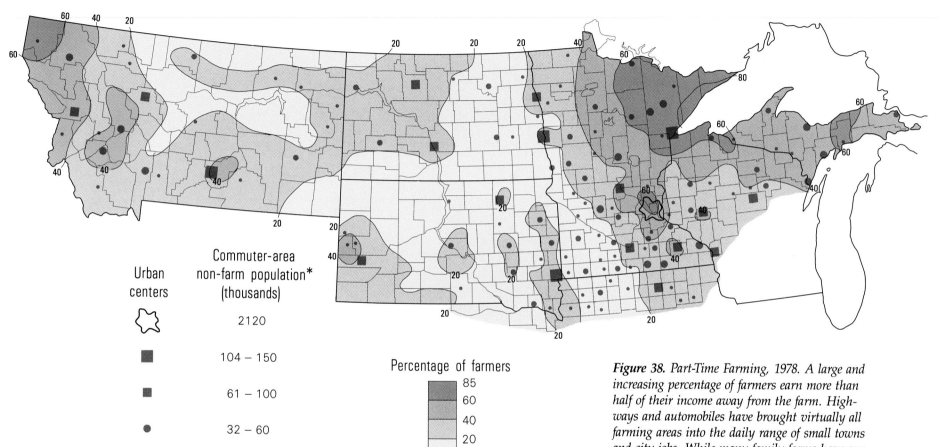

Urban
centers

Commuter-area
non-farm population*
(thousands)

2120

104 – 150

61 – 100

32 – 60

20 – 31

9 – 19

* See note with Figure 1.

Percentage of farmers

85
60
40
20
11

Figure 38. Part-Time Farming, 1978. A large and
increasing percentage of farmers earn more than
half of their income away from the farm. Highways and automobiles have brought virtually all
farming areas into the daily range of small towns
and city jobs. While many family farms have survived through heavy investment in more land and
machinery and often formed family-held corporations, may others have survived through partial
merger of the urban and farm labor force. Source:
U.S. Census of Agriculture, 1978.

horses was transformed into gasoline purchases and delivery for tractors, incidentally freeing an average of 20 percent of the crop acreage for other uses. Horse husbandry gave way to parts and repair shops; woodcutting to fuel oil, bottle gas, and electricity; voluntary road grading to highway maintenance shops and equipment fleets. An unprecedented rural commerce evolved in vehicles, machinery, motors, batteries, chemicals, feed, seed, additives, concentrates, in welding and metal shaping, power and phone line maintenance.

There were also gradual, subtle, but important multiplier effects. Professions, business services, financial institutions, public services, and construction gathered and grew around this emerging array of specialized, urbanized, former farmyard tasks. Here and there an office or a shop developed a specialty product and began to sell it though brokers in a regional or national market. Particularly impressive in the industrial directories of Upper Midwest states is the number of manufacturing firms that have sprouted from the metal and machine shops in the farm trade centers.

In the Corn, Dairy, and Wheat belts, farming evolved into a gigantic, highly capitalized industrial organization with an incredibly decentralized system of ownership and management and with an intense, efficient network of information. Within that structure the towns evolved as nerve centers, windows on the world, and entrepreneurial seedbeds. They were much more than that, of course, and to some people, much less.

REGIONAL MIGRATION

The off-farm movement triggered an avalanche that worked its way through the whole system of towns and cities. While its momentum accelerated in the tractor and trucking era, the avalanche began earlier, when the first generation of frontier children reached working age. The result was the rapid release of surplus quality labor and talent from the rural parts of this culture region for more than 50 years (Figure 40).

More than half the outflow spilled either directly or through the Twin Cities into the migration corridors to the rest of the nation and the world. But job growth in the Twin Cities both attracted and accommodated at least half a million immigrants from within the region. With the advent of low rural birthrates and increased dispersion of migration, both the quantity and sharpness of focus have decreased. But, for more than half a century, the regional migration system gave the Twin Cities special access to one of the nation's largest, highest quality surplus labor pools. It also established a dense network of personal and family ties that linked rural and metropolitan places, farms and mercantile offices. A regional community emerged.[60]

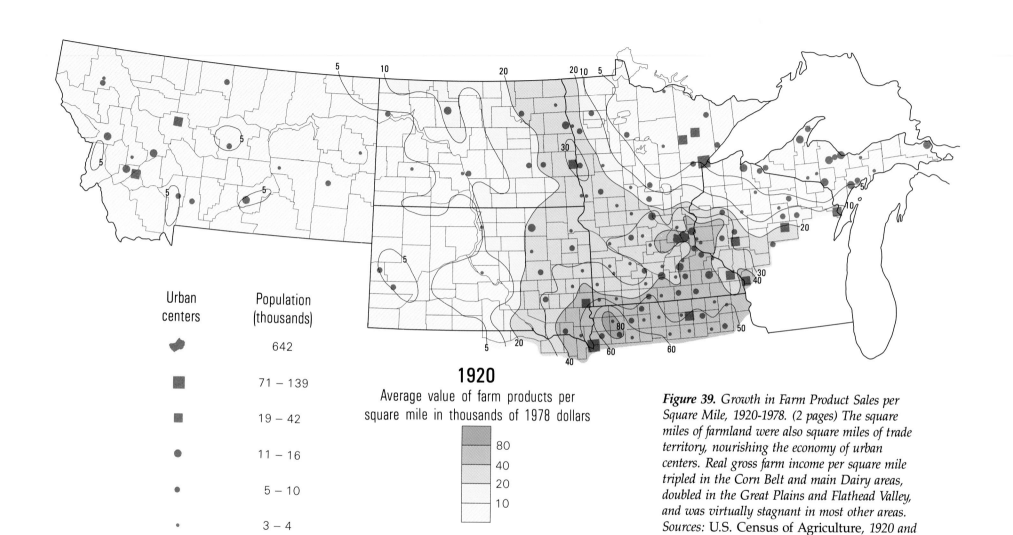

Urban centers

Population (thousands)

642

71 – 139

19 – 42

11 – 16

5 – 10

3 – 4

1920

Average value of farm products per square mile in thousands of 1978 dollars

80
40
20
10

Figure 39. Growth in Farm Product Sales per Square Mile, 1920-1978. (2 pages) The square miles of farmland were also square miles of trade territory, nourishing the economy of urban centers. Real gross farm income per square mile tripled in the Corn Belt and main Dairy areas, doubled in the Great Plains and Flathead Valley, and was virtually stagnant in most other areas. *Sources:* U.S. Census of Agriculture, 1920 and 1978.

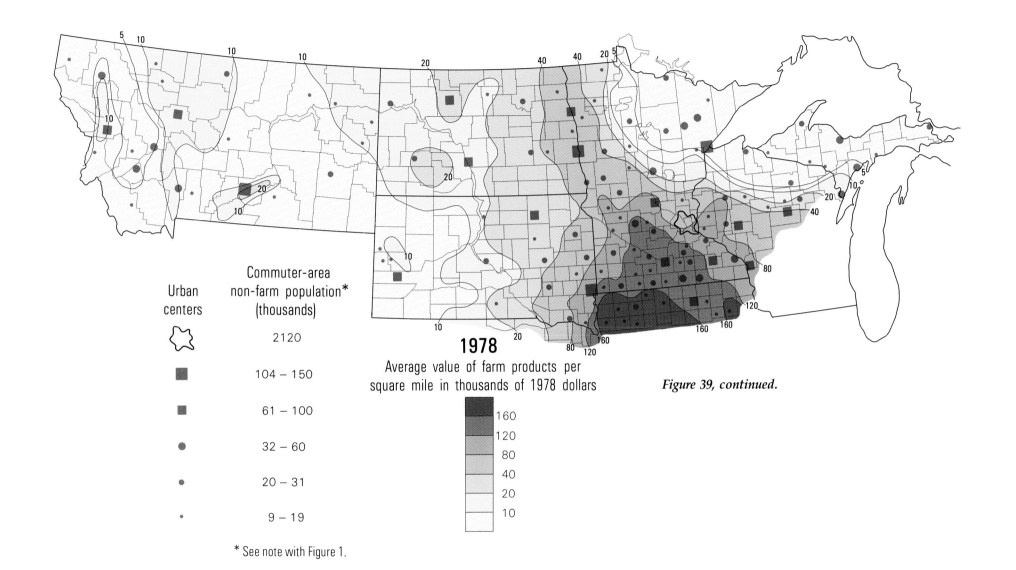

Urban
centers

Commuter-area
non-farm population*
(thousands)

2120

104 – 150

61 – 100

32 – 60

20 – 31

9 – 19

* See note with Figure 1.

1978

Average value of farm products per
square mile in thousands of 1978 dollars

160
120
80
40
20
10

Figure 39, continued.

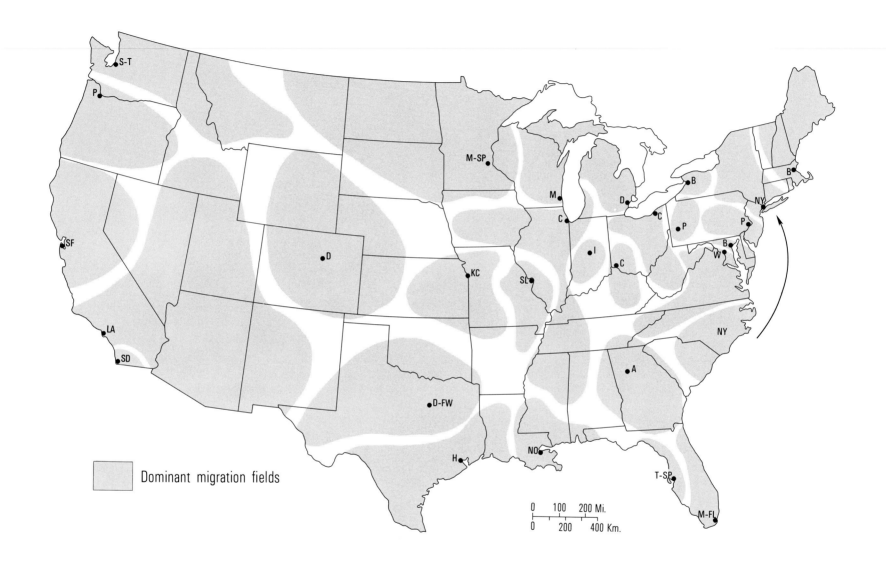

Figure 40. The Migration Field of the Twin Cities
in the U.S. Setting, 1960. The shaded area around
each high-order metropolis sent the largest number
of out-migrants to that urban area, 1955-1960.
Source: note 60.

CHAPTER 5

Concentration
of Nonfarm Growth

As the dust cleared from a half-century of spectacular off-farm movement, the geographic pattern of urban centers on the Upper Midwest map still looked remarkably familiar (Figure 41). Excluding Twin Cities suburbs, there were 138 urban places at the advent of the new era in 1920. At the close of the era in 1980, there were 134. Twenty places were deleted from today's map through consolidations into the Twin Cities metropolis or into hyphenated complexes such as Fargo-Moorhead, Marquette-Negaunee-Ishpeming, or Wahpeton-Breckenridge. Meanwhile, 16 places were added. One hundred eighteen were unchanged. The basic pattern had indeed been set in the railroad era.

Of course, that stable number of urban areas had to accommodate a flood of new nonfarm people. The result was a sharp increase in the geographical concentration of the region's population. Half of the urban centers were in just one-third of the region's counties (Table 3). Those counties accounted for 82 percent of the nonfarm growth between 1940 and 1980, and by 1980 they were home to nearly three-fourths of the region's total nonfarm population. The counties were mainly in clusters where historic location factors had seeded several cities in close proximity (Figure 42). In today's highway era, their labor markets and trade areas have become intertwined. In a few other cases, one or two counties form the principal commuter shed or labor market for an isolated major growth center, far from any others. Altogether, 18 of those major clusters were on the 1980 map.[61]

The Minnesota Core

The largest cluster of counties centered on the Twin Cities. More than ever, that cluster was the urban core of the Upper Midwest. With 2.7 million in nonfarm population in 1980, it accounted for 37 percent of the population of the entire region and 44 percent of the growth since 1940. The two Central Counties included the cities of Minneapolis and St. Paul and about half of the suburban population. A surrounding Commuter Ring of counties included virtually all the remainder of the commuter shed, or daily urban system. Beyond that, the Satellite Ring of counties included more than half-a-dozen partly independent urban centers, whose commuter sheds overlap the Twin Cities. Industries in the Satellite Ring included many branch plants of Twin Cities firms, and many manufacturers and distributors served primarily the Twin Cities market. A significant part of the retail and service trade was siphoned off to the Twin Cities. Cities in the Satellite Ring drew a substantial business conference trade from the metropolitan area, and lakes provided a large amount of weekend recreation for people from the Central Counties and Commuter Ring. The Central Counties retained 52 percent of the cluster's total population in 1980. But their growth in the preceding 40 years was only 64 percent, compared with 524 percent in the Commuter Ring and 137 percent in the Satellite Ring.

The Minnesota Lakes cluster, northwest of the Twin Cities, was the location of 40,000 vacation homes. There were 170,000 vacation homes in the Upper Midwest in 1980—one for every dozen households (Figure 43). Ninety-four percent of the total was located in the moraine-and-lake and Canadian Shield country from Minnesota eastward across Upper Michigan, and one-quarter of those were in the Minnesota Lakes area. The area's eight ur-

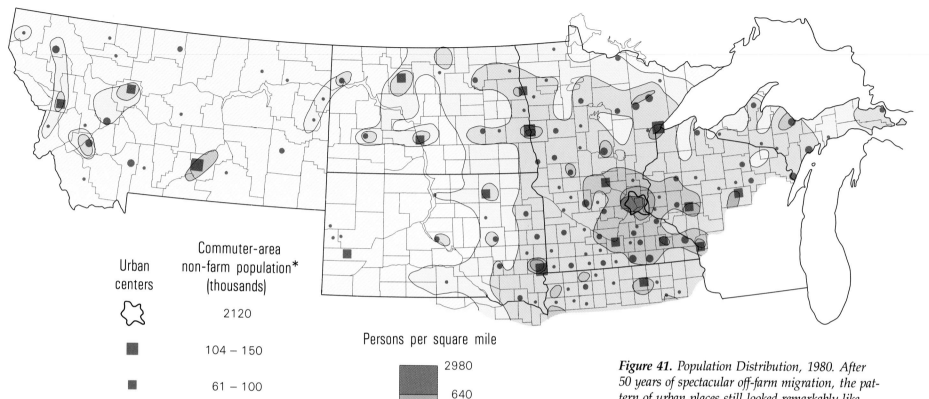

Urban
centers

Commuter-area
non-farm population*
(thousands)

2120

104 − 150

61 − 100

32 − 60

20 − 31

9 − 19

* See note with Figure 1.

Persons per square mile

2980

640

160

40

10

5

0.5

Figure 41. Population Distribution, 1980. After
50 years of spectacular off-farm migration, the pattern of urban places still looked remarkably like
that of the 1920s. But there had been important
differences in growth rates at different towns and
cities. More than four-fifths of all population
growth in the region was concentrated in areas of
more than 40 persons per square mile. Source:
U.S. Bureau of the Census, County and City
Data Book, 1982.

Non-farm population (millions)

Minnesota Core
   A: Central Counties
   B: Commuter Ring
   C: Satellite Ring
D: Southern Minnesota
E: Chippewa Valley-La Crosse
F: Upper Wisconsin Valley
G: Minnesota Lakes
H: Sioux Valley
I: Fargo-Moorhead
J: Grand Forks
K: Bismarck
L: Minot
M: Billings
N: Western Montana Valleys
O: Black Hills
P: Duluth-Mesabi Range
Q: Marquette Range
R: Gogebic-Menominee Ranges
S: Copper Range

Minnesota Core   Smaller Urban Clusters   Total/Primary Region   Total/Banking Region

Figure 42. Concentration of Nonfarm Population, 1940-1980. The bar graph shows that more than 80 percent of the region's nonfarm population growth since 1940 has been in major urban clusters of counties. The map outlines those areas, and Table 3 details the numerical population changes in each cluster. Source: note 61.

The core area of the regional metropolis spreads from downtown St. Paul (center) toward central Minneapolis (upper left), 10 miles to the west, in 1982. In 1862 the St. Paul and Pacific Railroad began at the riverboat landing, just upstream from the nearest bridge in the foreground, and crossed the wide-open spaces to its western terminal at the doorstep of Minneapolis. Photos, Cook's Aerial Photos, Minneapolis, MN.

Viewed from Gray's Bay, at the eastern end of Lake Minnetonka in 1982, these wooded suburbs in the western part of the Twin Cities metropolis resemble major resort areas of the Minnesota and northern Wisconsin lake districts. Photo, Cook's Aerial Photos, Minneapolis, MN.

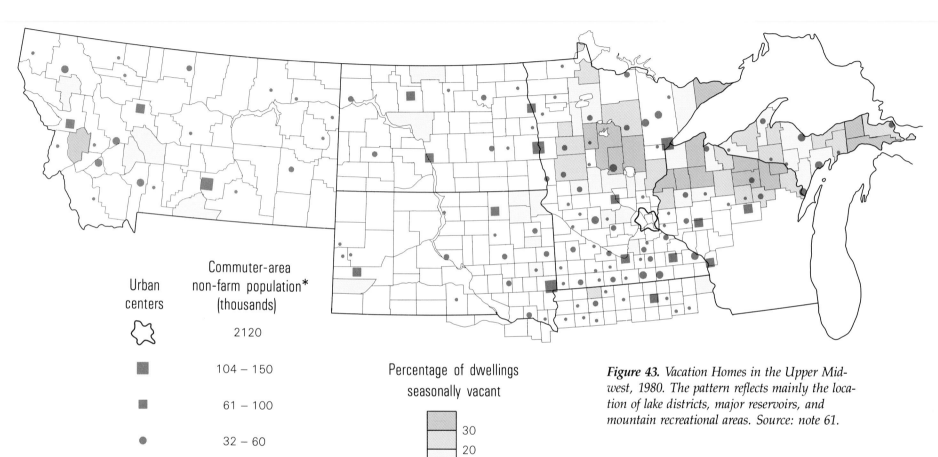

Figure 43. *Vacation Homes in the Upper Midwest, 1980. The pattern reflects mainly the location of lake districts, major reservoirs, and
mountain recreational areas. Source: note 61.*

ban centers provided the main streets and highway commercial strips for the recreational service business and also for local logging and dairy farming. An oversized array of boat, snowmobile, and ski sales, restaurants, beverage stores, gift shops, bars, and amusement facilities mingled with food and beverage warehouses, trucking terminals, woodworking plants, and farm stores along the strips. Of course, important variations emerged across the area. The logging and pulpwood influence increased toward the northeast, the commercial agricultural influence toward the southwest. Visitors from the Twin Cities dominated overwhelmingly toward the east, Dakotans toward the west. Canadian guests were numerous in the northwest, and visible on all the high-quality lakes was a sprinkling of vacationers from metropolitan Chicago and the midcontinent states.[62]

Year-round nonfarm population increased two and one-half times, to more than one-quarter million since 1940. The summer and winter weekend populations probably added another 50,000 to 150,000. Population growth was the result of three factors. One was the growing discretionary spending of vacation home owners and tourists. Another was the growing use of lakeshore houses and condominiums for retirement. A third was the entry of people who were in the urban labor force but self-employed and footloose. They wrote, ran conferences, sold schoolbooks, consulted, crafted musical instruments or pottery, and worked in myriad other occupations. Many of their occupations defied the federal government's 10,000-category Standard Industrial Classification scheme. Most lived on the lakeshores, but many occupied old farmhouses amid hilly, stony, brushy or wooded pastures and an occasional tamarack bog.

Table 3. Nonfarm Population in the Upper Midwest, 1940–1980

Area	1940		1970		1980		Total Growth, 1940–80
	No.[a]	% of Total	No.	% of Total	No.	% of Total	
Urban Clusters							
Minnesota Core	1,184	30.4	2,350	37.2	2,682	36.7	44.3
Central Counties	854	21.9	1,433	22.7	1,400	19.2	16.2
Commuter Ring	129	3.3	554	8.8	805	11.0	20.0
Satellite Ring	201	5.2	363	5.8	477	6.5	8.2
Minnesota Lakes	110	2.8	197	3.1	261	3.6	4.5
Southern Minnesota	128	3.3	246	3.9	283	3.9	4.6
Chippewa Valley–LaCrosse	154	4.0	242	3.9	287	3.9	3.9
Upper Wisconsin Valley	93	2.4	162	2.6	212	2.9	3.4
Fargo-Moorhead	56	1.4	110	1.8	130	1.8	2.2
Grand Forks Area	51	1.3	93	1.5	112	1.5	1.8
Sioux Valley	73	1.9	128	2.0	152	2.1	2.3
Bismarck-Mandan	29	0.7	54	0.9	75	1.0	1.3
Minot	22	0.6	54	0.9	55	0.8	1.0
Billings	32	0.8	84	1.3	105	1.4	2.2
Black Hills	33	0.8	79	1.3	98	1.3	1.9
Homestake[b]	17	0.4	16	0.3	17	0.2	0.0
Western Montana Valleys	125	3.2	272	4.3	342	4.7	6.4
Butte-Anaconda[b]	64	1.6	58	0.9	51	0.8	−0.4
Lake Superior Mineral Districts							
Mesabi-Duluth	219	5.6	274	4.3	278	3.8	1.7
Gogebic-Menominee	78	2.0	65	1.0	65	0.9	−0.4
Marquette	42	1.1	65	1.0	74	1.0	0.9
Copper Range	44	1.1	36	0.6	39	0.5	−0.1
Outlying Areas							
Corn Belt	554	14.2	718	11.4	866	11.8	9.2
Great Plains	547	14.0	667	10.6	707	9.7	4.7
Northern Forest	215	5.5	296	4.6	342	4.6	3.8
Montana Rockies	37	0.9	49	0.8	55	0.8	0.5
Total[c]	3,907	100.0	6,315	100.5	7,288	99.7	99.8

Sources: See note 61.

[a] In thousands.

[b] Mining district populations are separated from the remainder of Black Hills and Western Montana Valleys.

[c] Percentage totals contain minor discrepancies due to rounding.

In 1985 the towering Mayo Clinic buildings and related hospitals, hotels, and apartments dominate the downtown area of Rochester, Minnesota, beyond the winding Zumbro River. Aerial photo by K. Bordner Consultants, Inc., Minneapolis, MN.

Many also farmed their marginal land on a small scale, part-time.

South of the Twin Cities, six urban areas composed the Southern Minnesota cluster. All grew early as county seat trade centers on the fertile prairies. Rochester, Owatonna, Waseca, and Mankato stood along one east-west rail line between Chicago and South Dakota; Austin and Albert Lea on another. All six were located at intersections with north-south lines between the Twin Cities and the midcontinent. In the subsequent years, they were incubators for not only the Mayo Clinic and Hormel but also two dozen medium or large industrial and service companies. Non-farm population in the Southern Minnesota cluster more than doubled between 1940 and 1980, to nearly 300,000.

The Eastern Transition Zone

The Chippewa Valley–LaCrosse cluster in 1980 had a large element of long-established manufacturing industries, a strong trucking-based wholesale trade with the surrounding area and the Twin Cities, and several colleges and universities that shared in the post–World War II enrollment boom. The logging industry of the Chippewa Valley was a major factor in the early development of Eau Claire-Chippewa Falls and Winona. It also augmented the early role of LaCrosse as a river-rail transfer point. The commuter sheds of those four cities outline the modern urban cluster. Nonfarm population nearly doubled between 1940 and 1980, to about 340,000.

Still farther east, the logging industry gave rise to another line of towns at Wisconsin river power sites from Rhinelander southward through Merrill to Wausau. In 1980 they were the northern centers of the massive Wisconsin Valley pulp and paper industry. But Rhine-lander is also the principal service center for another major concentration of lakeshore homes and resorts. Three generations of southeast Wisconsin and Chicago vacationers have swarmed to the lakes between Toma-hawk, 25 miles downstream from Rhine-lander, and the headwaters area to the north. At the turn of the century, the visitors came by train on lines that were first built to haul lumber to Milwaukee and Chicago. Some families lived at the lakes all summer, and their bread-winners commuted in parlor cars and sleepers attached to local trains on weekends. Many another family made the long trip by daycoach to enjoy a hard-earned week in a rental cabin. In the 1920s, family automobiles on dusty roads began slowly, but surely, to empty the passenger trains. By 1980 the train tracks were rusting beside long lines of weekend traffic on wide ribbons of pavement. Many of the depots have disappeared or stand in ruins. A few have become items of renewed curiosity and restoration efforts. Like the Minnesota Lakes cluster, those towns have added many retirees and self-employed to a growing local service base. As a result, the nonfarm population tripled to about three-quarters of a million between 1940 and 1980.

The Great Plains

Where the Corn and Dairy belts give way westward to the wheat country, the urban pattern breaks into a half-dozen smaller clusters or isolated counties. Those clusters were home in 1980 to 70 percent of the entire urban population of the region's subhumid and semiarid plains.

Fargo-Moorhead and Grand Forks-East Grand Forks thrived at historic rail crossings of the Red River. The two centers shared North Dakota's major state university campuses. Grand Forks had drawn economic support from a large military air base for three decades. But Fargo, substituting trucking for rail, had continued its powerful century-old wholesale penetration from the Red River Valley to the Montana border. As in the other riverside twin cities of the Upper Midwest region, the larger growth at both Fargo and Grand Forks was on the west bank, facing the direction of initial frontier expansion. The Grand Forks cluster included the labor markets of Crookston and Thief River Falls, Minnesota. Sioux Falls, the state university town of Vermillion, the historic river port of Yankton, and the northwestern exurban fringe of Sioux City formed another cluster on the western edge of the Corn Belt. In the trucking era, Sioux Falls had displaced Sioux City in a substantial part of the South Dakota wholesale trade, while its manufacturing and services not only diversified but also extended to national markets.

In central North Dakota, Bismarck has been a vigorous growth center in the post–World War II years. Its site on commanding bluffs above the Missouri was enhanced by the big dams on the river. The upstream Garrison Reservoir traps the mud, clears the river, and minimizes the flood risk. Meanwhile, the downstream, Oahe Dam has placed the city at the head of a 200-mile-long recreational lake. Bismarck's government center has grown and attracted other service industries. Oil and lignite firms have selected the city for regional offices. The resulting growth has generated additional agricultural service and distribution jobs. Across the river, Mandan has more than offset declining railroad employment through the effects of oil and lignite activity and residential and commercial spillover from Bismarck.

Minot followed a different course. As a bigger railroad center, it had to absorb larger

LaCrosse has grown on a broad terrace above the Mississippi and below the bluffs and hilly upland of southwestern Wisconsin. Today's downtown district covers the city's initial site downstream from the marshy confluence of the LaCrosse River with the navigable Mississippi. New parkland and buildings had replaced some of the early port and warehouse area on the riverfront when this picture was taken in the early 1980s. The marina and recreational boating reflect a major and growing use of this scenic valley. Photo copyright 1986, Western Wisconsin Technical Institute, LaCrosse.

employment losses in its yards and shops. Its large government payroll came in the much more uncertain form of a military air base. Its transportation advantage for wholesaling shrank somewhat with the shift from rail to highway. While growth from 1940 to 1980 was substantial, it was also volatile. For example, the county nonfarm growth in the Bismarck–Mandan labor shed was 33 percent in the 1950s, compared with 46 percent for Minot. In the 1970s, it was 38 percent for Bismarck-Mandan, 2 percent for Minot.

Fastest growing of the Great Plains centers was Billings, which seemed to be emerging in the oil-trucking-service era as the metropolis of Montana. In its revitalized downtown, Billings developed the first suggestions of a traditional metropolitan skyline west of the Twin Cities. Meanwhile its burgeoning residential developments sprawled westward on former irrigated farmland between the Yellowstone and the rimrocks and up the wooded canyons in the breaks of the High Plains.

Though uneven, growth in all these plains nonfarm clusters was fast—154 percent between 1940 and 1980, to a total of nearly 630,000.

The Western Mountain Zone

Today's urban clusters in the Black Hills and Western Montana Valleys are mainly in the same counties as were the earliest settlements of ranchers and prospectors. Part of the Black Hills cluster is the historic Homestake gold-mining community, sprawled over ridgetops at Lead and jammed in the neighboring narrow canyon of Whitewood Creek, 2,000 feet below, at Deadwood. Rapid City and Sturgis stand where two sparkling creeks discharge from the wooded hills to the dry plains. The same streams once spread gold-

At Eau Claire, Wisconsin, in 1977, the railroad era city surrounds the early business core at the confluence of the smaller Eau Claire river with the Chippewa (upper center).

Post-World War II expansion adjoins the freeway bypasses to the east (upper right) and south (foreground). Aerial photo by K. Bordner Consultants, Inc., Minneapolis, MN.

In a 1978 picture, Moorhead and Fargo spread along the east and west banks of the Red River. Railroad-era industrial satellite communities at Dilworth, Minnesota (foreground), and West Fargo, North Dakota (top center), have become parts of the suburban fringe. Heavily wooded banks of the meandering Red River mark the Minnesota-North Dakota boundary, *from left to right (south to north) through the urbanized area. Warehouse-industry districts, formerly confined to the east-west rail corridor, sprawl into the grain fields, especially along the western freeway bypass. Aerial photo by K. Bordner Consultants, Inc., Minneapolis, MN.*

In this view west over Grand Forks in the autumn of 1979, the Red River, meandering north-south on the flat floor of glacial lake Agassiz, separates Minnesota (foreground) from North Dakota. The rail-era commercial core lies just downstream from the confluence of Minnesota's Red Lake River with the Red. Residential areas of the 1920s and earlier are marked by dense tree cover; the outer edge of post-World War II growth nibbles at the vast checkerboard of black soil and grain stubble of the Red River Valley. Aerial photo by K. Bordner Consultants, Inc., Minneapolis, MN.

Sioux Falls, South Dakota, 1979, spreads from the south loop of the Big Sioux River and the south freeway bypass (lower edge) to the northwest airport-industrial area (upper left). Rail-era downtown district and industries developed at an early river crossing point upstream from the falls (upper center). Aerial photo by K. Bordner Consultants, Inc., Minneapolis, MN.

The wide Missouri flows between Bismarck (foreground) and Mandan, North Dakota, in this 1980 picture. The historic transcontinental railroad axis winds from the left center to the upper center where it crosses the Missouri. The land rises from the rail corridor and downtown area northward toward the state capitol grounds (right center) and the bluffs overlooking the river. The extensive shopping mall and related expansion south of the rail corridor has spread across lower land, and its development followed initiation of flood control by the big dams on the Missouri. Aerial photo by K. Bordner Consultants, Inc., Minneapolis, MN.

A major highway heads north through Minot, North Dakota. Dense tree cover marks the area of residential growth during the 1920s and earlier, on the sheltered, but flood-risky, floor of the Souris River Valley. Post–World War II expansion had climbed the valley walls and spread to the upland plains by the mid-1970s. Aerial photo by K. Bordner Consultants, Inc., Minneapolis, MN.

Ponderosa pine-topped cliffs command a panoramic view northwestward across Billings in 1985. Downtown bank, oil, hotel, and civic buildings rise above the rail-industry corridor and Yellowstone River in the foreground. Residential areas spread across the flat terrace to the base of the Rim Rocks in the distance. Photo, High Plains Productions.

In the foreground of this 1985 view of Rapid City, South Dakota, the College of Mines and Technology campus lies between dry, grassy foothills and the tree-lined course of Rapid Creek. The pine-covered, deeply carved Black Hills dome rises abruptly west of the city. Aerial photography by Horizons, Inc., Rapid City, SD 57709.

bearing gravels before the Custer expedition's scientists and the prospectors who followed them, scarcely more than a century ago. Belle Fourche is the focus of a twentieth-century federal government irrigation project where the Belle Fourche River leaves the hills. Rapid City was the main railhead. With the help of a large air base, state enterprise, and the tourist traffic, it has become the metropolis of the area. Outside the mining district, total non-farm population of the cluster tripled to nearly 100,000 between 1940 and 1980. Meanwhile population of the Homestake district has been virtually unchanged at 16,000 to 18,000 for more than half a century.

The Western Montana Valleys also nearly tripled in nonfarm population from 1940 to 1980. The settlements include the Kootenai Valley around Libby, the Flathead and Bitter-root valleys from Kalispell-Whitefish-Columbia Falls south through Missoula to Hamilton, the Gallatin Valley around Boze-man, and the Missouri Valley from Helena to Great Falls. The Butte-Anaconda complex, in the upper reaches of the Deer Lodge Valley, is part of the same urban system.

In a small way the population growth of these valleys mirrors an important nationwide economic mystery. By traditional measures, it is not entirely clear what the whole economic base is; nevertheless, there are well-being and growth. To be sure, a traditional base is impor-tant. The state of Montana maintains its capital and three principal college campuses in four of the cities. Federal agencies are attracted to the area. Scattered small mines and a smelter still operate. Logging in the neighboring moun-tains sustains paper mills and sawmills. A small, but significant, farming enterprise works the irrigated valley floors. Augmented by the payroll of the city's large military air base, Great Falls business and professions

In this 1980 panorama, downtown Great Falls, Montana, ad-joins the historic Missouri River crossing above the great falls. Rail-era industrial development is concentrated on the north outskirts (left), near the falls. Wheat ranching country spreads 30 miles eastward between the city and the High-wood Mountains on the horizon. Montana Air National Guard photo by Msgt. Jack W. Carte.

serve the vast wheat and livestock ranching country on the plains of Montana's Triangle and High Line. There is a substantial recreation business. Between 5,000 and 10,000 vacation cabins hide in the mountain forests and dot the lakeshores. Perhaps a million people from the rest of the country pass through the valleys each year en route to Glacier and Yellowstone National Parks, the National Forest wilderness, and the ski resorts.

Yet, beyond that traditional base, there is a large component of footloose, self-employed people with a variety of skills, entrepreneurial talents, and survival instincts as well as a passion for a spectacular mountain setting for their activities. They live in urban neighborhoods, small towns, tumbledown gold camps, and mountain cabins. Few, if any, are wealthy by American standards. Instead of retreating from the Twin Cities or Chicago, as have most of their counterparts in the Minnesota and Wisconsin lake country, they have retreated from southern California and the Pacific Northwest, as well as nearby places—and in significant numbers from all around the country.

These people are the piece of the economic base that provides the mystery. Part of the base is risk capital imported with the immigrants. Sources of the capital are usually informal—often relatives; the investment might well be unorthodox, quite small, highly risky, or all three. Another part of the base could better be classed as long-term expenditures for personal consumption and leisure. Traditionally, individuals and households everywhere make a clear distinction between work and play. They make most of their expenditures for personal enjoyment in small amounts, over short periods of time, and in the locality where they live and work. There are frequent retreats to the restaurant, bar,

bowling alley, ball game, tennis court, pool, movie theater, and so on. Retreats to more distant places tend to be brief—weekends at the lake, a Las Vegas weekend, a week's excursion to the mountains. But it is also possible to package those expenses and pleasures in a quite different way. A household can live austerely for some years—drive 10-year-old cars, save intensely in many ways. Eventually the wage earners may quit their jobs and embark on a large expenditure for personal enjoyment, spread over a long period of time, in a remote place. They might buy a good four-wheel-drive pickup truck and other basic equipment, move to a mountain valley, buy a place, and settle there. Interest earnings or cannibalized savings might be augmented by a service job, part-time logging, guiding, art, handicrafts, roadside storekeeping, raising a few cattle, and hunting. Long-term stability depends not only on the combined value of the savings and the supplemental work but also on the durability of the spirit.

This mysterious phenomenon has at least two definitions. In one lexicon it is "alternative life style"; in another it is "economic base"—though, in the available data sources, any measure of it as economic base is buried at best as "miscellaneous" or "other" activities. This phenomenon has become part of the economy of almost everyplace in the United States. Measuring it seems less urgent in areas where most of the economy is traditional and institutionalized, and not understanding this mysterious sector leaves only a small part of the base unaccounted for. But the problem is more important in areas such as the Montana valleys and the Minnesota lakes, where the phenomenon explains a significant part of the population growth.

Meanwhile, the Butte-Anaconda area has thus far attracted little new economic activity

to shield it from the collapse of Anaconda Copper Company's Montana operations. The population there has declined more than 20 percent since 1940, with no respite in view, while the other places in the Western Montana Valleys have grown threefold in the same period to reach a 1980 population of more than one-third million. Population trends have been most volatile in the Great Falls urban area, because of the copper-refining shutdown, the loss of railroad employment with which James J. Hill once helped to launch the place, and the vicissitudes of the military air-base industry.

The Lake Superior District

At the opposite end of the region, in the Lake Superior districts, four more clusters have their urban roots in the mining industry. They are striking analogues to their geographically distant cousins at Butte-Anaconda and Lead-Deadwood. The most obvious similarity is non-growth or decline of population. From the beginning, these mining towns and ports grew in areas hostile to competitive commercial farming. They never had any significant relationship to the urbanization of agricultural work. Thus they missed that drama which provided so much stimulus to urban growth and diversification in most of the Upper Midwest.

The oldest commercial mining district is the Copper Range, on Michigan's Keweenaw Peninsula. Slashed from the forest and blasted from the hard-rock ridges high above Lake Superior, it was North America's leading copper producer by 1850. The need to get Keweenaw copper into the national economy triggered the building of the first Soo locks in 1855. The Keweenaw continued to lead all other copper-mining districts until Butte was developed in the late 1880s, soon after the Northern Pacific made that area accessible. Meanwhile the Marquette Iron Range became the country's leading source of iron ore in the 1870s, supplying the new, fast-growing Great Lakes steel industry. Later in the same decade, the Menominee and Gogebic iron ranges were opened. Across the lake the first Minnesota production came from the Vermilion Range in the 1880s. The Mesabi Range, centered on Hibbing and Virginia, opened in the 1890s. Mesabi ore production quickly eclipsed all others because its ore bodies were not only very large and high-grade but also easily mined by open-pit methods. Within two decades, the yawning open pits were strung like beads for 60 miles along the ore railroads from east of Virginia southwestward nearly to Grand Rapids.

That was the sequence of starting dates. Meanwhile, one by one the districts reached peak production then declined. Population fell not only because of declining production but also because of increasing mechanization. As in farming and forestry, the sharpest wave of change in the mining industry got under way around the time of World War I. Population decline began locally on the Copper Range in the nineteenth century and became pervasive in the 1910s. Decline began on the Michigan, Wisconsin, and Vermilion iron ranges in the 1920s. Stagnation of urban growth rates set in on the Mesabi in the 1920s. During World War II, demand for all-out production at any cost temporarily revived the best underground mines, while it nearly exhausted the much more accessible high-grade open-pit ores on the Mesabi. The two following decades saw the closing of virtually all underground mining and the rise of the colossal pelletizing industry for low-grade open-pit ores. Almost all of the pellet plants were built on the taconite deposits of the Mesabi, a single one on the Marquette. Today all active mines

Across from Houghton, Michigan, the Quincy Mining Company smelter and docks pressed against the north shore of the Portage Lake embayment of Lake Superior at Hancock in the early 1900s. The mine works were partly visible on the top of the hill. At that time, the Upper Peninsula of Michigan was the world's major copper producer and led the United States in iron ore production. Photo, Louis G. Koepel, Quincy Mining Company.

On a bright autumn day in 1982, the forested Keweenaw Peninsula rises above the deep trench of the Portage Lake channel. The historic downtowns of Houghton (left) and Hancock stand at opposite ends of the bridge. The Michigan Technological University campus dominates eastern Houghton (foreground). Suomi College (Finnish Lutheran Synod) and medical facilities are other major buildings. Quincy Hill rises above the old smelter site east of Hancock (extreme right). Photo, Keweenaw Tourism Council.

are on those two ranges; and the Vermilion, Gogebic, and Menominee, with the Copper Range, are abandoned.

Because the Iron Range urban communities have depended so heavily on mining, their fortunes have been kept on a roller coaster by war, depression, new discovery, exhaustion, mechanization, pelletizing, and world competition. But with each cycle, some momentum was lost at one place or another. Meanwhile, as the forest gradually recovered, the wood-based industries grew slowly in the neighborhood of some mining communities. Attracted by deep winter snow, the scenery of the glacier-scoured shield and Lake Superior coasts, and the unique history, the annual tourist stream grew from a few thousand in the rail era to hundreds of thousands in the auto era. But by 1980 that had not yet been enough to offset the mining declines.

The net result has been an auto-era growth history quite different from that of the other main urban population clusters of the Upper Midwest. The Lake Superior clusters were home to 524,000 people in 1980. But that reflected a growth of only 19 percent from 1940 to 1980. The inactive Menominee-Gogebic and Copper ranges declined 15 percent, and the active Mesabi-Duluth-Superior and Marquette areas grew 34 percent. The picture at Duluth-Superior was more complicated. The Twin Ports retained their massive tonnages, especially in ore, grain, and coal. But larger, faster, and more specialized ships and trains increased efficiency and cut employment in transportation. The lumbering decline had already reached bottom at the beginning of the auto era, and the stagnation of wholesaling and heavy industry that was portended at that time did indeed develop. The timing of Duluth-Superior's emergence in the nation's transportation evolution was not quite right.

Because of railroad improvements and the Panama Canal, the Great Lakes waterway never did develop as the major link in the northern transcontinental general cargo route. Thus the Zenith City did not materialize as the strategic location promised in early commercial dreams. Consequently, the growth rate was very sharply reduced from the boom years of the steel rail era. The Twin Ports had catapulted to one-fourth the population of the Twin Cities by 1920, but by 1980 they had fallen back to one-tenth.

Prolonged stagnation and shrinkage have produced selective abandonment, rehabilitation, and redevelopment in the Lake Superior urban areas. There has been an inexorable sorting of residential and business locations. Marquette, Houghton-Hancock, and Duluth-Superior have emerged as centers of maintenance or growth. Those urban areas house the state universities in the Lake Superior district, with accompanying income transfers from other parts of their states. They have also become the centers of health services, business services, shopping, and communication. The largest cities on the Mesabi Range—Virginia and Hibbing—have been similar centers of maintenance or growth. But they have been even more dependent on the mineral industry, and their fortunes even more subject to fluctuation and uncertainty.

Within the large, aging, slowly shrinking populations of these Lake Superior mineral districts, a core number of people is needed in the emerging basic economy. The cities are trying to adapt their legacy of land and buildings to fit that population. It is a gradual, fitful process of trial and error. But a new settlement pattern, emerging from the old, probably will suit both modern standards and the unique history and terrain of the district. It may also help to guide many other places nationwide

where similar problems are more recent or still in the future.

Outside the Clusters

Three-quarters of all Upper Midwest land and one-quarter of the nonfarm population are outside the main clusters of urban growth. Four large groups of counties make up those outlying areas. They include large parts of the Corn Belt, the subhumid and semiarid Great Plains, the more sparsely settled parts of the northern Great Lakes forest, and the more rugged parts of the Montana Rockies. Well over half the urban centers in the Upper Midwest—more than 70—are in these four outlying areas. Almost all are located in the main cropland corridor that stretches from western Wisconsin to northern Montana. Their emergence as urban centers reflects not only their legacy as county-seat trade centers but also the auto-era transformation of farm work into urban jobs and the concentration of the resulting urban growth at established centers.

The outlying urban centers are most numerous and closely spaced on the more productive land of the Corn Belt, fewer and more widely separated on the Great Plains, and virtually absent in the forest regions where there was little farming and, consequently, little farm-related urban growth. For example, in 20 counties of southwestern Minnesota and northwestern Iowa, there are 13 cities in the small and medium shopping-center size classes. Their trade areas cover 10,000 square miles altogether. Contrast that with only seven comparable-size centers with combined trade areas of 75,000 square miles in 28 counties of western North Dakota and eastern Montana. If you are a livestock feed representative driving out of Spencer, Iowa, it is only 30 to 50 miles to competing urban centers at Estherville or Storm Lake or Cherokee, or across the state line at Worthington, Minnesota. Small towns and hamlets spread out beside the highway every six miles or so along the route. But when you leave Dickinson, North Dakota, it is 100 miles or more to the nearest comparable neighboring city, with few small towns or hamlets to break up the panorama of rolling plains and rare river breaks along the way. When you pull up the hill above the Yellowstone Valley at the east edge of Miles City, Montana, a sign on U.S. 12 warns you that there is no service of any kind ahead for the next 68 miles. Similarly, in the northern Great Lakes forest, distances are as great between Sault Ste. Marie, Michigan, and its nearest comparable neighbors, or between Roseau and Bemidji, Minnesota. Only the scene changes as the roadside vegetation grows above eye level rather than below, and as sweeping panoramas of ranchland and sky are traded for close, dark walls of forest.

The urban centers in the outlying areas are mostly at the lower end of the size-rank order. Of the 70, only two are secondary wholesale-retail-service centers—Aberdeen, South Dakota, in the James Valley at the eastern edge of the Great Plains, and Mason City, in the Iowa Corn Belt. Both owe their relatively large size to legacies from the steel rail era. All the other outlying urban centers are in the lower three commercial size ranks.

Population growth rates outside the main urban clusters during the automobile era have been comparatively slow. Although the outlying counties have half the Upper Midwest urban centers and one-fourth of the nonfarm population, they accounted for less than one-fifth of the growth between 1940 and 1980. Net out-migration has been the rule. Growth rates were high in only a handful of counties. Two were in South Dakota. One was the urban area

of Brookings, whose strong growth reflected campus and industrial expansion as well as the attractiveness of the university community to service businesses. Another was at Pierre, which grew with the state government and related federal offices. Four counties, which included the cities of Williston and Dickinson, North Dakota, and Sidney, Montana, accounted for much of the volatile immigration to the Williston Basin oil fields. Two more counties reflected the exceptionally large increases in Indian population counts on the Turtle Mountain Reservation in northern North Dakota and the Pine Ridge Reservation southeast of the Black Hills.

In their way, the outlying counties also reflected the geographical concentration of population during the automobile era. As a result of the shift to the main urban clusters, their share of Upper Midwest nonfarm population has fallen from 34 percent to 26 percent since 1940. Meanwhile, that remaining 26 percent was concentrating more and more in the 70 urban centers.

Changing Fortunes of the Cities

So impressive and seemingly inexorable has been the population concentration process in the auto era that the mere recognition of it began to take on the aura of a social science law. The widespread notion developed that growth depended on size alone: growth begets growth; grow or die. Superficially, that noiton seemed to be true. There was a clear shift of population up the size-rank order, from the smaller to the larger. Between 1940 and 1980, the Twin Cities share of the region's nonfarm population grew 5 percent. Regional wholesale-retail-service centers captured an additional 3 percent. The share of the large and medium shopping and service centers held

steady, and that of the small shopping and service centers fell 6 percent.

But those were aggregate figures. That was too simple a model of growth and change. For example, in 1980 the 20 largest centers outside the Twin Cities had 60-year growth records that ranged from a high of 245 percent at Rapid City down to 23 percent at Duluth-Superior. Newcomers to the higher ranks, such as Rapid City, Missoula, Billings, Bismarck-Mandan, or Rochester, were in the top 20 because of recent strong boom periods. At the other end of the scale, Duluth-Superior and Mason City were in the group only because they boomed so strongly at the turn of the twentieth century. Most of the lower-order centers were smaller because their booms had been smaller or shorter. But some of today's smaller centers are smaller despite the fact that they once had very large booms. They are in the lower ranks today because of their exceptionally prolonged and deep obsolescence in the national economy. Butte and the Michigan Copper Range cities are the Upper Midwest's notable cases. Their 60-year population changes were −25 percent and −29 percent, respectively.

Recall that, between 1870 and 1890, Boom, slowdown, decline, and instability had become part of the scene. Each class of places contained many cities that were only temporarily in that class. Some cities were passing through a particular class on the way up, others on the way down—each for its own reasons. If that was true for the 76 urban centers on the 1890 map, it was even more true for the 134 centers on the 1980 map. The complex causes and fickle results of growth had already begun to unfold between 1870 and 1890. As fickle and complex as the process of change had become by 1890, so it continued to be fascinating and frustrating to the boosters, lead-

In Mason City, Iowa, 1980, scattered limestone quarries and clay pits–both active and abandoned–of the historic cement, brick, and tile industry adjoin the built-up area. Otherwise, the city is an urban island in a sea of cornfields. Aerial photo by K. Bordner Consultants, Inc., Minneapolis, MN.

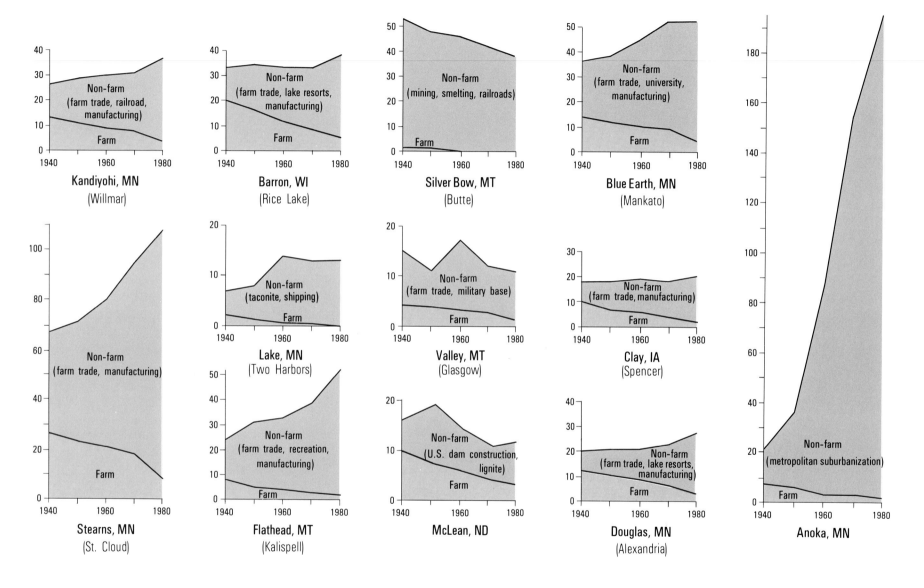

Figure 44. *Changes in Farm and Nonfarm Populations, 1940-1980. The relationship between the two trends has varied in different parts of the region. Nonfarm growth has been more erratic and unstable than farm decline. Instability of growth rates therefore became greater as urbanization in-* *creased. With the county name on each graph, the principal urban center is shown in parentheses for each county except two. (1) McLean county, North Dakota, has no center large enough to be classed as an urban place by the U.S. Census Bureau. It includes the communities of Riverdale, Under-* *wood, and Washburn, near the Garrison Dam on the Missouri River and large lignite-fired electric power plants, midway between Bismarck and Minot. (2) Anoka county, Minnesota, embraces several large northern suburbs of the Twin Cities. Source: note 61.*

ers, and many others in the automotive era.

In contrast with the long-term disturbances of the order in the settlement system are the even more chaotic, complex, and unpredictable short-term fluctuations. In the great farm-to-urban metamorphosis of the past half-century, there was a great deal of variation from one part of the region to another in the relation between farm population decline and nonfarm population growth. To be sure, that variation reflected in part the concentration of most of the nonfarm growth at a relatively few urban centers. Farm population declined in every county while the compensating gains in nonfarm population were much more unevenly distributed. But a great deal of variation emerged within each county from one decade to another. Nonfarm growth has been more erratic and unstable than farm decline. As a result, the shift from the farms has been accompanied by increasing fluctuation and uncertainty in overall population-change rates in almost every county across the region (Figure 44).

During the 1970s, some short-term trends departed notably from the path of long-run changes during the auto era. One departure appeared at the regional metropolis. While the population of the Twin Cities area, including the Commuter Ring and the Satellite Ring, climbed from 2.4 to 2.7 million, for the first time in a century its share of the Upper Mid-west total population dropped slightly, from 38 to 37 percent. Growth in the suburbs and satellite areas increased, but not enough to offset the losses in the old central-city cores. Thus auto-era reduction in density continued, while overall growth slowed. Some observers classed that trend a turnaround from long-term concentration in the metropolis. Others viewed it as a slowdown of the concentration process. To still others, it was only a temporary pause in the stampede to the big cities. Also during the 1970s, already-fast growth accelerated still more in the Minnesota Lakes, Upper Wisconsin Valley, and Western Montana Valleys. Again, some viewed that increase as the other half of the turnaround—a reversal at last of auto-era rural population decline. But others saw it as metropolitan sprawl continued and enlarged. There were also sharp increases in the already-strong concentrations of growth at urban centers in the semiarid and subhumid western farming country.[63]

All these changes lay within the range of fluctuations observed in previous decades. Hence no one can be certain whether the region must prepare to cope with a new era or only patch up the aftereffects from yet another unexpected decade. The longer we watch the process of differential growth and development, the more it seems that nearly everything is explainable, if one waits long enough for adequate hindsight—but almost nothing is predictable. The process is indeed fascinating and frustrating.[64]

Meanwhile, what is the effect on community spirit of this added turbulence that boom and decline bring to the swirling demographic stream? On the one hand; in the fast-growth centers, immigrants outnumber emigrants by a ratio of 2:1 or 3:1. Young households add relatively high birthrates to an already large inflow. Acres of new commercial development, new subdivisions, and mobile-home courts are prominent in the landscape. There is a challenge to maintain a spirit of community and the current of continuity in so turbulent a demographic stream. But optimism, vigor, and expanding wealth support the effort. On the other hand, in the nongrowth centers, emigrants outnumber immigrants 2:1 or 3:1. A relatively large proportion of older households results in a relatively low birthrate to further dampen an already-low inflow. Acres of weedy and littered open space, hollow business facades, patched-up monumental Victorian buildings, and plain ruins are prominent on the land. In urban areas of clearly visible abandonment, community spirit and continuity must be tested most severely. We wonder where the best lessons are learned—in boom or adversity? Perhaps the results of those tests are as uncertain as the booms and declines that cause them.

◀ CHAPTER **6** ▶

Reorganizing
the Cities

Community responses to boom and adversity were reflected in the changing maps of individual cities. Booms were accompanied by explosive expansion and drastic geographical reorganization. In the auto era, urban land and floor space grew two or three times as fast as population. The effects of simple population growth were multiplied and complicated by increased travel, exchange, and material consumption. In the country as a whole, while the number of households tripled, trade and service employment grew sevenfold, and floor space per person more than doubled. The avalanche of personal vehicles, and the space needed to accommodate them, soon became obvious and gradually became legendary. But, aside from personal vehicles, the sheer physical volume of goods stored and used by an average household increased at least ten fold. Per-capita use of outdoor urban space for schoolgrounds, playgrounds, and residential lots rose in similar proportions.

Meanwhile, the effects of obsolescence and decline were more extensive and more visible than they had ever been before. The

railroad era had brought a vast increase in economic activity and wealth and, consequently, in the amount of construction. By the 1970s, railroad-era structures still accounted for more than one-fourth of the buildings standing in the nation and in the Upper Midwest. A half-century of auto-era changes in technology and geography had hastened the obsolescence of most of those structures. A high proportion of them were poorly maintained, worn-out, or even abandoned. Never before had a generation of Americans found itself living amid so many buildings and other structures which logically called for demolition, better maintenance, replacement, or rehabilitation. Demolition was usually nobody's responsibility. Maintenance required more money than the occupants of most old or obsolescent buildings could afford to spend. Replacement structures were usually built in more accessible or attractive locations. Rehabilitation depended on a strong, persistent demand for an old location. All of those problems were present in every settlement, and they were isolated in stark relief in areas of population decline.[65]

Growth Centers in the Prairies
and the Plains

Maps of the change in five cities from 1920 through the 1970s illustrate the auto-era's reshaping of growth centers outside the Twin Cities. Fairmont, Minnesota, was a strong-growth, medium-size shopping and service center in the Corn Belt (Figure 45). Fargo-Moorhead, Sioux Falls, Bismarck-Mandan, and Billings were leaders among the places that emerged as new census metropolitan areas (Figure 46–49). Their populations grew from three- to sevenfold during the half-century, and their subdivided, urbanized areas grew at more than twice that rate.

While each municipality greatly enlarged its limits, it also dramatically reshaped itself to meet the explosive increase in land requirements.[66] Expansion of city limits responded at first to accelerated auto-era growth in directions of previous development. With the general increase in affluence, residential growth concentrated in the established directions of high-value housing—on the right side

139

Fairmont, Minnesota, and its chain of lakes contrast with their Corn Belt suroundings, about 1980. The lakeside site is typical of many small towns and cities in the eastern half of the Upper Midwest. Pioneer settlers built at the present downtown location (center). In the 1880s, the railroads ran east to west at the north edge of downtown. A century of residential growth expanded away from the tracks and parallel to the lake shores. Photo, Fairmont Photo Press, Inc., Fairmont, MN.

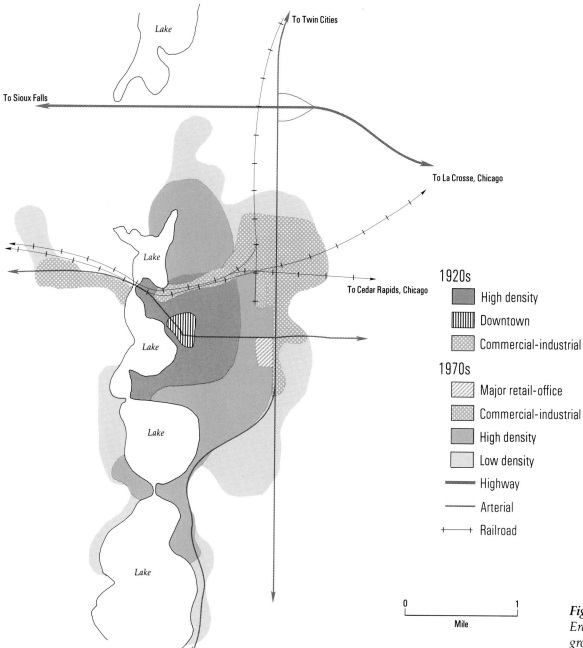

Lake

To Twin Cities

To Sioux Falls

To La Crosse, Chicago

Lake

Lake

To Cedar Rapids, Chicago

Lake

Lake

1920s

High density

Downtown

Commercial-industrial

1970s

Major retail-office

Commercial-industrial

High density

Low density

Highway

Arterial

Railroad

0   1

Mile

Figure 45. Land Use Change during the Auto Era: Fairmont, Minnesota. Most residential growth followed the pre-auto middle- and upper-income bias away from the railroad tracks and near the lake shore. Industrial and commercial expansion sprawled along the outskirts in the areas with best highway and rail access. Source: note 66.

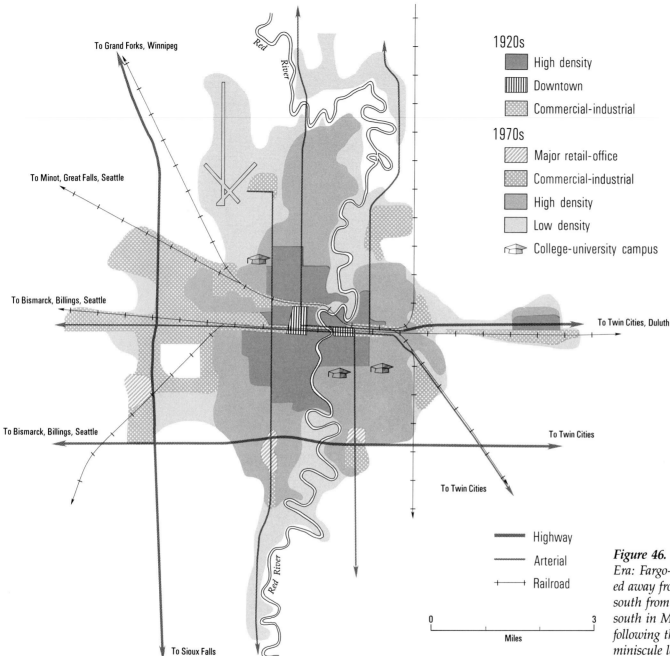

To Grand Forks, Winnipeg

To Minot, Great Falls, Seattle

To Bismarck, Billings, Seattle

To Bismarck, Billings, Seattle

To Sioux Falls

To Twin Cities, Duluth

To Twin Cities

To Twin Cities

Red River

Red River

1920s
- High density
- Downtown
- Commercial-industrial

1970s
- Major retail-office
- Commercial-industrial
- High density
- Low density
- College-university campus

Highway
Arterial
Railroad

0   3
Miles

Figure 46. Land Use Change during the Auto Era: Fargo-Moorhead. Residential growth expanded away from the railway corridors, north and south from the central business district in Fargo, south in Moorhead, with high-value areas mostly following the narrow belt of natural woodland and miniscule local relief along the Fargo side of the Red River. Exponential growth of the city's already large farm supply and wholesale business resulted in explosive development on the outskirts, especially along the western freeway bypass. Source: note 66.

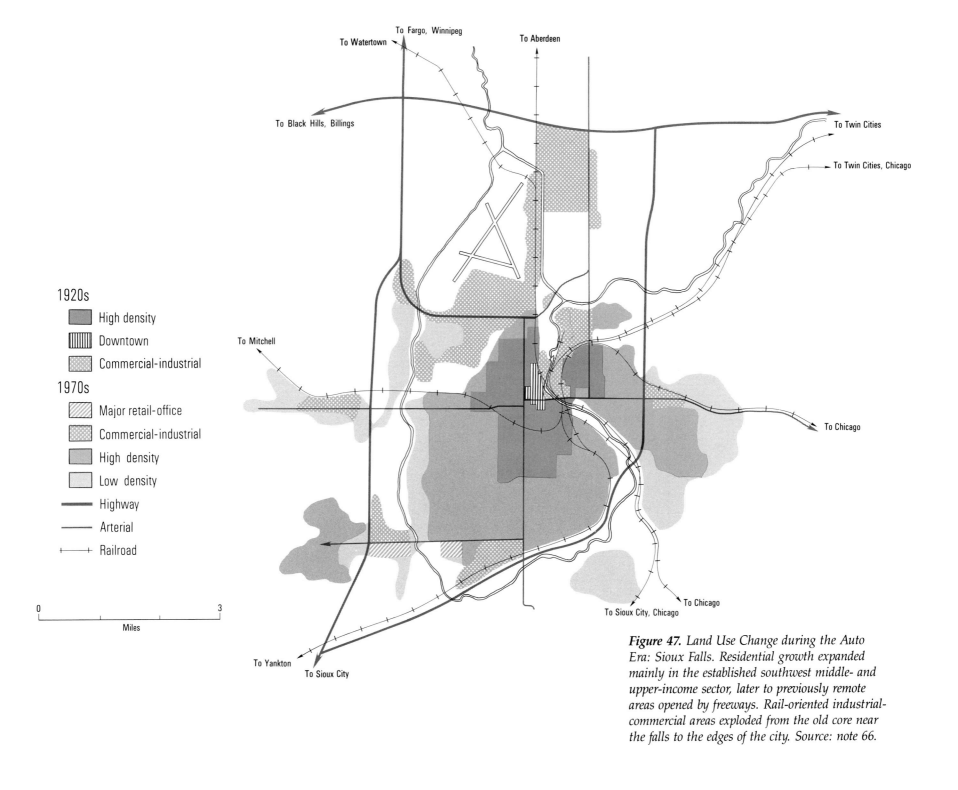

To Fargo, Winnipeg
To Watertown
To Aberdeen
To Black Hills, Billings
To Twin Cities
To Twin Cities, Chicago
To Mitchell
To Chicago
To Sioux City, Chicago
To Chicago
To Yankton
To Sioux City

1920s

High density

Downtown

Commercial-industrial

1970s

Major retail-office

Commercial-industrial

High density

Low density

Highway

Arterial

Railroad

0 Miles 3

Figure 47. Land Use Change during the Auto Era: Sioux Falls. Residential growth expanded mainly in the established southwest middle- and upper-income sector, later to previously remote areas opened by freeways. Rail-oriented industrial-commercial areas exploded from the old core near the falls to the edges of the city. Source: note 66.

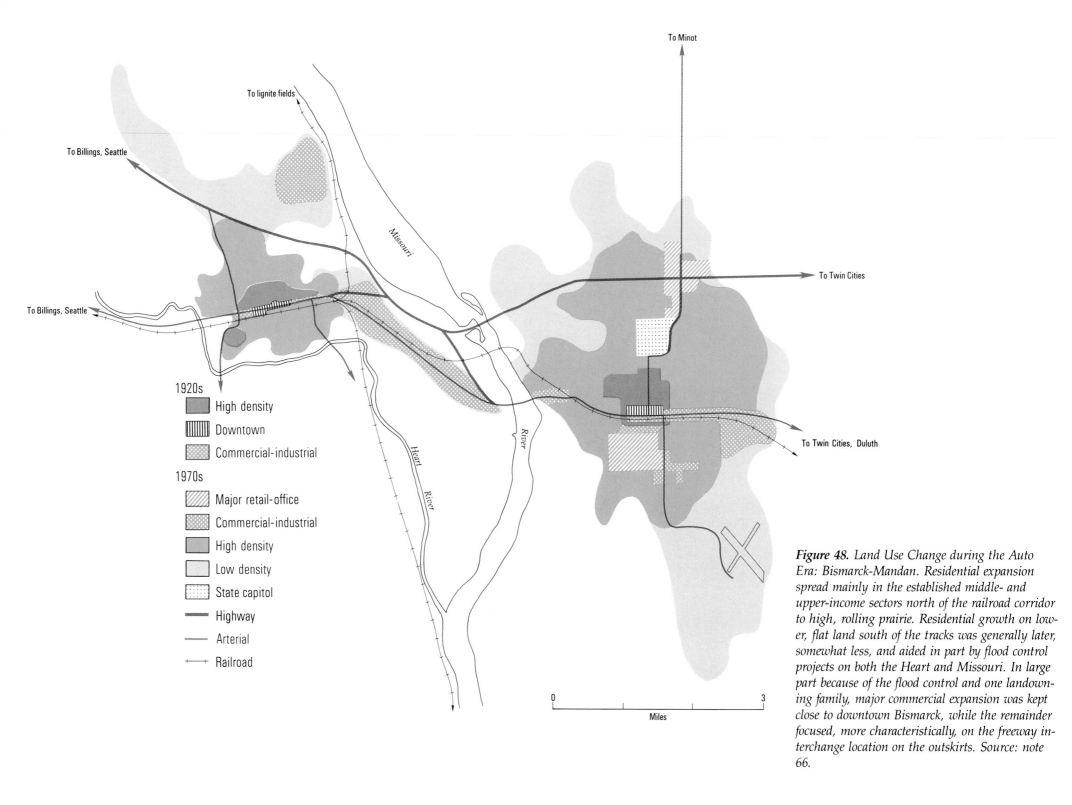

To Minot

To lignite fields

To Billings, Seattle

To Billings, Seattle

Missouri

To Twin Cities

To Twin Cities, Duluth

1920s

High density

Downtown

Commercial-industrial

1970s

Major retail-office

Commercial-industrial

High density

Low density

State capitol

Highway

Arterial

Railroad

Heart

River

River

0   3

Miles

Figure 48. Land Use Change during the Auto Era: Bismarck-Mandan. *Residential expansion spread mainly in the established middle- and upper-income sectors north of the railroad corridor to high, rolling prairie. Residential growth on lower, flat land south of the tracks was generally later, somewhat less, and aided in part by flood control projects on both the Heart and Missouri. In large part because of the flood control and one landowning family, major commercial expansion was kept close to downtown Bismarck, while the remainder focused, more characteristically, on the freeway interchange location on the outskirts. Source: note 66.*

To
Twin Cities,
Omaha

To
Twin Cities

To
Black Hills,
Chicago

R i m r o c k s

R i m r o c k s

C l i f f s

To
Butte,
Seattle, Denver,
Great Falls

N

0   3 Mi.

Figure 49. *Land Use Change during the Auto Era: Billings. While population grew sixfold, the subdivided or built-up area expanded by nearly 11 times, following the level benchlands and probing* the canyons along the broken edge of the High Plains. Downtown rebuilding has been accompanied by outlying development of shopping centers and commercial strips. Warehouse-industry *growth exploded from the area around the downtown railway stations to extensive highway-trackage areas well outside the rail-era city. Source: note 66.*

of the tracks, that is, on the downtown sides of river or rail-yard barriers to city traffic flow, and toward the natural amenities of high ground or lakeshore. Thus residential growth pushed mainly south and southeast in Fairmont, north and south from downtown Fargo, southwest from downtown Sioux Falls, north in Bismarck, and west in Billings.

City limits were also enlarged to accommodate industrial expansion along the railway lines leading into and out of the city. Those developments were often explosive in scale because of the land needs of modern one-story factory and warehouse buildings, trucking, parking, and sometimes even landscaping; and they usually pushed in directions away from high-value residential land. The results are evident in the developments east from the business center of Fairmont, in the remarkable lengthening and widening of the rail-industry strips along the historic Northern Pacific main line through Fargo-Moorhead, Bismarck-Mandan, and Billings, and in the extensive flatland development northwest of the old rail-industry core of Sioux Falls.

Further letting-out of corporate limits and dramatic reshaping resulted from freeway and highway building. Most of the major highways bypassed the rail-oriented, older, congested city. That avoided an immediate, obvious disruption of the existing patterns of land use and circulation, and it held down right-of-way acquisition costs for the highway departments. But it gradually became obvious that avoiding long-term disruption of the old city was impossible. The new bypasses became the major force in the location of industrial expansion, airport development and related hotel construction, and major shopping malls. Nearly every mall was located at an interchange in the direction of major high-value residential growth. Thus it could easily pene-

trate the most lucrative market in the older city, capture the trade from the largest and most affluent areas of auto-era expansion, and invade the trade areas of neighboring smaller towns. In some cases, the new highways also spurred development of attractive residential land that had been avoided throughout the railroad era because it was on the wrong side of the tracks or the wrong side of a river barrier. Now new large-scale subdivisions ignored previous constraints, leaped over old outskirts or slums, and capitalized access to new, highway-oriented job locations. The results of those forces are evident in the development patterns of all five cities.

The U.S. Army Corps of Engineers also played an important role in three of the cities. At Fargo-Moorhead, on the flat Lake Agassiz plain, their dikes flood-proofed the land next to the low banks of the Red River of the north. The dikes not only protected the pre-1920 city but also encouraged development of the open lands that followed the river into the countryside both north and south from the old core of Fargo and far to the south and southeast of central Moorhead. In Sioux Falls, the army engineers dug a canal to divert the Big Sioux River from its sluggish, sinuous course almost entirely around the city. The canal bypassed the falls and dumped floodwaters into the deeper valley downstream from the city. In this fickle climate, near the semiarid margin of the Midwest, the flood risk from occasional spring and summer storms far outweighed the waterpower advantage from a small, unreliable river. Though it was the reason for the city's location, waterpower was long outmoded and unimportant. But the flood risk was an important problem for airport and industrial development on the flatland northwest of the city. At Bismarck and Mandan, the giant Missouri River dams had stabilized the flow of the river. As

a result, potential industrial lands were floodproofed in Mandan. On the Bismarck side, former sloughs and frequently flooded, unused bottomland became the location for a new public zoo, recreational areas, and marina. Slightly higher floodplain land immediately south of the central business district became a feasible area for urban expansion. The result was a major redirection of growth which partly restored the centrality of the rail-era downtown.

Enlarging and reshaping those growing cities was clearly a complex community task. The larger cities added an average of 100 to 200 acres of new land per year. Even Fairmont added an average of perhaps 40 acres per year. Land was subdivided, permits issued, buildings erected, streets and utilities extended. The community had to orchestrate a continuing procession of development decisions, actions, and reactions—both public and private, local and regional. Such a process had characterized city building from the beginning; but the rate, scale, and number of actors increased sharply in the auto era.

In the midst of each booming city there was also decline. The cities had been turned insideout. The original central areas became museums of the rail and streetcar era: derelict railway stations, wall-to-wall multistory buildings with narrow frontages, little parking space—all separated from the freeways by many congested blocks. As the threat of deterioration became clear, leaders in the cities began in the 1950s and 1960s to try to define the problems and the community actions that looked practical. Fargo and Moorhead were among the country's first cities in their size classes to enter the long, trial-and-error struggle toward central area renewal. Organized city and private actions came a little later in Sioux Falls, Bismarck, and Billings. Large out-

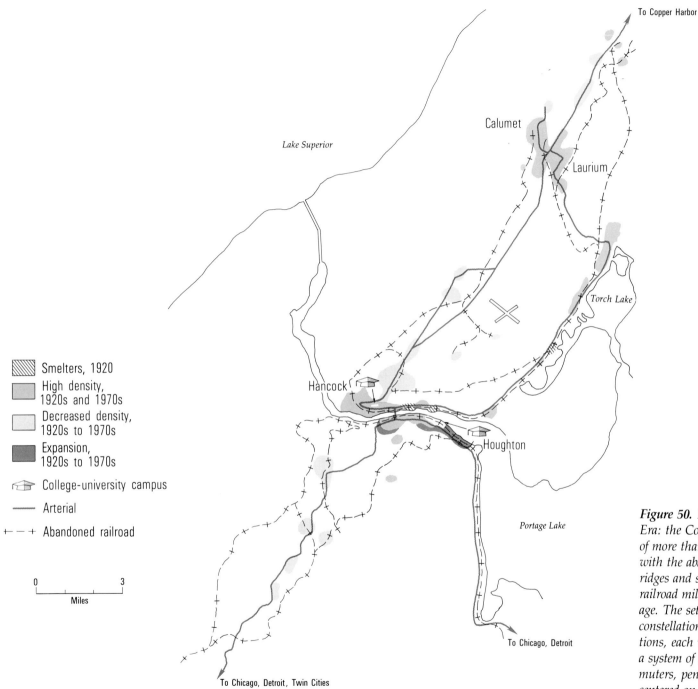

To Copper Harbor

Calumet

Lake Superior

Laurium

Torch Lake

Hancock

Houghton

Portage Lake

To Chicago, Detroit

To Chicago, Detroit, Twin Cities

Smelters, 1920

High density,
1920s and 1970s

Decreased density,
1920s to 1970s

Expansion,
1920s to 1970s

College-university campus

Arterial

+ — + Abandoned railroad

0   3
Miles

Figure 50. Land Use Change during the Auto
Era: the Copper Range. The map reflects the loss
of more than half of the 1920 population, together
with the abandonment of mines on the upland
ridges and smelters on the waterfront. Abandoned
railroad mileage exceeds the arterial highway mileage. The settlement pattern has evolved from a
constellation of mining, smelting, and port locations, each with nearby workers' neighborhoods, to
a system of scattered residential clusters of commuters, pensioners, and local service employees,
centered on Houghton and Hancock. Source: note
66.

lays of private and government funds, both local and federal, helped to stimulate the activity. The results were extensive clearance of marginal business blocks and fringe residential areas; experiments with assistance in relocating people and small businesses; rehabilitation; street improvements; and construction of public buildings, high-rise apartments, hotels, office buildings, and new retail developments. The task is still far from complete. The reasons for delay are familiar: abundant, good-quality new housing on the open land in the outer areas; difficult access to central areas from the freeways; railroad blight; difficulty in bringing together enough large institutions to generate a downtown office boom. The development process was controversial and educational. The need became clear for not only a long-term strategy but also a long-term community-wide commitment, a great deal of money, and two or three decades of time. On a smaller scale, Fairmont joined dozens of other cities in rehabilitating and redeveloping its original central area.

Transformation of Lake Superior Cities

Maps of the Copper Range complex and Duluth-Superior present a much different picture. Changes in the Copper Range reflected both the total loss of the original economic base and the partly counteracting gains from tourism and interregional income transfers by state and federal governments through Social Security, medical programs, education, and construction projects (Figure 50).

From 1920 to 1980 total population of dozens of small mining locations plummeted from 53,000 to 23,000. In the mid-1980s, the remains of those compact, pre-auto villages were strung along today's highways and back roads and also along miles of abandoned railroad grades. Some nineteenth-century, frame miners' houses and tiny clumps of brick business buildings were still in use. But on many vacant lots only a few overgrown foundations and cellars remained. Some of the mine locations are marked today by one or two houses or a historical plaque. On the surrounding ridges and swales, the cutover landscape of stumps, brush, and saplings has given way to a revived forest that once more softens the horizons and hides the excavations and waste-rock dumps.

While some of the remaining houses showed signs of dilapidation and austerity or poverty in the 1980s, the majority had been maintained and modernized with income from jobs in the principal range cities, logging, or tourist trade. The history and the cool Lake Superior climate attracted summer tourists from sultry cities to the south. Autumn leaves, hunting, and exceptionally deep snow for skiing drew visitors from the same markets in other seasons. Small flocks of former residents and their descendants, returning for village and township reunions, added to the summer tourist inflow. Scores of Copper Range expatriates gathered at places where only a handful live today, to recall or learn about old times. They came from California, Texas, the urban Midwest and Northeast, and the retirement colonies of Floria, as well as many other places in the United States and abroad.

Perhaps the most striking monuments to the past mining booms were at Calumet, near the northern end of the Copper Range. Partly devoted to boutiques and exhibits in the early 1980s, the sprawling cavernous stone shops and offices of the once-mighty Calumet and Hecla Consolidated Mines brooded over several hundred partly subsided acres of derelict railway grades, foundations, waste-rock dumps, and rusting frames. Hundreds of miles of partly collapsed, water-filled tunnels honeycombed the underlying bedrock. Nearby, impressive blocks of monumental brick and stone buildings reminded curious visitors that the downtown once served a local market of 20,000 inhabitants. The frame homes that remained around the downtown in the 1980s housed scarcely 1,000. A monument on the library grounds recalled the philanthropy of Alexander Agassiz, the Bostonian who ran the Calumet and Hecla after the Civil War. In the 1870s, at about the time Minnesota naturalist and historian Warren Upham was naming glacial Lake Agassiz for Alexander's father, Louis, Alexander was donating civic improvements to his temporary hometown out here on the frontier. Local place-names such as Atlantic Mine, Boston, and the famous Quincy Mine reflect the early importance of Boston capital and initiative in the Copper Range. The resulting philanthropy came to rest more on the Harvard campus than in the Range. And most of the earnings—perhaps inevitably—moved into America's massive, fast-growing stream of investment capital through Eastern trusts.[67]

In contrast with most of the other places, the population of Houghton-Hancock was steady from 1920 to 1980, at about 12,000. Employment in retail trade held barely constant, while service-employment doubled. Service employment growth reflected in part the rising tourist trade, but other factors even more. There was diversification and expansion of the historic state college of mining technology and expansion of medical and social services by both federal and state governments. Especially important were services to the elderly, who made up a large part of the Copper Range population. Along the once-busy ship channel, extensive restoration in the 1980s was

Great lakes and ocean cargo ships ride on lower St. Louis Bay, the harbor of Duluth-Superior, on a summer day in 1983. Grain terminals are prominent in the lower foreground on the Superior waterfront. Duluth's general cargo and grain terminals occupy Rices' point (center). The main entrance to the harbor (upper center) cuts through Minnesota Point, which protects the bay from the open water of Lake Superior. Duluth's redeveloped waterfront and downtown lie to the southwest (left) of the base of Minnesota Point. The central and eastern residential districts of Duluth climb the escarpment to the forested, rocky highlands of Minnesota's Arrowhead Country. Iron and coal docks are out of the picture to the west (left) and east (right). Photo, Basgan Photography and Seaway Port Authority of Duluth.

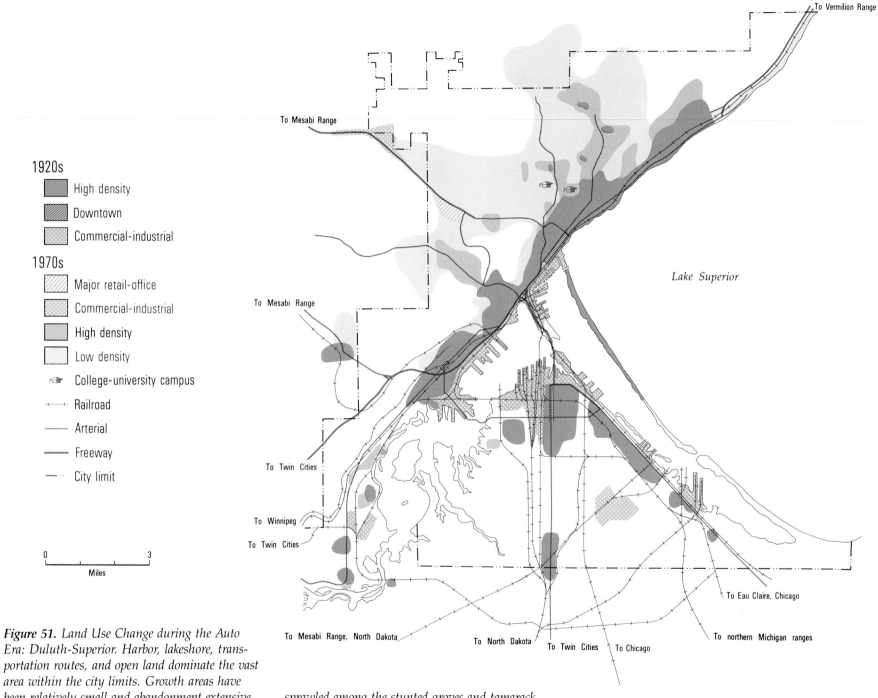

1920s

- High density
- Downtown
- Commercial-industrial

1970s

- Major retail-office
- Commercial-industrial
- High density
- Low density
- College-university campus
- Railroad
- Arterial
- Freeway
- City limit

0   3
Miles

To Thunder Bay
To Vermilion Range
To Mesabi Range
Lake Superior
To Mesabi Range
To Twin Cities
To Winnipeg
To Twin Cities
To Mesabi Range, North Dakota
To North Dakota
To Twin Cities
To Chicago
To Eau Claire, Chicago
To northern Michigan ranges

Figure 51. Land Use Change during the Auto Era: Duluth-Superior. Harbor, lakeshore, transportation routes, and open land dominate the vast area within the city limits. Growth areas have been relatively small and abandonment extensive in the pre-auto rail and heavy industry areas of Superior and western Duluth. In contrast, substantial new growth—based on service jobs—has sprawled among the stunted groves and tamarack bogs and captured spectacular panoramic views, on the rocky uplands above central and eastern Duluth. Source: note 66.

changing the face of Houghton's downtown. Well-maintained old housing was terraced up the steep hillsides on both sides of the channel. A few new subdivisions, mainly on the gentler slopes around the university, accommodated some of the replacement housing built since World War II. Other auto-era housing was scattered along the highways at scenic spots among forested, rocky ridges and coastal coves, or on the edges of the small towns along the west side of Torch Lake. Those one-time settlements of mill workers had become suburbs of Houghton-Hancock. Between the towns stood the stark ruins of the world's greatest stamp mill and copper smelters. Between the ruins and the open lake lay extensive flat, low, slowly revegetating deltas built by a century of tailings discharge from the mills into the lake.

The Copper Range had a drastic change in urban structure from 1920 to 1980. It lost almost as much population as some of the large, fast-growing urban areas of the Upper Midwest gained. Census population data suggested a debacle. The visible ruins added to that impression. Yet, eventual depletion of the copper ores was always a certainty. Earnings from exploiting the deposits have been spread among a vast and varied array of developments worldwide. The people who lived on the Range in 1980, and those who returned for summer reunions, were both intellectually and materially much better off than the immigrant laborers and perhaps even their schoolteachers, ministers, doctors, and merchants in the rough-and-tumble settlement of the 1860s and 1870s. For thousands of families, the Keweenaw was a way station on geographically twisting, economically upward paths from scattered origins in Europe to equally scattered destinations in America. While they lived and toiled there, they con-

tributed to the world's swelling stream of capital. We can only speculate or wonder what the situation would be if the people and capital had been less mobile.

The Twin Ports of Duluth-Superior presented a more striking picture of maintenance and growth amid obsolescence and abandonment (Figure 51). Centerpiece of the urban area in 1980 was still the spacious harbor. A nineteenth-century whaleback freighter near the modern hotel and yacht basin on Superior's waterfront is only one small part of the harbor's living museum.

Some of the great, dredged promontories on the bay were vacant and overgrown, edged by rotting pilings, washed by the waters of quietly silting slips. Hundreds of acres of railway yards were used at a fraction of their capacity. Other hundreds of acres were virtually abandoned. Nearly 5,000 transportation jobs had disappeared between 1929 and 1980, as trucks took over a large share of the grain traffic and new railway equipment reduced turnaround time for grain, coal, and iron shippers. Near the head of the bay, the steel mill was cold and rusting away—as it did while hundreds of jobs disappeared during its last decade of operation. The neighboring cement plant was silent because it lost its source of raw material when the steel mill closed.

Yet there was much activity at scattered locations along the sprawling harbor. Even in a depressed steel economy, millions of tons of taconite pellets moved through the ore docks in western Duluth and the southeastern outskirts of Superior. Tens of millions of bushels of grain moved through the elevators on Rice's Point and along the Superior waterfront, and a new terminal transshipped Montana coal to the lower Great Lakes. Duluth's post–World War II general cargo terminal on Rice's Point served dozens of freighters at the upper end of

the Great Lakes–St. Lawrence Seaway. Widely scattered industrial plants, including a large, new papermill, enlarged on nineteenth-century traditions in wood- and metalworking.

There was also much uncertainty. Changing steel requirements and foreign competition made iron pellet shipments more variable. The volume of grain shipments was also increasingly variable as more of the flow was directed to international markets, with resulting competition from Pacific and Gulf ports. The general cargo port was competing against the much larger market and more frequent sailings at Chicago. Post–World War II residential expansion in areas around the bay had been miniscule. Much of it had been in the vicinity of Morgan Park—once a planned company community, designed and built at the time the steel mill opened in 1910. Though the mill was defunct, the carefully designed residential area had kept its amenities and enhanced its status.

In contrast with many port-rail-industry areas, maintenance, or even growth, was prevalent in other districts—notably central and eastern Duluth. Employment had grown on the campuses on the east side, in the services and light industries downtown, and fitfully around the airport during temporary periods of military expansion. On the downtown Duluth waterfront, some of the big, multistoried buildings that housed the great hardware and grocery wholesalers at the turn of the century were subdivided, rehabilitated, and partly occupied by a new generation of light industry and offices. Impressive rehabilitation and redevelopment was gradually lifting the face of the railroad-era business district. Energy for those improvements came from generous federal construction grants as well as the downtown economic base. The central and eastern high-density residential area had expanded one-third since 1920. Additional low-density development had sprawled across another dozen square miles. The expansion resulted from replacement. Although the net total of metropolitan population growth was near zero, new housing in the central and eastern heights had continually replaced deteriorated housing in the old cores and industrial west end. Newer dwellings had replaced perhaps one-third of the units in use in 1920.

With the help of generous federal and state funds, a network of modern highways and spectacular bridges was gradually stitching together the sprawling and varied metropolitan patchwork; and a long-enduring planning program kept nudging the pieces into place.

The Twin Ports in 1980 presented an unusual and dramatic view of the powerful auto-era thrust of service growth, federal and state expenditures, industrial transformation, and international interdependence. Because the metropolitan area was not buried in layers of recent growth, it offered an exceptionally clear exposure of the obsolescence and maintenance problems that have beset most cities in the auto era. The problems have not been unique to the Twin Ports, only more prominent because of the slow counteracting growth. Nor was the growth experience here unique among America's more than 300 metropolitan areas. In the years since 1920, only eight have experienced such chronic nongrowth as Duluth-Superior. But 30 more have experienced little or no growth during three or four consecutive decades, and another 130 have had one or two decades of nongrowth. The historical geography of the northeastern United States and other areas around the North Atlantic is replete with cases of prolonged nongrowth of cities. The record

suggests that the Twin Ports might feel an occasional resurgence, but it also suggests that their nongrowth experience could be shared by many other cities in the coming decades. The Duluth-Superior communities were indeed coping with obsolescence. But they were also running an urban laboratory experimenting with the future.[68]

The Regional Metropolis

In all the transformation of the Upper Midwest in the auto-air-electronic age, the most dramatic and intense changes came in the regional metropolis. The changes incorporated both boom and obsolescence on massive scales. In the auto era, the Twin Cities area absorbed half the net out-migration from the rest of the Upper Midwest. It accounted for more than half of the employment and population growth in the entire region. Its daily commuting area in 1980 covered more than 10,000 square miles. In many ways the metropolis had become a region in itself.[69]

In a little more than half a century, the urbanized area—including the scattered subdivisions on the outskirts—grew from 160 square miles to 880 (Figures 52–53). Population of the urbanized area grew from 670,000 to 2 million. The total outlay for construction of all kinds was more than $20 billion at the prices current at the times of development. In constant 1980 dollars, the investment was probably over 40 billion. If it were to be replaced at 1985 standards for roads as well as residential, commercial, and public structures, the outlay would surely exceed $60 billion; and those figures do not include the cost of interest on borrowed money. The building took place along 3,000 miles of new streets and roads on about 500,000 parcels of land into which the 1920 farms had been subdivided. Thus the billions

were invested as a result of hundreds of thousands of decisions of families, corporations, and governments. It was a kind of community project; almost everyone was involved. Together they created an outer city, surrounding the older inner city.

Auto-era expansion has taken place in three stages: the building boom of the 1920s and the following hiatus of the Great Depression and World War II; the post–World War II building boom (and baby boom) from 1945 until about 1960; and the subsequent period of maturation of the outer city.

THE 1920s BUILDING BOOM

This boom was the first in American history to be affected by automobiles, and even then their potential impact was still in some doubt for many investors. In the Twin Cities, most auto-era development before World War II followed the directions of earlier streetcar expansion. In fact, much of it filled in vast areas in the outer parts of Minneapolis and St. Paul that had been subdivided in the previous boom and not yet built upon. But there were suggestions of other changes that would come in the future on a massive scale. Abundant credit encouraged construction of new dwelling units faster than new households were formed. As a result, there was a high rate of replacement building, and the surplus new units could replace old ones which could then be discarded. While new areas boomed, it was possible to abandon some of the least desirable, oldest housing. The abandonment showed up in the city residential cores. It reflected the accelerated obsolescence of many older houses, with primitive wiring and piping, on small, crowded lots. Central heating and garages had become standard; and burgeoning demand for major appliances had created the need for modern plumbing and

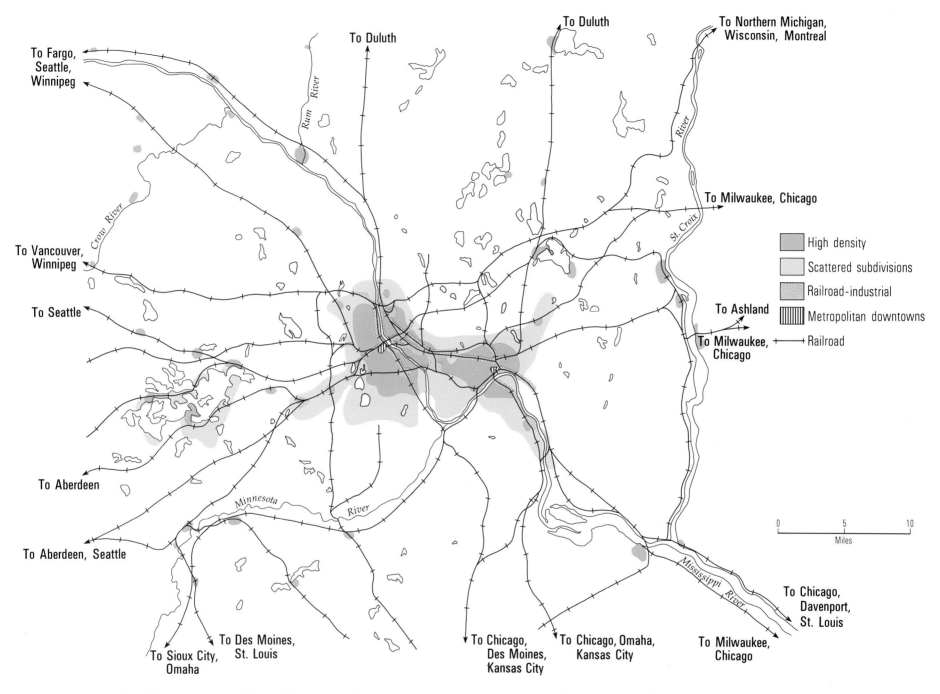

Figure 52. *Land Use in the Twin Cities, 1920. The Upper Midwest metropolis was a compact streetcar city. Most of its 670 thousand people lived within about 80 square miles focused on the* job locations in the main railroad corridor from north Minneapolis to South St. Paul. The halo of low density settlement on the outskirts reflected the scant beginning of automobile commuting. Ex- *cept for the streetcar and summer cottage suburbs around Minnetonka and White Bear lakes, the bountiful supply of shoreland and rolling glacial terrain was still used for farming. Source: note 66.*

Legend:
- High density
- Scattered subdivisions
- Railroad-industrial
- Metropolitan downtowns
- Railroad

Map labels:
To Fargo, Seattle, Winnipeg
To Vancouver, Winnipeg
To Seattle
To Aberdeen
To Aberdeen, Seattle
To Sioux City, Omaha
To Des Moines, St. Louis
To Chicago, Des Moines, Kansas City
To Chicago, Omaha, Kansas City
To Milwaukee, Chicago
To Chicago, Davenport, St. Louis
To Duluth
To Duluth
To Northern Michigan, Wisconsin, Montreal
To Milwaukee, Chicago
To Ashland
To Milwaukee, Chicago

Rum River
Crow River
St. Croix River
Minnesota River
Mississippi River

0 5 10 Miles

Rail-Era Core

High density

Rail-industry

Metropolitan downtowns

Auto-Era Expansion

Pre-World War II

Post-World War II

Major office, retail, industrial

Freeway

Arterial

To Northern Wisconsin, Michigan

To Lakes, Mesabi Range

To Lakes, Mesabi Range

To Duluth, Mesabi Range

To Fargo, Seattle, Winnipeg

To Eau Claire, Wausau, Milwaukee, Chicago

To Sioux Falls, Black Hills, Sioux City

To Des Moines, Kansas City, Omaha

To Rochester, La Crosse, Chicago

Rum River

Crow River

St. Croix River

Minnesota River

Mississippi River

0   5   10
Miles

Figure 53. Land Use in the Twin Cities, 1980. The streetcar city was engulfed in more than 800 square miles of auto-era subdivision and develop- *ment. Homes and work places for an additional 1.3 million people had spread over former farmland and along rural lakeshore of 1920. A* *500-mile web of freeways had extended and reinforced the rail transportation network. Source: note 66.*

wiring. With the 1920s skyscrapers, the downtowns were building more upward than outward. The result was a widening "gray zone" of accelerated obsolescence and some abandonment in the older housing stock, surrounding the downtowns. Then the first large department stores to be located outside the downtowns opened their doors in connection with the giant Sears and Montgomery Ward mail-order houses in south Minneapolis and in the St. Paul Midway. Thus the forces of change had appeared, but they were slowed by the 1929 crash and the decade of the Great Depression that followed.

THE POST–WORLD WAR II BOOM

Explosive growth erupted in 1946, following fifteen years dominated by depression and wartime austerity. Employment was growing rapidly. There was pent-up demand from the long period of under-building. The Congress insured liberal home-financing credit for veterans, who accounted for most males in the family-forming age group. And this time almost every household owned an automobile. To be sure, the automobiles could not get out of the city very far or very fast on the remarkably primitive highway system of that time. At the end of World War II, no more than three dozen narrow, mostly two-lane paved roads reached even 10 miles outside the Minneapolis–St. Paul city limits. As hundreds of feeder streets were graded for burgeoning subdivisions, congestion began to develop on the limited number of arterials. Nevertheless, it was a big improvement over walking from the end of the streetcar line in the 1920s. In 1920 only 250 square miles of land area lay within one hour of travel time, by a combination of trolley car and walking, from the nearest downtown. With auto travel, the one-hour

area exploded to about 2,000 square miles. As a result, hundreds of previously inaccessible square miles had suddenly come into the urban real estate market. The consequence was relatively cheap land, larger lots, and lower density compared with earlier expansions—the sprawl of the 1950s.

In the frenetic effort to grade streets, run electric power lines, complete homes, and do basic landscaping, there was little time or money left over. First priority for the remaining funds went to building elementary schools as the baby-boom youngsters reached age six. Most of the remainder went to pave the streets and equip playgrounds. Residential growth advanced well ahead of employment. Suburban businesses consisted mainly of building-supply yards and convenience retail centers. Many of the centers were little more than enlarged hamlets from the recent agricultural past. Growth also ran far ahead of sewer and water extensions. At the peak, about 300,000 people in the first ring of suburbs were dependent on their own wells and septic tanks.

When the baby boom ended about 1958, a sea of single-family homes had filled all the partly developed outskirts of the 1920s and pushed a few miles farther into the countryside. The main thrusts followed level land north and south from Minneapolis, into southwestern St. Paul, and surrounded a few old streetcar suburbs. Most builders stayed with flatland to hold down excavation costs, or near the edges of older municipalities for access to water systems. But most of the fast-growing suburban population was using inadequate roads and city streets to reach central-city jobs, doctors, shopping, and entertainment. Downtown crowding, sewer problems, highway needs, and school construction were demanding further attention.

MATURATION AND CONTINUED GROWTH

Meanwhile, new forces had been gathering through the mid-1950s and emerged dominant in the 1960s. An unprecedented rise in real income was affecting most households in the Twin Cities, as it was in the nation as a whole. *The Exploding Metropolis* had yielded to *The Affluent Society* as best-selling nonfiction. Suburbs had emerged as a major market, labor force, and tax base with large, urgent demands. Freeway plans were nearing completion, and construction of the network was under way in the late 1950s. With those plans in mind, Dayton's department store in Minneapolis built the world prototype enclosed suburban shopping mall, Southdale in Edina. General Mills and 3M began to create two of the nation's earliest suburban corporate office and research campuses. Freeway construction sparked much more highway improvement. As the new network gradually approached completion through the 1960s and 1970s, more and larger shopping malls, office parks, and industrial parks developed near the main interchanges. The belt freeways, girdling the metropolitan area, interconnected the new mass of homes, shopping areas, and job locations. The belt lines also joined the entire suburban ring with the major radial highways that led not only inward to the downtowns but also, more importantly, outward to the rest of the region. The outer city could now become a new focus for both the metropolitan area and the regional economy.[70]

Long-gestating community improvements soon accompanied the highway and business investments. Suburbs initiated large, new sewer and water systems. Suburban school districts consolidated and built mammoth new high schools. Suburban congregations moved from temporary quarters in grade

Central Minneapolis, viewed from east to west in 1983, was in transition. The falls of St. Anthony—constrained by dams and concrete aprons, bypassed by locks—and the historic bridging point at Nicollet Island lie upstream from the center of the picture. The transcontinental rail corridor was busy, but large old yards were being abandoned in response to changes in railroading and pressure for redevelopment. Once a child of the falls and rail lines, the downtown had become a focus in the freeway system and the locus of massive new construction and rehabilitation. The expanded University of Minnesota campus straddled the river between the downtown and the major concentration of grain elevators (foreground). Aerial photo by K. Bordner Consultants, Inc., Minneapolis, MN.

Also in transition was central St. Paul, viewed from northeast to southwest, 1985. Oversize parking ramps for automobiles from today's converging freeways occupied the riverside location (left center) of the former Union Depot train sheds—once the focus of the region's rail network. With the river dammed and dredged, and the entire frontage improved, the original landing below the Union Depot was an incon-spicuous spot amid barge fleeting and pleasure craft operations. New towers rose among restored, old structures in the downtown core. Around the edges, extensive redevelopment and rehabilitation combined to change the face of "Lowertown" (lower center), the state capitol area (right), and the hospital-public arena complex (above). Aerial photo by K. Bordner Consultants, Inc., Minneapolis, MN.

schools, quonset huts, and taverns to monumental new churches. The Airports Commission made its first round of massive improvements, and Wold-Chamberlain Field became Twin Cities International. The new suburban municipalities built civic centers, libraries, and fire stations to replace sagging, nineteenth-century, wooden rural town halls. Finally, city and county parks, private and public golf courses, and state junior college campuses occupied some of the remaining gaps in the development pattern.

Amid these changes, support rose for coordinating the public improvement programs of the scores of local governments, state agencies, and special districts that made up the metropolitan area. Together they were using public revenue collected by local, state, and federal governments to build the basic skeleton of the outer city. The support grew out of both the frustrations of the frenetic boom years and the obvious, growing management problems now that the community was catching up with the backlog of major public construction. Thus the Minnesota legislature created the Metropolitan Planning Commission in 1957, then strengthened, broadened, and renamed it the Metropolitan Council in 1967. Within a short time, the council had to make influential decisions on eventually unsuccessful proposals to build a new super-airport on the Anoka Sand Plain and to build a new subway system focused on the central-city downtowns. Both projects would have made important shifts in the location of public capital investments within the metropolitan framework, whether or not they would have affected the overall pattern of growth. The council then produced its metropolitan development guide in 1970 and first defined the urban services line, to limit the rate

and sprawl of the sewer and water network, in 1974.[71]

The housing market also changed in the 1960s. The array of choices became more diverse as the share of new housing construction in single-family units dropped from nearly 100 percent in 1955 to about 60 percent during the following decade. Apartments, then condominiums, made up the other 40 percent. Also, the replacement rate rose to an unprecedented level. That is, new houses continued to be built at a high rate, although the rate of new household formation declined. As a result, more people all the way down the housing chain could move up into new quarters more quickly, and old housing at the bottom of the chain could be abandoned at an unprecedented rate. Most of the new housing was built in the outer city, and virtually all the abandonment of older and dilapidated housing was in the inner city.

THE NEW OUTER CITY

By 1980, a new outer metropolis indeed existed. It had been built to accommodate 1.7 million people, or more than half a million households, with automobiles. It included all the suburbs plus the post-1920 edges of the central cities. It spread across rolling land, around hundreds of lakes and ponds, among tens of thousands of acres of woodlands, with abundant parks and playgrounds. On its inner margin were the major parks which had been developed from farmland nearly a century earlier, and 50,000 acres of recently created regional parks and preserves lay in its outer margin. The new outer metropolis was bound together by the nation's highest per capita metropolitan freeway mileage and a highly developed grid of arterials. The outer city focused on eight major shopping malls and the

vastly upgraded metropolitan airport. It also included several sprawling assemblages of offices, hotels, and industrial parks around the principal interchanges on the belt freeways.

Of the one million jobs in the metropolitan area in the early 1980s, more than half were located in the auto-era outer city. Metropolitan area retail sales rose from $1.3 billion in 1958 to $7.3 billion in 1977. But in the same period, the downtown shares of the total had fallen to 5 percent in Minneapolis and one percent in St. Paul, while the major shopping malls had captured 12 percent. Fifty-two percent of all sales were in the garish suburban commercial strips, where there had been virtually nothing in 1920. In addition to hundreds of new firms, nearly 300 industries from Minneapolis and nearly 50 from St. Paul had moved to more spacious quarters in suburban industrial parks between 1960 and 1977. In 1982, the auto-era ring contained 31 million, or well over half of the 58 million square feet of metropolitan area office space less than 15 years old. The downtowns were home to the office headquarters for most of the largest business firms with the greatest assets and also for the largest government offices. But the suburban ring, with generally lower development costs, housed more of the young fastest-growing firms and the greatest number overall.[72]

Impressive as the outer city had become, older parts here and there were already beginning to come unraveled. Some early post–World War II commercial strips were obsolete. Their locations had poor access to the freeways, vacancy was high, building maintenance was neglected, and parking spaces were broken and weedy. The giant sports stadium, opened in the late 1950s, replaced in 1982 by the downtown Minneapolis dome, was abandoned and awaiting eventual clearance and

Twin Cities International Airport, 1983, grew from a grass field and small frame hangar on the site of a defunct auto-racing track of the 1920s to be one of the country's major hub airports. The complex occupies the flat peninsular plateau west of the Mississippi (upper right) and north of the Minnesota River (bottom). Historic Fort Snelling stood at the confluence, just east of the present airport. Several square miles of sprawling runways, ramps, terminals, and major airline headquarters made up the air-age version of the rail-era downtown depots, yards, and railroad company offices. The airport succeeded the rail terminals, the riverboat port, and the old fort as the fourth generation of regional transportation nodes. Office-industry-hotel developments (lower left) follow the freeway about seven miles west to the Edina interchange, shown in the following picture. Aerial photo by K. Bordner Consultants, Inc., Minneapolis, MN.

The nearly uninterrupted level plain south of downtown Minneapolis (upper right), which accommodated most streetcar-era growth, contrasts with the rolling, lake-studded moraine land, the scene of most auto-era expansion. Roughly the lower two-thirds of the area pictured in 1984 was built up since World War II. Western and southern legs of the first belt freeway around Minneapolis intersect in Edina and Bloomington, in the foreground. The high-rise concentration in downtown Minneapolis (top center) is eight miles to the northeast. Aerial photo by K. Bordner Consultants, Inc., Minneapolis, MN.

redevelopment. Schools built for the baby boom of the 1950s were redundant.

NEW ATTENTION TO THE INNER CITY

In the center of the 800-square-mile suburban ring lay the 50-square-mile inner city, entirely within Minneapolis and St. Paul. To be sure, all the inner city was not literally pre-auto. Although all of it was subdivided and settled before the auto age, parts of it had been rebuilt at least once. The downtowns were the scene of frequent though fitful and partial replacement of old buildings by new ones almost from the beginning. There have been major redevelopments over the years in some of the central cities' outlying districts, notably the Honeywell headquarters complex, the hospital zones, the University of Minnesota campus, and the public clearance and housing projects.

But redevelopment had accounted for less than one-tenth of the inner-city area. From the 1920s through the 1960s most of the pre-auto city had been the scene of creeping obsolescence and abandonment. The obsolescence was coupled with deferred maintenance on many buildings and streets. Abandonment was coupled with deferred clearance or redevelopment. There was a general spreading of low income and low investment.

The situation was the result of a stubborn syndrome of problems. Except for the federally financed interstate freeways, highway improvements did not penetrate the inner city "lump." Even the interstate freeway penetration was slow. Higher welfare and police costs accompanied the changes in population and land use, while costs also rose for even minimal care of aging improvements. Those expenses kept real estate taxes high. And before anything new could be built, costly demolition and removal had to take place. Consequently,

in competition with the suburbs, inner-city land suffered from less accessibility, higher taxes, and higher land preparation costs for new development. In one way, the lump of older, obsolete structures was part of the pervasive American solid waste problem. Unlike cans and bottles, the buildings could not simply be tossed out of sight. But they could be left behind as the metropolis turned its back and faced outward. Yet, if you believed that the Twin Cities metropolis was here to stay, perhaps you had to believe that this relatively small area in the middle of it merited recycling.

Beginning in the late 1950s, strong counterforces began to develop and converge on the inner-city malaise. They came from different sources, partly related, partly coincidental. Together their effects were truly impressive. With 90 percent federal financing, the interstate freeways penetrated the inner city in the 1970s. Costs had been high and delays lengthy because of the need for demolition, resettlement, and compensation for a wide range of unprecedented social, economic, and physical damages. But eventually the freeways restored metropolitan accessibility to the downtowns. The freeway plans, coupled with other federal aid opportunities, sparked comprehensive plans for redevelopment. The St. Paul Capitol Approach plan took on new life, and the Minneapolis Metro Center plan evolved rapidly. Basic hopes and themes reappeared from the proposals of a half-century earlier—monumental central-city cores, riverfront development and beautification. This time action quickly accompanied the planning.[73]

City government, large corporations with local control and inner-city headquarters, major hospital and medical centers, and neighborhood resident organizations soon joined in the effort. Major developers were attracted

from other centers of investment capital in the United States and Canada. The city governments and specially created authorities funneled federal subsidies to target areas. Money went to realign and improve streets, build parking ramps, improve public buildings and parks, and subsidize new housing and home improvements as well as subsidize interest rates on bonds for new major construction. The cities borrowed heavily to buy land, clear it, prepare it for new development—and to make accompanying public improvements and embellishments. The private organizations, in turn, made heavy commitments to new construction. And the neighborhood organizations labored to keep a share of the public improvement funds flowing into residential areas and a share of the subsidies directed to family housing. Plainly, with the complexity of the script and the diversity of actors, a great deal of learning and negotiation was necessary to evolve the plans and translate them into action. The resulting boom has been peaking in the 1980s.

Meanwhile, in the late 1970s the post-World War II baby-boom generation entered the housing market. That happened at a time of unprecedented national inflation. With building costs high and interest costs rising, the new generation could not do what their parents had done in the housing crisis of the late 1940s: go to the outer fringe and build a rambler. Instead, they turned inward. They bought into the vast, older housing stock in the transition zone between inner and outer city and set out to improve it. Thousands of households were soon burning the lights late at night, pouring "sweat equity" into older houses and yards, just as their parents had with new ones three decades earlier. While public outlays were important in bringing new life to those older neighborhoods, private outlays were far greater. Although most of the activity was the result of average young families renovating average old houses, some involved higher-income young families renovating fine old mansions and gentrifying historic, once-prestigious neighborhoods near the edges of the downtowns and in the lake districts. Thus the central cities' ring of deterioration was shrinking and even partly dissolving in the 1970s. A new wave of downtown improvement and gentrification was pressing against it from the inside, and a wave of house-painting, cabinet-installing, carpet-laying younger families pressed from the outside. As a result, abandonment came virtually to a halt, and there was more crowding of the lowest-income and the transient populations.

A historic preservation movement also converged on the inner city in the 1970s. If housing is an indicator, the average life expectancy of a building in the United States is about 80 to 100 years. The first large wave of construction of monumental buildings in the Twin Cities began with the rise of the Northwest Empire after completion of the northern transcontinental railroads. That was in the 1880s and 1890s. Eighty to 100 years later, Twin Citians faced for the first time the abandonment and destruction of hundreds of architectural monuments that commemorated important people and institutions in Upper Midwest history—office buildings, warehouses, churches, homes. Consequently, other forces coalesced on the stage. At first there were protests and rallies. Then buildings were surveyed and classified. City and federal tax subsidies were aimed at helping private investors restore high-priority, well located structures. The oldest, most durable, monumental, and well-situated structures were in or near the downtowns. For at least the first round of historic preservation, the major targets were in the inner city.[74]

As a result of these converging forces, the inner city in the 1980s was probably in the best physical condition in its history. Increasingly the downtowns were impressive collections of restored old facades, tastefully remodeled interiors, gleaming towers, fountains, designed open spaces. Forty- to 60-story towers dwarfed the rail-era skyscrapers of 12 to 18 floors. The buildings were monumental and their functions diverse: offices, hotels, shops, pedestrian malls, auditoriums, sports arenas, concert halls, theaters, housing, enclosed skyways. The Metropolitan Council estimated that resident population in and adjacent to the downtowns would grow by 25,000 in the 1980s and early 1990s. The boom had produced at least $2 to $3 billion in private and public investment in the inner city. A large share was downtown, but the flow to housing and public improvement in the neighborhoods was also large. New construction in the central cities accounted for perhaps one-third of the metropolitan total from the mid-1970s to the early 1980s. While the greater part of residential building continued in the suburbs, all new housing in the inner city was for replacement. There was no net population growth. The result was a very high replacement rate. At the same time, nearly half of the office space expansion in the 1970s, and more than half of that projected for the 1980s, was located in the inner-city downtowns.

The chronology suggests three historical-geographical stages in post–World War II metropolitan development. The first stage was an all-out effort to house the war veterans' families after 15 years of neglected construction. In the second stage, while residential growth continued, the new outer city caught up with the backlog of nonresidential construction needs that had been postponed during the frenetic postwar housing boom. Through both stages operation of the metropolis continued to wear out the inner city, while it concentrated on building the outer city. In the third stage, attention turned to rebuilding the inner city. Never before had the problems of aging, maintenance, preservation, and replacement been recognized so clearly and attacked with so much coordination and money.

The Urban Countryside

While cities were realigning internally to adapt to auto-era changes, there was additional realignment in the neighboring countryside.

Good roads not only got the farmers out of the mud, but also brought whole counties or multicounty shopping trade areas into easy commuting distance from urban centers. As a result, many people moved to the rural areas to live. Many others, who had grown up in rural areas, found work in the cities but established their homes on familiar soil and began to commute. In an earlier generation, they would have migrated to the city; in the auto era they were long-distance commuters.

As a result, cities could not expand their boundaries far enough, fast enough to encompass the dispersal of urban population. The region's urban centers, with populations over 2,500 in 1920, enlarged their city limits to accommodate 1.2 million more people by 1980. But that was less than half the nonfarm population growth in their own counties during that period. Urban population obviously burst out of the municipal cage, especially in the densely populated eastern half of the region and the Western Montana Valleys.

More than half of the dispersal occurred in the Twin Cities area. Minneapolis, St. Paul, and the suburbs already incorporated in 1920 added only 350,000 population from 1920 to 1980. Meanwhile the seven-county area added 1.3 million. The two central cities made almost no significant changes in their boundaries, and most of the streetcar suburbs changed very little. Obviously, about 900,000 population spilled into previously unincorporated territory.

Similar dispersal occurred around the smaller urban centers. For example, in the Southern Minnesota urban cluster, Owatonna let out its corporate belt to accommodate a population increase of 11,000 in 60 years. But annexation did not encompass all the growth. Another 5,000 built new homes in farm wood-lots and on gentle hillsides among the corn fields, converted old farmhouses, pumped new life into small towns and hamlets, or hooked up in mobile home courts on the outskirts. Another example, in the Minnesota Lakes urban cluster, Brainerd city population grew only 2,000 from 1920 to 1980, but more than 20,000 were added to the nonfarm popu-lation of the surrounding county. Ninety per-cent of the urban area's growth followed the blacktop arterials and sand side roads to lakeshore and pine woods outside the city limits. Even the declining areas experienced similar urban dispersal.

In every case growth spread into rural townships, hamlets, and small towns alike. Most of the urban pioneers in the Twin Cities area quickly organized new municipalities to resolve mounting community problems—to pave streets, lay sewer and water lines, build schools. But at lower densities around the smaller cities, few people felt any need to or-ganize new municipalities. As a result, many state and county roads became in fact the streets of extended urban areas. Consolidated school districts reflected extended urban com-munities. County sheriffs' offices began to operate urban police services for urban areas dispersed outside the city limits. Utilities and merchants had to adjust their rates and charges to be able to provide urban services in rural areas. Each of these communities reor-ganized to provide a framework for urbaniza-tion of the countryside.[75]

Thus community decisions and actions, both private and public, provided the frame-work for dealing with growth and decline. The decisions and actions were needed in the medium and large growth centers, the declin-ing or nongrowth cities, the regional metropo-lis and the urbanizing countryside.

In the process of settlement, the map of places and populations became a map of geo-graphic communities. Each community was anchored to its place by the long life-expec-tancy of the buildings that people have put there, by the commitments of people there to one another, and by their affection for the place itself. When a crisis makes part of the place obsolete, some individuals can adapt by moving on to another place. But a community rooted in a place cannot move. The core of the community turns out to be the group that is anchored there at any given time by the build-ings and by fixed commitment and affection. That group has to provide the current of con-tinuity in the turbulent demographic stream. And it is that group, at any given time and place, who creates the framework for dealing with problems of growth and decline.

CHAPTER 7

Reorganizing the Region's Work

In 1929, employed people in the Upper Midwest numbered 2.3 million, or 37 percent of the total population. By 1980 the numbers had grown to 3.6 million, or 43 percent (Table 4). Throughout the years, employment, with population and income, was one of the most-used indicators of the changing material health of communities and regions. Changes in the description and location of jobs were part of the process of adaptation and transformation in the auto era.

Jobs on the transportation and communication lines, on the farms, and in the mines, factories, trade, and service organizations are all parts of a vast productive system. Maps of circulation and settlement patterns are geographical diagrams of the system. And the purpose of the system is simply to enable people to work together to use the earth's resources and to enhance the quality of their lives. The system is unique because of its size and complexity—and because it is built from the inside by people who are a part of it. Hence, the productive system keeps evolving as part of a continuing quest for a better life, with both the inertia of human institutions and the uncertainty accompanying human curiosity and in-

novation. In that evolution, commitments and affections for places are always under review—continually tested by changes in the size, wealth, and functions of each community. The world market makes different demands on each place at different times, and the local people invent ways to meet the demands and even to change them. Thus employment keeps changing as the productive system evolves.

A New National and Global Environment

A host of new circumstances in the auto era demanded profound adjustments in Upper Midwest employment. The long-run decentralization of American population and industry from the historic Northeastern core region was accelerated toward the South and West. In that realignment, the region's share of the nation's industry and income increased, while its share of the population declined. But the biggest shifts went to other parts of the country, and the Upper Midwest had to adapt to the emergence of major new market opportunities and competition in both the Southeast

and the Southwest. Meanwhile, it joined other American regions in coping with new international opportunities and competition.

Improvements in transportation technology also promoted new job specialization and faster exchange of the nation's growing volume of goods, capital, and information. Waves of new products, services, and knowledge crashed incessantly across the marketplace, and with each wave came opportunities for new occupations and business firms. As a result, a continuous flow of entrepreneurs had to come into the marketplace to organize resources, labor, production, and distribution—to create organizations and jobs.

Dun and Bradstreet counted a net increase nationwide of nearly one million new business firms from 1920 to 1980 (Figure 54). The increment was somewhat slower and much more unsteady than it had been before 1920. But the net growth figures masked a far more turbulent process of business formation, growth, decline, and demise. More than 9 million different firms were incorporated during that 60-year period, but only one million grew to even the very modest size and stability necessary for listing by Dun and Bradstreet. On the

Table 4. Breakdown of Upper Midwest Employment by Industry Group, 1929 and 1980 (In Thousands)

Area	Agriculture[a]		Manufacturing[b]		Circulation[c]		Construction		Trade		Services		Total[d]		Public[e]	% of 1980
	1929	1980	1929	1980	1929	1980	1929	1980	1929	1980	1929	1980	1929	1980	1980	Total
Urban Clusters																
Minnesota Core																
Central Counties	11	5	89	155	40	36	25	32	79	167	111	337	356	731	107	15
Commuter Ring	48	20	11	76	4	20	4	18	9	85	15	144	91	363	56	15
Satellite Ring	73	27	15	44	6	8	6	13	13	46	26	84	140	222	39	18
Minnesota Lakes	46	12	6	14	4	4	2	7	6	24	15	46	79	106	24	22
Southern Minnesota	30	12	8	32	3	5	4	6	9	31	26	54	81	140	20	14
Chippewa Valley–LaCrosse	25	12	17	28	5	5	4	7	11	31	17	56	79	138	22	16
Upper Wisconsin Valley	28	12	13	21	2	3	2	5	7	20	10	34	62	96	12	13
Fargo-Moorhead	9	4	3	6	3	3	1	4	5	18	8	32	29	66	10	15
Grand Forks Area	15	5	2	4	2	2	1	2	4	13	7	23	32	49	11	23
Sioux Valley	15	5	5	11	2	4	2	4	6	19	10	35	39	79	12	15
Bismarck-Mandan	6	3	1	2	1	2	1	4	2	9	4	19	14	38	7	19
Minot	5	1	1	1	1	1	1	2	2	6	3	10	13	22	4	17
Billings	4	2	2	4	1	4	1	4	2	14	3	22	12	50	7	15
Black Hills	5	2	1	4	1	2	1	3	2	9	3	17	12	36	7	20
*Homestake	2	2	1	1	...	...	...	...	1	2	1	3	5	8	2	19
Western Montana Valleys	19	11	9	15	7	7	4	11	8	35	16	71	62	150	35	24
*Butte-Anaconda	1	1	5	1	2	1	1	1	4	4	7	10	20	20	5	25
Lake Superior Mineral Districts																
Mesabi-Duluth	23	13	15	12	16	8	6	7	16	25	27	47	102	111	22	20
Gogebic-Menominee-Copper Ranges	24	2	4	3	3	...	2	2	5	6	8	12	45	25	8	31
Marquette	6	4	3	1	2	1	1	1	2	6	4	14	17	26	8	30
Outlying Areas																
Corn Belt	211	88	21	68	18	15	16	31	41	95	69	150	376	447	61	14
Great Plains	281	105	16	18	23	16	22	24	41	76	79	140	464	378	76	20
Northern Forest	56	12	25	32	10	5	6	8	13	28	25	52	135	137	25	18
Montana Rockies	9	4	1	1	2	2	1	1	2	4	4	8	19	20	5	25
Total[d]	951	364	272	554	160	151	113	197	288	770	499	1,419	2,283	3,455	585	17
Upper Midwest % of U.S.																
Total Employment	9.0%	10.5	2.3	2.5	4.1	2.4	7.6	3.2	4.7	3.9	6.2	3.6	5.5	3.6	3.5	

Sources: See note 78.

[a] Includes Forestry.

[b] Includes Mining.

[c] Includes Transportation, Communications, and Utilities

[d] Totals contain minor discrepancies due to rounding.

[e] No data were available for 1929. Public employees, extracted here, are included in all industry groups.

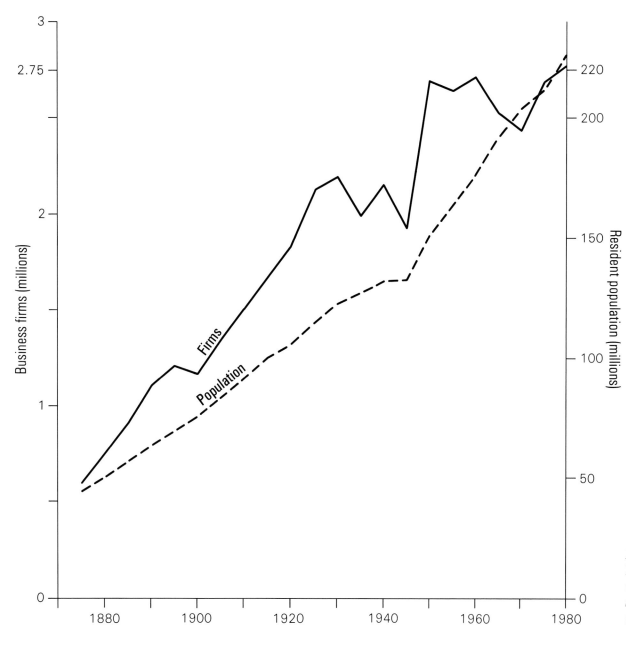

Figure 54. Growth in the U.S. Population and Number of Business Firms, 1875-1980. Since 1920 the growth rate has become much more variable, and the average number of firms per unit population has gradually declined. Source: note 76.

Figure 55. Absorption of U.S. Labor Force Growth, 1960-1980. In those two decades, jobs had to be created for an unprecedented 37.3 million new entrants into the labor force. Source: note 77.

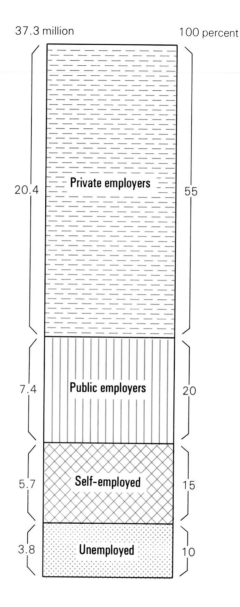

other hand, while millions merged, failed, or sold out, hundreds had phenomenal growth and moved up into the ranks of the 1,000 or so largest corporations in the country. Those newcomers, in turn, replaced big-time drop-outs. Of the nation's 1,300 largest corporations in 1920, only one-third were still intact 50 years later.[76]

Entry of the post–World War II baby-boom generation into the labor force provided another example of the complexity of employment growth and change (Figure 55). In the 1960s and 1970s, jobs had to be created for 37.3 million new entrants into the American labor force. Never before had there been anything like that lump for the job market to swallow. Business firms created 20 million jobs, a little more than half the number needed. A million of those were in research and development working on new products to create still more organizations and occupations. Public agencies expanded to absorb another one-fifth. Fifteen percent—about one in every six—created their own jobs. They were self-employed. The remaining 10 percent were unemployed. Those groups, of course, were very dynamic. Uncounted hundreds of thousands of individuals shifted between private corporations, government, and self-employment. They were accounting for a substantial part of the job creation drama—the innovation, organization, spin-off, reorganization, growth, failure, merger. To be sure, ordinary population and market growth accounted for a large amount of employment increase within the framework of existing companies and public agencies. But the organizations that were largest, on the average, in 1960 provided less than their share of the new jobs. The greater share came from the growth of smaller firms and the creation of new ones.[77]

Americans also made some big changes in

the nature and location of government employment. Amid fast-growing income and wealth, they raised the level of investment in every aspect of education in an effort to broaden the opportunities for their children in an increasingly sophisticated world. They committed governments to build and maintain a paved road and street system that links virtually every driveway with all others, and to build airports and improve waterways. Thus, the public took over construction and maintenance of way for the greater part of the transportation system. They also created a complex array of social insurance and subsidies in repeated efforts to gain security in a world of increasingly complex financial uncertainty. They supported a sevenfold increase in peacetime military employment in an effort to reduce their insecurity in a world of turbulent, and increasingly visible foreign contacts. Finally, they wanted more and better records and accounting of the changes in population, business, and government itself.

Regional Adaptation

The Upper Midwest did adapt to these dramatic auto-era changes in its environment. Growth in nonfarm employment not only compensated for the 600,000 lost farm jobs but added another 1.2 million in the bargain (Figure 56). Manufacturing employment doubled as a result of both decentralization and development of new products. The number of construction jobs nearly doubled, despite slowed population growth, in response to the region's growing wealth and capital improvements. Retail and wholesale trade employment more than doubled, and service employment tripled, reflecting the nationwide specialization and acceleration of exchange.

Transportation employment declined slightly. Thousands of railroad jobs fell victim to greater efficiency and private auto competition, but thousands of new jobs appeared in trucking, airlines, and utilities. Employment dropped much more in the mineral industries, but it also shifted from the troubled iron and copper ranges to Great Plains oil and coal fields. A remarkable Upper Midwest seedbed and crop of entrepreneurs invented ways to serve not only the regional market but also distant national and world markets. They expanded older firms and started new ones. They created jobs that otherwise would not have been here and income that otherwise would not have come here.

Government employment increased fourfold in 50 years, from 150,000 to nearly 600,000. The share of all Upper Midwest jobs on public payrolls grew from an estimated 7 percent to 17 percent. The public sector accounted for nearly half of the increase in service and transportation and utilities employment. The Upper Midwest was often in the vanguard of government programs in education, transportation, and welfare—perhaps because relatively homogeneous culture and comparatively rapid economic growth made it easier for state populations to act as communities.

Employment adaptation varied from one part of the region to another. Gains and losses were in different locations. The Twin Cities and the other major clusters of urban growth gained 1.4 million nonfarm jobs between 1929 and 1980, while they lost about 200,000 farm jobs from the suburbanization or consolidation of farms—seven nonfarm jobs gained for every one farm job lost. In contrast, in the mining districts 41,000 jobs were added in the services and trade, but 40,000 were lost in mining and related industries. With the help of

manufacturing expansion in many medium-sized cities, nonfarm growth more than offset the loss of 123,000 farm jobs in the Corn Belt. Mainly because of increases in the recreation and paper industries, nonfarm employment growth slightly exceeded the loss of jobs through farm abandonment in the northern forest areas. But in the semiarid and subhumid Great Plains, out-migration and farm consolidation were very large, and urban centers were few and widely dispersed. As a result, nonfarm job growth was scarcely half as large as farm job loss.[78]

The Surviving Farm Jobs

Farm households decreased from more than one-half million to about one-quarter million in the auto era. Total employment, including hired hands, dropped from 951,000 in 1929 to 364,000 in 1980. The 1980 total included about 250,000 farm operators and a little more than 100,000 other farm family members and hired workers. A small fraction—perhaps 2 percent—of the hired workers were seasonal immigrants.

The farmers who remained after a half-century of transformation were vastly more highly capitalized and productive than their predecessors two generations earlier. Value of farmland and buildings in 1982 was nine times the inflated post-World War I figures of 1920, 10 times the depressed values of the mid-1920s. The change reflected the mushrooming in the 1950s through the 1970s of new buildings for livestock, grain and equipment storage, large machinery, cars and trucks, as well as pens, fencing, tanks, drainage or irrigation works, and new or enlarged and improved housing. In the region's cropland corridor from western Wisconsin and northern Iowa to

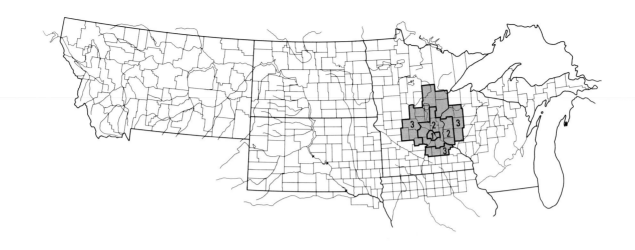

Jobs (thousands)

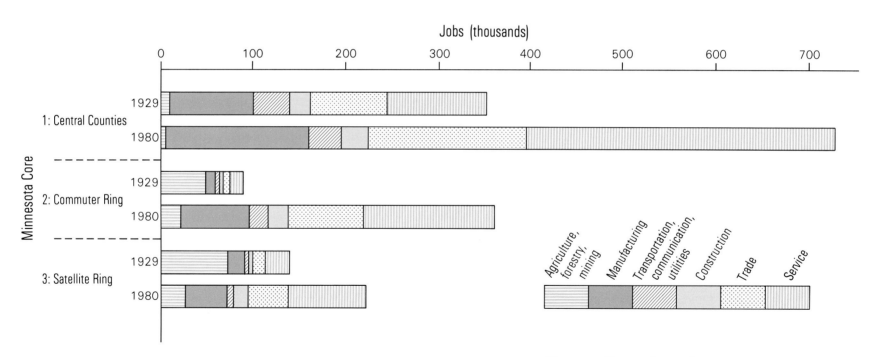

Figure 56. *Changes in Employment, 1929-1980. (4 pages) The bar graphs dramatize the overall employment growth and shift from farming to service, trade, and manufacturing in the auto era. The graphs also point up contrasts and similarities between the different urban clusters and outlying areas identified on the maps. Source: note 78.*

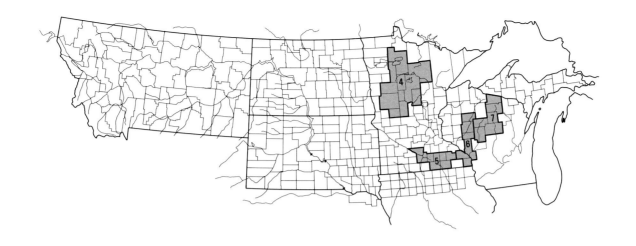

Jobs (thousands)

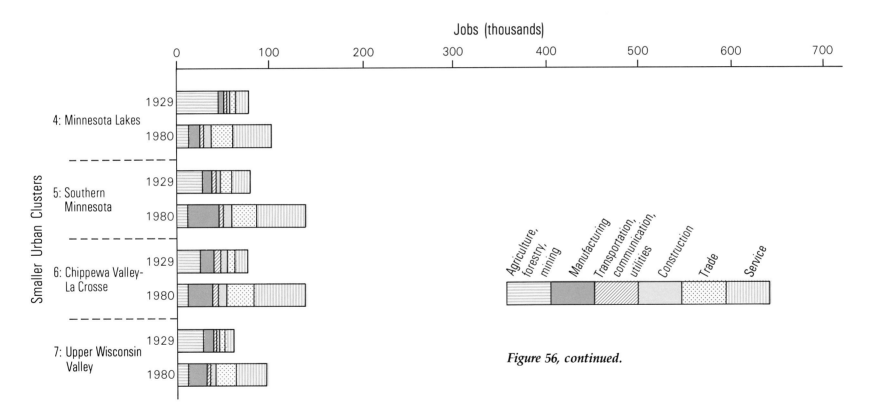

Smaller Urban Clusters

4: Minnesota Lakes
1929
1980

5: Southern Minnesota
1929
1980

6: Chippewa Valley-La Crosse
1929
1980

7: Upper Wisconsin Valley
1929
1980

Agriculture, forestry, mining
Manufacturing
Transportation, communication, utilities
Construction
Trade
Service

Figure 56, continued.

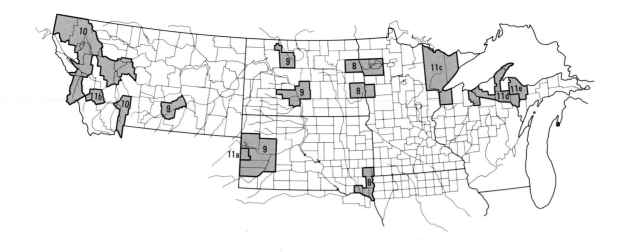

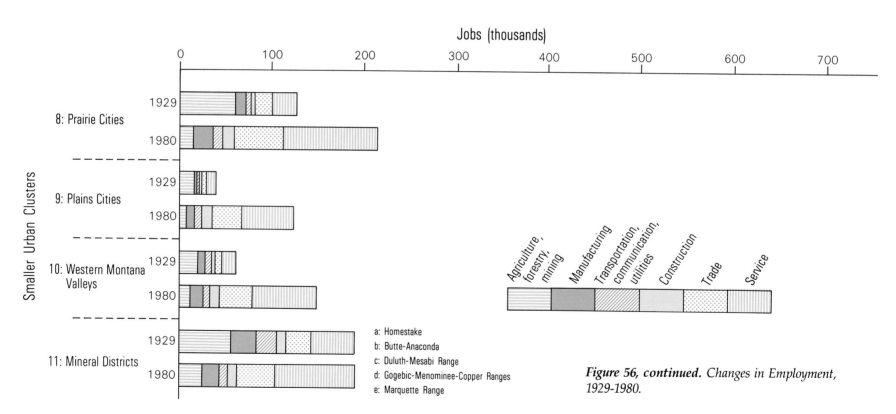

Jobs (thousands)

Smaller Urban Clusters

8: Prairie Cities
1929
1980

9: Plains Cities
1929
1980

10: Western Montana Valleys
1929
1980

11: Mineral Districts
1929
1980

a: Homestake
b: Butte-Anaconda
c: Duluth-Mesabi Range
d: Gogebic-Menominee-Copper Ranges
e: Marquette Range

Agriculture, forestry, mining
Manufacturing
Transportation, communication, utilities
Construction
Trade
Service

Figure 56, continued. Changes in Employment, 1929-1980.

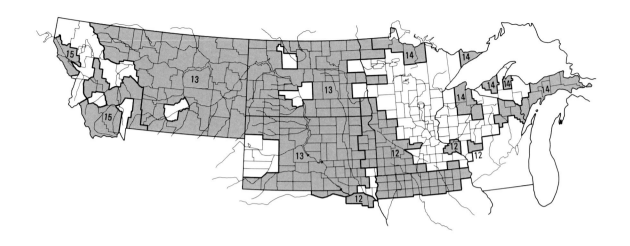

Jobs (thousands)

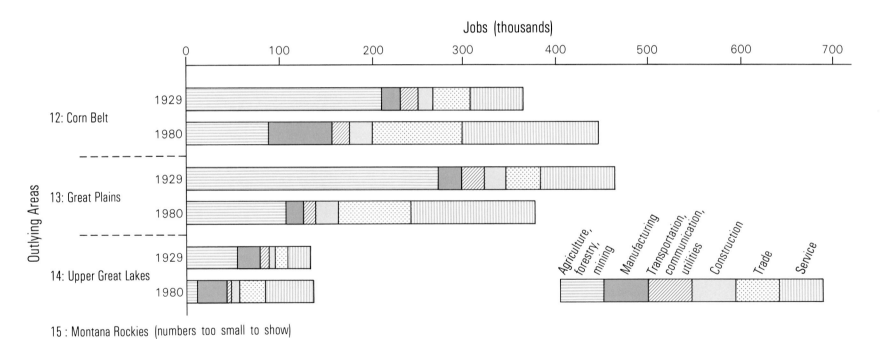

Outlying Areas

12: Corn Belt

13: Great Plains

14: Upper Great Lakes

15 : Montana Rockies (numbers too small to show)

Agriculture, forestry, mining

Manufacturing

Transportation, communication, utilities

Construction

Trade

Service

Figure 56, continued.

northern Montana, land and buildings on the average fulltime farm were valued at around half a million dollars in 1982. In addition, the average place had $75,000 to $100,000 worth of equipment and machinery. That equaled the value of crops and livestock sold from the average fulltime farm in the preceding year (*See* Figure 42, Figure 43). The investment in land, buildings, and machinery per farm worker was about $390,000! But two-thirds of the workers were also owners, managers, and executives of their own enterprises.

With its enormous gross earnings and heavy capital outlays, farm employment continued to undergird a major share of the Upper Midwest economy. In North and South Dakota, Minnesota, and eastern Montana, 70 percent to 80 percent of the economy depended ultimately on the handling and processing of farm products for export to the rest of the nation and world. In the region as a whole, the economy depended perhaps one-third on agriculture, in the Twin Cities, perhaps 15 percent.[79]

Yet the 1980s saw growing concern about the future of agricultural employment. The industry depended increasingly on grain exports in the international markets. Earnings were becoming more variable and uncertain. Competition was increasing from other regions of the developed world and from some developing countries. Need for the region's bulging output of grain, meat, and dairy products was still high in many overpopulated, underfed areas of the world, but shipments to those areas generally required American subsidies, and there was always uncertainty about future public support. Farms continued to grow in average size, with an accompanying reduction in the number of fulltime farms and farm jobs. As a result, both rural and urban

people felt uneasy about the outlook for family-owned, family-operated farms.

Family farms were believed to be the hearth and bastion of basic values in the society of America in general and of the Heartland in particular. Sheer reduction in the number of farms was threat enough. But beyond that, to many observers increasing size and capitalization pointed toward an inevitable shift away from owner-occupants toward absentee ownership and control by large business organizations. The fears were aggravated during periods of financial adversity.

While the family farms had developed a mythos, they had also played a major, real part in shaping the remarkable transformation of the Upper Midwest in the automobile era. To be sure, the changes in that era had greatly increased the farmers' productivity and their participation in the world's system of specialization and exchange. The resulting increase in gross farm income would have occurred in any case. But the decentralized, local ownership and control of the industry meant that the flow of earnings, expenditures, and savings would be channeled and revolved through the local communities to a much greater extent than would have been probable with more centralized, absentee control, at that stage in American development. On the resource side, soil management practices were probably better than they would have been otherwise, because the majority of owners expected to remain on their land and pass it along to successive generations.

In fact, the region's family farms, with those of the nation as a whole, appeared to be diverging from the historic norm along two different lines: industrialization and urbanization. Neither trend was new. Both had been running throughout the auto era.

On the one hand, farming had become ever more industrial in character—bigger fields, more land, more and bigger machines, more modification of the natural resource through drainage, irrigation, and chemicals. The industrializing units tended to be owned and run by operators who earned most or all of their income from farming. While most still lived on their farms, a significant number of "sidewalk farmers" lived during much of the year in a nearby urban trade center for greater convenience to schools and other services. The number of these fulltime farms dropped by 59 percent from the 1920s to the 1980s.

On the other hand, farming had also become more urban in character. Not only had many farm tasks shifted to the towns; but also growing numbers of farm operators were earning more than half of their income from nonfarm employment (*See* Map 41). The number of those part-time farmers actually increased about 10 percent between the 1920s and 1980s. The trend reflected the greater accessibility of farming areas to jobs in the towns and cities. It offered an opportunity for increased income as well as increased stability from diversification. The average part-time farmer's total net income, including off-farm earnings, was more than that of the average fulltime operator.

The opportunity to diversify reached both ways. It appealed to farm families with skills that were marketable off the farm, and it appealed to urban workers and their families who wanted to live in the countryside and employ their farming skills. The urban occupations of both groups ranged from laborer to business proprietor to professional. For example, small farmers became factory workers or independent technicians in the towns; urban computer programmers and auto mechanics bought small farms and worked them evenings and weekends. A prosperous farm family might buy an automobile dealership, and a prosperous auto dealer might buy a farm. For what it was worth, many values of the idealized family farm appeared alive and well in the statistical profile of the average part-time farm: self-reliance, large families, children participating in farm work and growing up in the open country.

Part-time farming was growing mainly within commuting range of the region's main urban employment clusters and in the lake and mountain regions. By 1982 the operators who earned most of their living off the farm accounted for one-fourth of the region's farms, 9 percent of the value of land, buildings, and machines, and about 7 percent of the value of farm products sold. Thus, the part-time farms averaged about one-third the size of the fulltime operations.

No near, practical limit to the urbanizing trend in agriculture could be foreseen. Much more farmland could shift into the part-time category if necessary. And the trend seemed to pose no clear threat to the family farm as a social institution. However, the need persisted to adopt large-scale industrialization of fulltime farms yet somehow to maintain family ownership and occupance, decentralized management and control. Thus, the number and character of jobs in the region's most important basic industry depended on creative organization and entrepreneurship.

Trading New Jobs for Old in the Circulation System

Despite the transportation and communications explosion, the number of workers operating the Upper Midwest transportation, communications, and utilities systems changed hardly at all from 1929 to 1980 (Figure 57). There was a net decline of 2.5 percent, from 159,000 to 154,000. But beneath the calm statistical surface a metamorphosis occurred.[80]

At hundreds of small and medium-size cities, towns, and hamlets the transformation was gradual and simple. The railroad station agents and the operators of horse-drawn drayage and livery services disappeared. The local truckers graduated from four-wheelers to 18-wheelers and extended their range from the neighboring towns to the neighboring states. Operation and maintenance of the growing electric and phone utilities compensated for jobs lost in railroading. Most of the compensating jobs tended to locate at the county seat, no matter where in the county they had been earlier. Thus, despite many internal changes, the net loss of transportation and utilities jobs was small in most counties. In fact, in 289 of the region's 342 counties, with 54,000 transportation and utility jobs in 1980, there had been a net loss of only 4,000 in the half-century since 1929. A similar substitution of new occupations for old took place in some larger centers. The main rail lines operated sprawling yards and shops at La Crosse, Eau Claire, Mason City, Minot, Grand Forks, Aberdeen, and Great Falls. The confluence of rail lines had given those places much of their momentum in the first place. Now, employment growth in trucking and utilities roughly offset the sharp decline in railroading. Total transportation and utilities employment in those seven cities was about 11,000 in 1929, and it still stood at 10,000 fifty years later.

But the changes were dramatic in a few places. In the Twin Cities and nine new, fast-growing outlying metropolitan areas, transportation and utility employment rose 12 percentage points, from 33 percent of the Upper Midwest total to 45 percent. At the same time, the iron and copper country and highly specialized railroad towns dropped 12 points, from 24 percent of the total to 12. In those cases, too, jobs gained equaled jobs lost. But the gains and losses were located hundreds of miles apart.

In the iron- and copper-mining districts and the Great Lakes ore-shipping ports, employment on trains, docks, and tugs was lost because of larger and faster equipment. Mine and ore dock shutdowns added to the losses. Counteracting growth occurred in trucking and utilities, but it was mainly in the larger centers of population and wholesaling: Duluth-Superior, the Mesabi Range cities, and to a much smaller extent Butte and Marquette. Overall gains compensated for no more than one-third of the losses.

Declines also greatly exceeded gains in the small cities and towns at railroad division points. Those were the places where a single main line broadened to form a swath of 10 or 20 parallel sidetracks that spread over as much land as the town itself. In the 1920s, at those points through trains changed crews, locals originated and terminated, and equipment was serviced. An oversized two-story station housed a cadre of clerks and dispatchers who monitored and directed traffic over a hundred miles or more, by telegraph and handwritten orders. Many of the workers lived in the town, but many of the crews were transient. A two- or three-story hotel near the depot dominated the Main Street facade. Night and day, winter and summer, crewmen crossed the polished lobby floor, paused at the brass cuspidors and tobacco stand, and headed upstairs for some sleep before the next run.

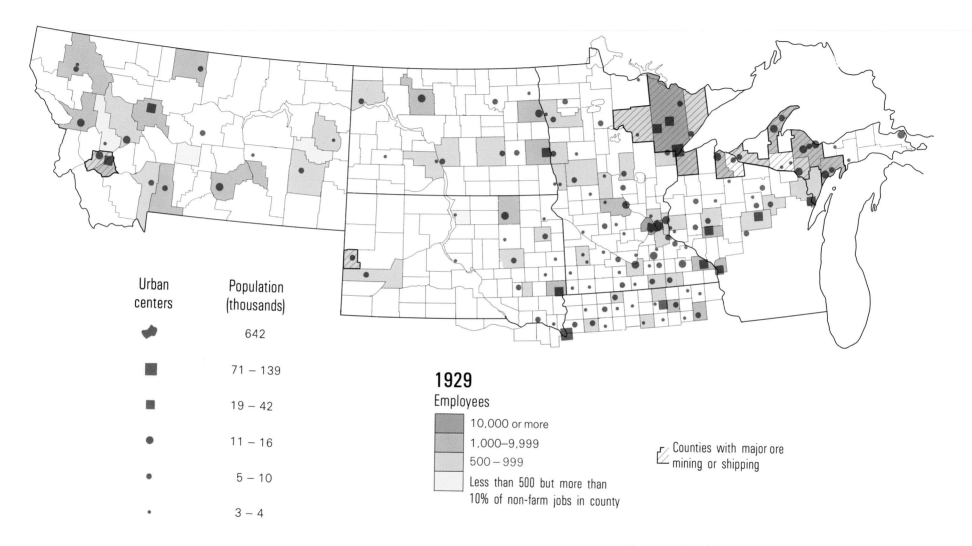

Urban
centers

Population
(thousands)

642

71 – 139

19 – 42

11 – 16

5 – 10

3 – 4

1929

Employees

10,000 or more

1,000–9,999

500 – 999

Less than 500 but more than
10% of non-farm jobs in county

Counties with major ore
mining or shipping

Figure 57. Employment in Transportation-Communications-Public Utilities, 1929–1980. (2 pages) Growth was concentrated at important urban centers on the highway grid. But, in the mining districts and about a dozen smaller railroad centers, it was not enough to offset the loss of railroad jobs. Source: note 80.

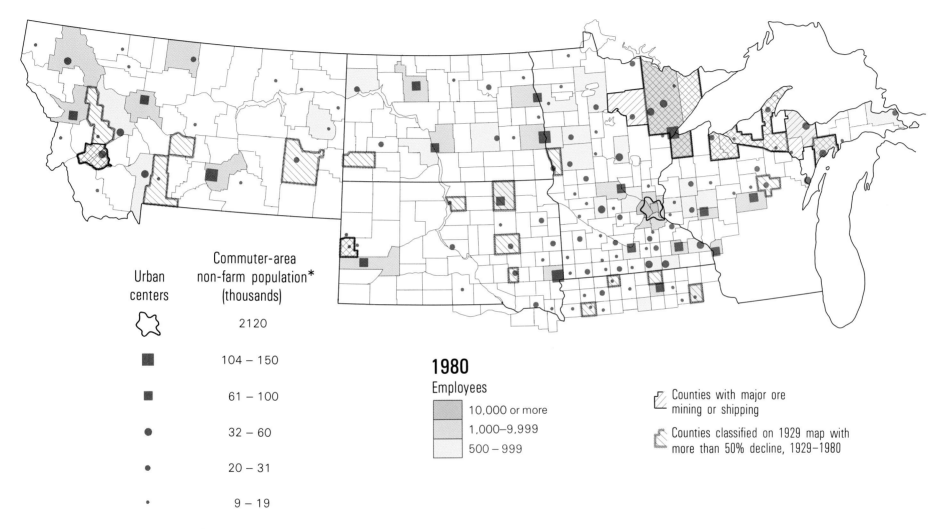

Urban
centers

Commuter-area
non-farm population*
(thousands)

2120

104 – 150

61 – 100

32 – 60

20 – 31

9 – 19

1980

Employees

10,000 or more

1,000–9,999

500 – 999

Counties with major ore
mining or shipping

Counties classified on 1929 map with
more than 50% decline, 1929–1980

* See note with Figure 1.

Figure 57, continued.

On the 1929 map, 24 of those towns were strung along the transcontinental corridor and along the prairie and North Woods lines from Chicago. They lost nearly half of their 1929 transportation employment by 1980. Strong railroad activity continued at Glendive, Montana, and strong growth of trucking went on at a few other places in the group. But the strength of those places fell far short of compensating for the collapse of railroading at Oelwein and Cherokee in Iowa, Huron and Mobridge in South Dakota, Miles City and Three Forks in Montana, Tracy and Staples in Minnesota, and perhaps a dozen more towns.

Of course, the main lines were far from dead. Only the labor force and trackage were cut back. Trackside offices, though smaller, were new or refurbished. Modern electronic communication helped to control traffic over longer segments of line. Hundred-car trains sped between more widely separated, automated yards. Their specialized cars were loaded with long-haul cargo: Upper Midwest grain for Duluth, Gulf, or Pacific ports; Montana coal for the Midwest; Pacific Northwest building materials for the Manufacturing Belt; Manufacturing Belt machinery and automobiles headed west; Japanese automobiles headed east; overseas containers en route from Japan to Europe or from Taiwan to Chicago—and countless other examples of national and international exchange. The locals and the passenger trains were only memories. But fewer, far longer, and heavier trains hauled a greatly increased tonnage as they rumbled through rusty yards on upgraded main tracks.

Seven of the nine fast-growing new metropolitan areas—St. Cloud, Sioux Falls, Fargo-Moorhead, Bismarck-Mandan, Billings, and Missoula—had also been important rail centers. But their smoky yards, roundhouses, and shops were replaced—in other parts of the city—by modern, even more extensive, but equally utilitarian steel truck terminals and blacktop parking lots. In bright but simple new offices, both at the truck terminals and trackside, the ratchet sound of computer printers had replaced the clacking depot telegraphs. Air-conditioning, cable TV, and banks of vending machines in the truckers' caravansaries replaced the stale-air austerity of the trainmen's hotels.

The Twin Cities were the scene of the biggest transformation. Within today's seven-county metropolitan area, the number of transportation and utilities jobs increased from 27,000 in 1929 to 34,000 in 1980. While thousands of jobs were lost in the railroad corridors through the central cities, nearly 2,000 railroad corporate office jobs remained in the downtowns. The airport, with its terminals, major overhaul bases, and airline corporate headquarters, accounted for more than 10,000 new jobs. Trucking companies spawned thousands of new jobs in the central wholesale districts and the Midway, then shifted and expanded into the suburbs. With the development of the Upper Mississippi River locks and dams and the stable nine-foot channel in the 1930s, commercial navigation revived; and the resulting new barge and towboat jobs concentrated at the port of St. Paul. Employment in communication and electric utilities grew with the metropolitan population, reinforced by central offices at the focus of the regional communication network.

By 1980, transportation and utilities employment was concentrated more than ever in the Twin Cities, and the concentration had increased strongly in the fast-growing, smaller metropolitan areas as well. Meanwhile, the transportation and utilities share of employment in all cities showed different patterns: it was about steady in the Twin Cities, while it rose sharply in the fast-growing smaller metropolitan areas and in scores of small cities and towns. The Twin Cities were shifting increasingly to capital-intensive components of the circulation system: air transport, electronic communications, long-haul freight. The smaller cities involved in shipping goods were doing more of the labor-intensive trucking: shorter hauls, smaller shipments, general cargo. As a result of decentralized trucking operations, most of the trade centers outside of the Twin Cities became more specialized in hauling the region's goods than their counterparts had been a half-century earlier. In fact, the number of places dependent on trucking for their living was greater than the number dependent on railroading in 1929; moreover, the dependency on trucking was greater than that on railroading had been. As a symbol of the livelihood of those places, the semi had replaced and surpassed the boxcar.

Shrinking and Unstable Employment in the Mineral Industries

From the 1920s to 1980, the total number of jobs in the mineral industries declined from over 50,000 to 24,000. Most jobs had always been located in just a few distinctive parts of the region—a few unique natural resource concentrations rich enough and big enough to appear on world maps. To be sure, the sand, gravel, and crushed-rock industries employed several thousand people in the production of construction aggregate at hundreds of widely scattered deposits. More localized were the quarries supplying the region's three cement plants, several brick and tile works, and the parent plant of the country's major producer of granite building-stone at Cold Spring, Minnesota, near St. Cloud. Except for several hundred employees in the granite quarries, those jobs were an integral part of the construction industry within the region. In contrast, the metallic ore and mineral fuel industries in the 1980s were more than ever parts of worldwide industries centered outside the Upper Midwest.[81]

Major metallic ore deposits are clustered in the Montana Rockies, the northern Black Hills, and the Canadian Shield. The richest have been the copper deposits of the Butte district in Montana and the Keweenaw Peninsula in northern Michigan, and the iron ores of the ranges around Lake Superior. The most important coal and oil deposits are in the massive accumulation of layered sedimentary rocks that underlie the semiarid Great Plains from the Missouri River in North Dakota to the eastern base of the Rockies in Montana.

Between the 1920s and 1980, copper, iron, and gold mining lost 33,000 jobs, while coal, oil, and gas gained 6,000. Sharp, temporary booms and recessions sometimes obscured the long-term trends.

LONG-TERM DECLINES

Copper-mining employment at Butte and the Copper Range locations declined from 18,000 in the 1920s to zero in 1980. The problems were declining quality and increasing depth of the ore, together with competition from foreign areas with comparable or better ore and a fraction of the labor costs. Most of the change came during the Great Depression of the 1930s. After World War II, there was a shift to open-pit mining at Butte in an effort to cut costs by taking advantage of the great gains in size and efficiency of earth-moving machinery. But that was still not enough in the long run, as world copper prices kept falling. By 1980 a few hundred jobs remained in the White Pine copper mine and smelter at the eastern base of Michigan's Porcupine Mountains, but those jobs also appeared to be threatened.

Iron-mining employment fell from 30,000 to 15,000 between 1920 and 1980. The industry retreated from the smaller, less accessible deep deposits, even though they were high-grade. As a result, employment of the Gogebic and Menominee ranges—centered on Ironwood, Iron River, and Iron Mountain, Michigan—fell from 6,000 to zero.

Production was consolidated on the large, shallow ore bodies and open-pit operations, although those ores were lower in average quality. By the 1970s, 95 percent of the production came from Minnesota's Mesabi Range, the remainder from the Marquette Range in northern Michigan (Figure 58). In both cases the industry opened new, highly mechanized mines and invested heavily in very large-scale plants to crush, grind, and pelletize the low-grade ores. The first of the mammoth plants, at Silver Bay on Lake Superior's north shore, was named for E. W. Davis, University of Minnesota engineering professor who spent his professional life in development of the process. The pellets provided a standard, high-quality feed for the iron and steel furnaces on the southern edge of the Great Lakes and in the Ohio Valley. In 1980 dollars, the plants represented an outlay of 3 to 4 billion—more money than all but the largest steel company could raise alone. Some of the nation's biggest corporations found themselves burying long-standing rivalries in favor of joint venture, to borrow hundreds of millions for construction and equipment. As a result of the change from natural ore to pellets, less tonnage had to be shipped down the lakes, and the average quality rose from around 50 percent iron to 62 percent.

There had been a strong case for investment in pellet plants. The substitution of capital for labor would shift from a larger number of unskilled jobs to a smaller, but it was hoped, more stable, number of higher-paying, more skilled jobs—the end of pick-and-shovel work, the beginning of more operation and maintenance of complex plant and equipment. When the plants were planned and initiated, Cold War psychology was especially pervasive. In contrast with rejuvenated Cold War thinking in the 1980s, greater emphasis then fell on national self-sufficiency. There was no question about the importance of self-sufficiency in iron and steel. The demands of World War II had seriously depleted reserves of high-grade natural ore. But vast reserves of low-grade ore, suitable for pelletizing, would last at least one or two centuries. Everyone concerned agreed that the investment should be made.

The steel industry could behave differently from the copper industry because it seemed to be less vulnerable to world competition. The iron-ore resources near Lake Superior were among the richest and largest known in the world. The coal resources of the Appalachians, not far from the southern shores of Lake Erie, were—and are—the world's largest high-quality reserves for metallurgical purposes. Between the two lay the natural waterway of the Great Lakes. And the southern part of that extraordinary natural complex lay in the path of expansion westward from the Middle Atlantic Seaboard. The result was a combination of market accessibility and naturally endowed production efficiency that was overwhelming.

The southern Great Lakes region had emerged quickly in the late nineteenth century as the dominant center of steel and heavy machinery fabrication in the western hemi-

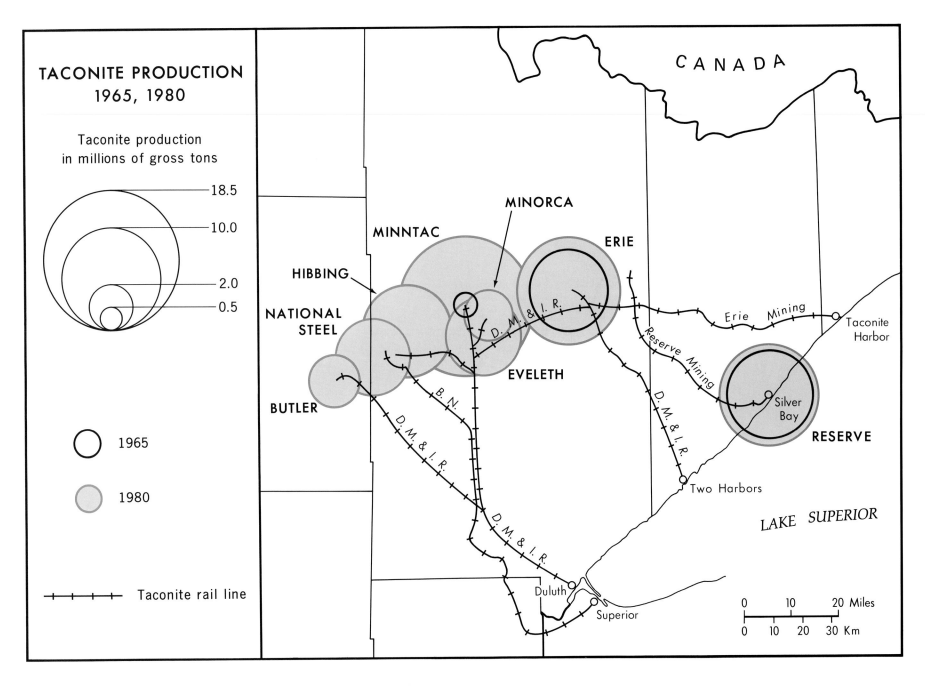

TACONITE PRODUCTION 1965, 1980

Taconite production in millions of gross tons

18.5
10.0
2.0
0.5

○ 1965

● 1980

+—+—+—+ Taconite rail line

CANADA

MINORCA

MINNTAC

ERIE

HIBBING

NATIONAL STEEL

BUTLER

EVELETH

D. M. & I. R.

B. N.

D. M. & I. R.

D. M. & I. R.

Erie Mining

Reserve Mining

D. M. & I. R.

Taconite Harbor

Silver Bay

RESERVE

Two Harbors

LAKE SUPERIOR

Duluth

Superior

0   10   20 Miles
0   10   20   30 Km

Figure 58. Minnesota Taconite Production, 1965 and 1980. By the 1970s, 95 percent of taconite tonnage came from the Mesabi Range. Source: J.R. Borchert and Neil C. Gustafson, Atlas of Minnesota Resources and Settlement (Minneapolis: University of Minnesota Center for Urban and *Regional Affairs, and Minnesota State Planning Agency, 1980).*

sphere. A regional oligopoly developed which included finance, management, and labor—protected by seemingly unassailable natural advantages. Not until the 1970s was a challenge visible. The quality of overseas machinery products had become high enough, while labor costs had remained low enough, that the Great Lakes area's natural endowment alone could no longer provide the competitive edge. At the same time, the uncertain price and supply of oil had conspired with foreign styling to squeeze Americans into smaller, lighter cars with a greatly reduced steel content. Growth in the South and West had changed the market position of the Great Lakes region. A potential flood of high-quality natural foreign ore from the tropics was waiting for new steel mill construction in tidewater locations to open wide the American market. Now everyone agreed the Great Lakes region was in big trouble. But by that time the pelletizing plants were built, and so were the homes and communities of the workers to run them.[82]

Black Hills gold-mining employment has been operating in a still different world environment. The Homestake, at Lead, South Dakota, is America's largest gold mine. The federal treasury has provided a stable market and floor price for its product, although profits have fluctuated with the effects of depression, inflation, and the rocketing in the 1970s of the world price of gold. The labor force has remained quasi-constant in the neighborhood of 2,500 for the past half-century, while the shafts have gradually gone more than a mile deep, and the honeycomb of tunnels has kept expanding.

OFFSETTING GAINS

While ore mining declined overall, the giant American fuel mineral industry expanded in the Upper Midwest part of the northern

Great Plains. Montana oil and gas production began early in the auto era in the Shelby–Cut Bank area along the Great Northern High Line east of the Rockies, near Baker in the eastern part of the state, near the Wyoming boundary southwest of Billings, and in the Cat Creek district in the center. In fact, when Jack Dempsey defended his world title in 1923, he boxed not in New York but in the unlikely location of Shelby, Montana—a small farm trade center then in the midst of a free-spending oil boom.

With deeper drilling, improved exploration science, and ever-increasing demand, those early fields were extended, especially after World War II. But the most important developments of the 1940s and 1950s came in the Williston area of northwestern North Dakota. Another burst of exploration and drilling followed the oil shortages and price increases in the mid-1970s. Employment in the oil and gas fields rose from virtually zero to a census figure of more than 4,000 in 1980—perhaps two to three times that many, if all of the directly related business and production services were added. Upper Midwest oil production was about 2 percent of the nation's total.

Long before the oil rigs came to the northern Great Plains, railroads and a few small local companies—and even a few farmers and ranchers—were digging coal and lignite. Immigrant laborers worked the bituminous coal deposits near Roundup, Red Lodge, Great Falls, and a few other locations in Montana, and the lignite deposits at Beulah, in North Dakota's Knife River Valley. Altogether no more than 900 paid employees worked in the widely scattered mines.

By 1980 the number of employees was nearing 3,000 and rising. The old underground mines were all closed. A comparatively small number of miners, working open pits with gigantic excavation and conveyor equip-

ment, were producing between 5 and 10 percent of the nation's coal. There had been major expansion of lignite production in western North Dakota's Knife Valley to supply a half-dozen large, immediately adjacent thermal-electric plants on the regional power grid, as well as a federally subsidized, $2-billion gasification plant to produce synthetic fuel for new pipelines to Chicago and Detroit. More electric power and hydrocarbon conversion plants were planned although soft prices on the world oil market made all plans tentative. Extensive new strip mines had been opened on the low-sulfur bituminous coal deposits in eastern Montana. The major operations were at Colstrip, southwest of Miles City, and Decker, southeast of Billings in the Tongue River Basin. The thick seams extend beneath picturesque ranching country and lands of the Cheyenne and Crow Indians. Both centers are less than 50 miles and little more than a century removed from the Custer battlefield. About one-tenth of the coal produced in 1980 was burned at two large generating stations at Colstrip. But unit trains carried the great bulk of the output to power plants in major Midwest markets, where it was mixed with high-sulfur Ohio valley and northern Illinois coal to meet air quality requirements. The largest flow moved from Colstrip to the historic transcontinental Northern Pacific line in the Yellowstone Valley at Forsyth, Montana, then eastward. Unit trains hauled about 1,500 carloads daily into Minnesota, two-thirds for in-state power generation, most of the remainder for shipment from Duluth-Superior down the Great Lakes.

SHORT-TERM UPS AND DOWNS

Short-term instability was just as striking as long-term decline. Metallic ore-mining employment has risen and fallen with production and demand. On the Mesabi, for example, average yearly production nearly doubled during World War I, fell back 20 percent at the end of the war, rose 25 percent at the peak of the 1920s boom, dropped nearly 70 percent in the worst years of the Great Depression, rose 500 percent during World War II, dropped 20 percent after the Korean War in the late 1950s, rose 11 percent to the peak taconite pellet production year in 1979, and fell 50 percent by 1983 in the face of recession and the auto-making crisis. Thus, in the early 1950s the mines were working overtime to feed Korean War and Cold War demands piled on top of the suburban growth boom. Managers invented a three-day, 40-hour shift to make it possible to draw commuting labor from farm and forest areas as far away as 200 miles. Commuters shared makeshift sleeping rooms on the Mesabi, attended to affairs back home on four-day weekends. Contrast that with the early 1980s. Then hundreds of unemployed tradesmen from the mines worked on construction projects as far away as the North Dakota lignite fields and commuted back to their Mesabi Range homes and families on weekends. At the Beulah gasification plant construction site, they shared barracks with skilled workers laid-off from southern Michigan's automobile factories, in a symbolic display of the problems of the Great Lakes economic complex and both groups' close linkage within it. The ups and downs have been dramatic indeed.

Meanwhile, Mesabi production has shifted from one part of the district to another as older mines were exhausted and new ones opened (Figure 59). That process began very early in the history of the Iron Range. While production locations were shifting, workers were buying homes and settling down. Increasing numbers of miners were reluctant or unable to move as the jobs moved from one location to another. As population and income grew, shopping and recreation facilities expanded at the larger urban centers, especially Hibbing and Virginia. There was more and more need for mobility along the axis of the Iron Range. At the beginning of the automotive boom around 1920, a Boston-backed electric interurban streetcar line was already 13 years in operation. The locally backed corporate embryo of the Greyhound Bus Company was four years old and destined to drive the trolley line out of business within a decade. By 1980 the electric railway was hardly even a memory. Greyhound was a nationwide bus operation and nucleus of a multi-billion-dollar conglomerate based in Phoenix, Arizona. And the state of Minnesota had built—with high priority and federal aid—an expressway to facilitate the still greater number of commuting and shopping and recreation trips along the length of the Iron Range.[83]

Short-term instability was also a feature in other districts and other sectors of the mineral industry. When they operated, the copper ranges had experienced similar fluctuations in overall employment, internal shifts in job locations and work trips, and a similar streetcar line running much of the length of the Range. Employment in oil and gas boomed with initial discovery in each field and again with the flurry of activity during the energy crisis of the 1970s. It declined after development in each field and again with the weakening of world oil prices and the slowed growth of American energy consumption in the 1980s. The gold mines have experienced less short-term instability, along with their smaller long-term changes. The price of their product was supported after 1933; and gold is really a deeply ingrained social institution, while iron and copper are mere economic necessities. Only a temporary order by the War Production Board during World War II seriously interrupted the steady flow of precious metal and the steady penetration of shafts and tunnels into the bowels of the Black Hills beneath Lead, South Dakota.

Employment trends during the auto era in the mineral industries of the region have been complicated. Different production centers are widely dispersed. Ore production has differed from fuel production. Copper trends have differed from iron, and both have differed from gold. Open-pit operations have differed from underground. The Great Plains have differed from the Shield and the mountains. Timing and technology have been different.

But the various places have also had important features in common. Each has been almost inflexibly specialized in the production of a single commodity. Each has experienced long and continuous substitution of capital for labor. Although each production center is part of the Upper Midwest service and distribution network, its basic function has always been integral to a separate, far-flung, specialized industrial complex. All of the places are in sparsely populated parts of the region. There have been no ready local substitutes for jobs lost in mining. The mineral industries are exploitive. The resources they recover are nonrenewable. In the communities, the sense of permanence has been diluted with uncertainty about how long the resources might last in both the earth and the marketplace. The result has been a half-century of fluctuating and fitful overall employment decline amid some of the world's most awesome industrial landscapes.

Expansion and Change in Manufacturing

While auto-era changes in farming, mining, and railroading illustrate how jobs were

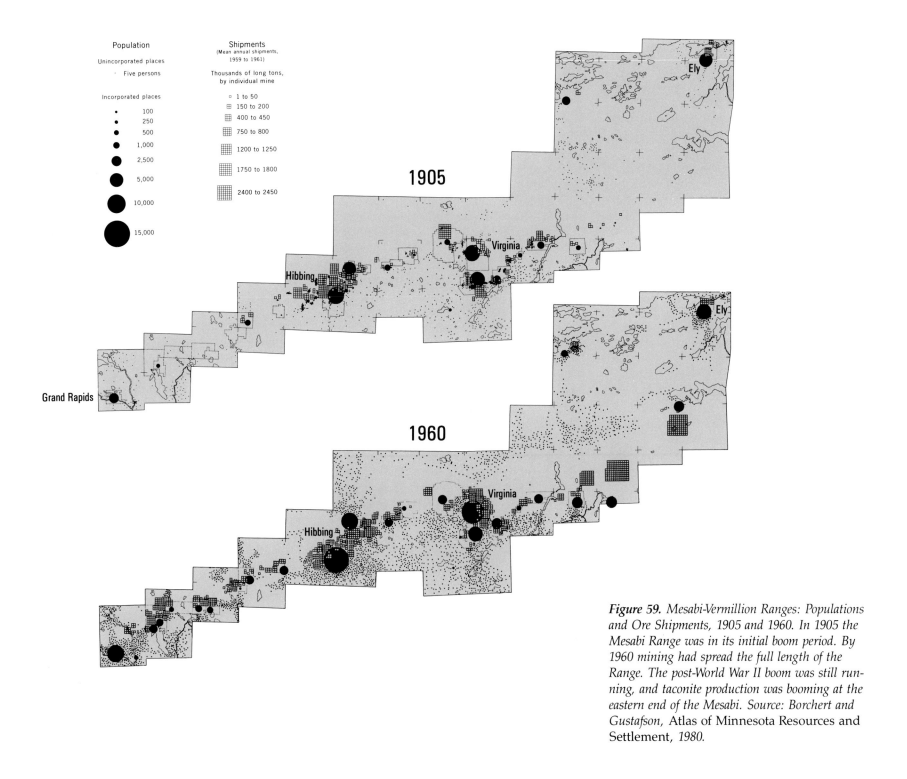

Population

Unincorporated places

· Five persons

Incorporated places

· 100
· 250
● 500
● 1,000
● 2,500
● 5,000
● 10,000
● 15,000

Shipments
(Mean annual shipments, 1959 to 1961)

Thousands of long tons, by individual mine

▫ 1 to 50
⊞ 150 to 200
▦ 400 to 450
▦ 750 to 800
▦ 1200 to 1250
▦ 1750 to 1800
▦ 2400 to 2450

1905

Ely

Virginia

Hibbing

1960

Ely

Grand Rapids

Virginia

Hibbing

Figure 59. *Mesabi-Vermillion Ranges: Populations and Ore Shipments, 1905 and 1960. In 1905 the Mesabi Range was in its initial boom period. By 1960 mining had spread the full length of the Range. The post-World War II boom was still running, and taconite production was booming at the eastern end of the Mesabi. Source: Borchert and Gustafson,* Atlas of Minnesota Resources and Settlement, *1980.*

lost, manufacturing changes begin to show how the jobs were gained. Upper Midwest manufacturing employment increased from 272,000 in 1929 to 554,000 in 1980 — about 6 percent above the national growth rate.

The growth was part of a national decentralization from the American Manufacturing Belt to the rest of the country. But it was different from the shift to most of the South and West. Industrial growth in those two regions accompanied major growth in their share of the nation's population, and a great deal of it came from establishment of branch plants from other regions. In contrast, the Upper Midwest's share of national population dropped, from nearly 5 percent to 3.1 percent. Despite that decline, the region's share of manufacturing employment rose slightly, and almost all the growth was generated by local entrepreneurs and locally based companies. The exceptional performance was not the result of traditional locational advantages. To be sure, the region did embrace 10 percent of the nation's market for farm supplies and equipment, but it remained well removed from even that market's center of gravity in Illinois. Average production wages were below those in the heart of the Manufacturing Belt but above much of the rest of the country, especially the South. Regional energy resources were significant but remote and still small in comparison with the major producers.[84]

Thus Upper Midwest growth had to come from unusual development in two fields. One possibility was export industries which did not depend on cheap labor, cheap local energy resources, or low-cost transportation to major national markets. The other was substitution for products otherwise imported from national manufacturers within the limited regional market.

THE 1920s: LEGACY AND PROSPECT

Manufacturing employment in the 1920s was mostly in the Twin Cities, the region's oldest agricultural areas in central and southern Minnesota and north-central Wisconsin, and the Lake Superior cutover and mining district (*See* Figure 60). The cutover district had a legacy of lumber milling at major waterpower and port cities, and smelters still operated on the Copper Range. Small metal-working industries supplied parts and equipment for the loggers, sawmills, and mines. World War I defense contracts had stretched the lives of some plants, but with the depletion of the forest, most of the complex was in decline. Duluth was an important exception; it was holding steady. With a relatively large, stable labor force, the district's largest city and port had a million-ton steel mill that supplied wire and posts to fence the agricultural hinterland and blast furnaces that supplied iron to Upper Midwest foundries. The region's largest horseshoe factory was converting to production of handtools. Other plants were established producers of shipboard and dock gear for the Great Lakes, and there was an array of small printing, food, and garment industries. Other exceptions to the general decline were the major waterpower sites and lumber-shipping ports, where some of the region's largest sawmills had converted to pulp and paper to use second-growth timber.

In contrast with the northern forest area, the older, eastern part of the Corn Belt and the dairying areas on the forest fringe contained important urban seedbeds for new industrial growth. The main centers were at historically important, small waterpower sites and intersections in the regional rail grid. At those locations, flour mills, large creameries, and breweries were legacies from pioneer settlement,

and meat packing had become well established by the twentieth century. Vegetable canning was already in its second decade in the Minnesota River Valley, where the jolly Green Giant had become an established resident. Small and moderate-sized plants that served the regional market turned out machinery, harness, belting, chains, and many other farm supplies. Brick, tile, and cement came from the well-established regional center at Mason City, tile and nationally famous pottery from what had been a pioneer crockery and tile works at Red Wing, Minnesota.

In the larger centers a few companies were beginning to diversify, and others had specialized for the national market. Notable firms produced machinery, auto parts and tires, and rubber apparel. Their plants dominated the industrial districts of Eau Claire, LaCrosse, Wausau, and even as far west as St. Cloud, where an electrical equipment manufacturer had occupied most of the ill-fated Pan Motor Company's sprawling auto manufacturing complex. Paper mills had replaced the much older sawmilling industries on the northern forest fringe of the Dairy Belt, along the upper Mississippi above St. Cloud, the Chippewa River at Eau Claire and northward, and the Wisconsin River from Wausau to Rhinelander. They could take advantage of both waterpower and the labor of European immigrant stock leaving marginal farms by the thousands.

The whole range of industries came together at the region's metropolis and primary market. The Minneapolis flour-milling industry had been the established leader. But it had begun to decline in the 1920s as a result of the loss of its preferential freight rates and competition from the hard winter wheat region of the southern Great Plains — from Kansas to the Texas panhandle. General Mills, newly formed from one of the great industrial mergers of that time, Pillsbury, and a few others were not only emerging as dominant companies but also embarking on nationwide programs of acquisition and innovative marketing. All-American housewife Betty Crocker and all-American boy Jack Armstrong, selling Upper Midwest cake mix and breakfast food, were pioneer advertising creations on the newly organized coast-to-coast radio networks. While milling headquarters were growing in Minneapolis, production was expanding elsewhere. The Twin Cities had the region's largest meat-packing plants, breweries, and millwork companies. There were large manufacturers of tractors, threshers, plows, and a great variety of farm hardware and supplies. The "Minneapolis" automobile was stillborn, but large-scale assembly of Fords had just moved in 1925 from a multistoried plant in Minneapolis to a much larger ultramodern industrial park in St. Paul. Twin Cities entrepreneurs had been among the first in the nation to see the possibilities of both central heating and electrical energy. The Minneapolis Heat Regulator Company had joined forces with an Indiana competitor named Honeywell. Franklin and Seeger were making mechanical refrigerators; although the big, absentee-owned Mazda Lamp plant had just closed. The Minnesota Mining and Manufacturing Company (3M) was beginning to diversify from its booming sandpaper business. In addition, hundreds of small shops were supplying the larger plants, the growing regional business services, and the regional market for consumer products: drugs and cosmetics; boots and shoes; apparel; printing and publishing of regional trade journals, religious books, calendars, playing cards. The shoe and apparel industries had suffered the loss of western markets after the completion of the Panama Canal, but the religious publications market was beginning to follow the swelling stream of Upper Midwest migrants to Pacific Coast states. Brown and Bigelow were building up the remarkable calendar sales force for international marketing of the products from their newly built lithography park in the Midway district. More than 100,000 manufacturing employees worked in the Twin Cities complex. It was a bustling mixture of legacies and newcomers. Yet its largest industry, flour milling, was reorganizing in the face of apparent decline, and all were about to face the test of the Great Depression.[85]

Industrial jobs were few and widely scattered in the rest of the region. The cities and towns of the western Corn Belt and Great Plains were creatures of the steel rail era. While the railroads brought settlement and trade, they did not bring the kind of local manufacturing growth that had accompanied the westward movement of the frontier up to the 1870s. Instead, with improved long-haul speed and capacity, they simply enlarged the hinterlands already served from the established centers, especially Chicago and the Twin Cities. The western cities were busy centers of distribution with little export manufacturing. To be sure, there were small, ubiquitous industries at all the wholesale-retail centers to serve their local territories: feed and flour mills, bakeries, meat packers, leather-goods makers, candy factories, and a host of others. Some grew large enough to go to the regional or national market—notably the grain and meat processors and a few beet sugar mills operating on the irrigated oases along the Yellowstone and Belle Fourche rivers. Additional important industries appeared on the scene in the mountain valleys of Montana and the Black Hills: the mammoth Anaconda smelting and refining facilities at Butte, Anaconda, and Great Falls; lumber mills in the Flathead-Bitterroot trench, and the Homestake mining and lumbering interests around Deadwood and Lead, South Dakota.

FIFTY YEARS OF ENTREPRENEURSHIP AND ADAPTATION

By 1980 the picture had changed dramatically (Figures 60–61). The greatest absolute growth occurred at the Twin Cities, where the central and suburban counties had a quarter-million manufacturing jobs, compared with 100,000 a half-century earlier. Their share of the Upper Midwest total had risen slightly, from 37 percent to 41 percent. However, the big net gain masked some losses and substitutions.

Only four flour mills were still running. Only one—that in the far outer suburbs—had been enlarged since 1920. The tractor and harvester plants had been sold, closed, and consolidated with one in Iowa. The big packing houses were closed, victims of decentralization to newly designed plants in smaller, lower-cost labor markets nearer the sources of livestock. Large, long-established refrigeration equipment plants had been sold, and the operations either moved or were about to be moved to the South or to smaller cities in the Upper Midwest. The millwork and apparel industries had declined, consolidated, and decentralized. Breweries had declined and consolidated. Most of those events reflected pervasive national trends.

Another set of industries had undergone a metamorphosis, with significant net growth. Jobs, products, and even companies had disappeared; while others had formed and grown. The vastly expanded business services

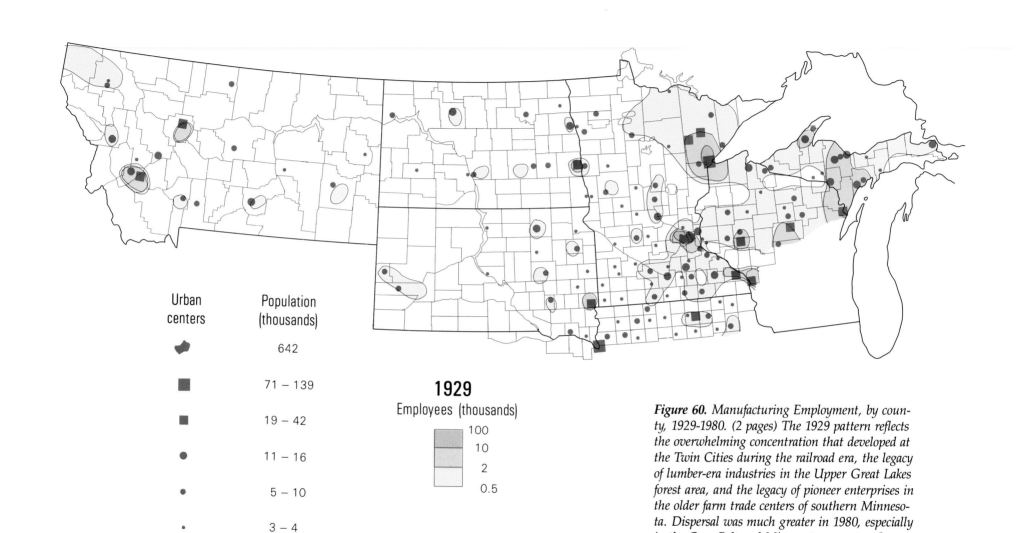

Urban
centers

Population
(thousands)

642

71 — 139

19 — 42

11 — 16

5 — 10

3 — 4

1929

Employees (thousands)

100

10

2

0.5

Figure 60. Manufacturing Employment, by county, 1929-1980. (2 pages) The 1929 pattern reflects the overwhelming concentration that developed at the Twin Cities during the railroad era, the legacy of lumber-era industries in the Upper Great Lakes forest area, and the legacy of pioneer enterprises in the older farm trade centers of southern Minnesota. Dispersal was much greater in 1980, especially in the Corn Belt and Minnesota core area. Source: note 84.

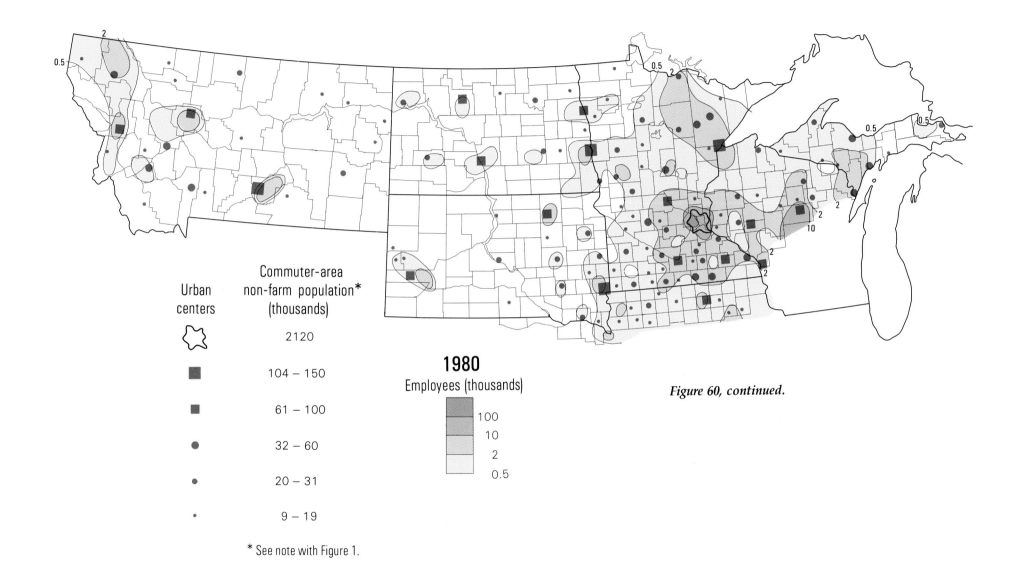

Urban
centers

Commuter-area
non-farm population*
(thousands)

2120

104 – 150

61 – 100

32 – 60

20 – 31

9 – 19

1980
Employees (thousands)

100
10
2
0.5

Figure 60, continued.

* See note with Figure 1.

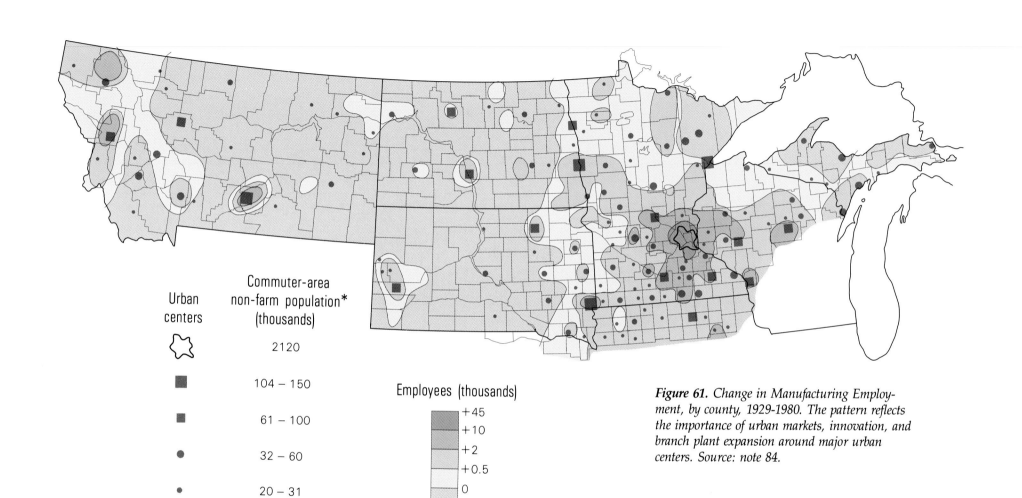

Urban
centers

Commuter-area
non-farm population*
(thousands)

2120

104 – 150

61 – 100

32 – 60

20 – 31

9 – 19

Employees (thousands)

+45
+10
+2
+0.5
0
Decline

Figure 61. Change in Manufacturing Employment, by county, 1929-1980. The pattern reflects
the importance of urban markets, innovation, and
branch plant expansion around major urban
centers. Source: note 84.

* See note with Figure 1.

proved community, with relatively high standards of maintenance.[89]

The region's industries have in fact been a dynamic succession of start-ups, expansions, mergers, sell-outs, acquisitions, conversions, adaptations. A varied flow of products, skills, and ideas has poured from a wellspring of individuals and organizations. Concentration on a few famous products has continued (Figure 64). But the other hallmark of the region's industry has been growth and innovation. Above-average innovation has been necessary to sustain growth, in the face of competition from areas with longer histories, better market accessibility, or lower wages.

The vast majority of the industries have been homegrown. To be sure, the people who created them were not necessarily homegrown. Perhaps half were. The others were immigrants from other parts of the United States or abroad. Nor has industry managed to keep all of the local talent it would need. Skilled people left when growth was slow, returned when it picked up. In 1960 the personnel director of a major Twin Cities electronic firm told me, "When we are expanding, we find that the best place to recruit is in southern California. That's where we find the largest number of people from this region. And they don't have to be sold. They known the place." A quarter-century later, the president of a Twin Cities research and development firm told a newspaper reporter that one recruiting strategy would be "locating Midwesterners working in California's Silicon Valley." Both could have added that they would gladly have taken anyone else who qualified and wanted to become familiar with this mysterious part of America. In an era of high mobility and intensely interactive society, the whole country has become a temporary reservoir for the export surplus of skilled people from any region

at any given time. But the Upper Midwest has long been a leading producer and exporter, and the rest of the country has long been storing a part of the region's reserve labor supply.

Thus the Upper Midwest became a fertile seedbed of entrepreneurship; home base of a somewhat dispersed skilled labor force; adopted home to self-selected migratory entrepreneurs, professionals, and technicians; focus of a commitment to build, maintain, improve, and rebuild. It appears that an industrial community emerged on the circulation network that ties together the region's farms, towns, cities, lakes, forests, plains, and mountains. Industry provided a current of continuity in the turbulent demographic stream.

Wholesale and Retail Merchants

As the rail era drew to a close in the 1920s, 290,000 people worked in wholesale and retail trade in the Upper Midwest. About one-fifth of those jobs were in wholesaling, the others in retailing. By 1980 the total number had grown to more than 750,000, with little change in the proportions of wholesale and retail jobs. Perhaps one-fifth of the 50-year employment increase was the result of population growth. The other four-fifths reflected the vast growth of purchasing power and available goods. The basic task of the merchants remained the same: to link producers with consumers, to organize and smooth the flow of goods through a very complex system.[90]

THE LEGACY OF RAIL-ERA PATTERNS

One large, distinctive group of wholesale merchants in the 1920s included the assemblers and forwarders of farm products. They were mainly in the grain and livestock business, and they were located all along the rail lines in places of every size from sidetrack

hamlets to the Twin Cities. Grain flowed by the wagon- or truckload from farms to country elevators with typical capacities of 25,000 to 50,000 bushels. From there it moved by rail carload to much larger terminal elevators at major junctions in the region's cropland corridor. Or it went to Duluth-Superior or the Twin Cities where elevator capacity was 50 to 100 million bushels. Grain not milled in the region was likely to move by the trainload from the Twin Cities to distant milling centers in the Midwest and East, or by the shipload from Duluth-Superior to Buffalo. Livestock were assembled at pens and ramps at hundreds of towns along the rail lines, herded into cattle cars, and shipped to central yards. Most of the shipments moved east, through markets at Fargo, Sioux Falls, and South St. Paul, or on to Sioux City, Omaha, or Chicago. From those places the animals were sold to Corn Belt farmers to be fattened or to the packing houses to be slaughtered. Twenty thousand to 30,000 cattle, hogs, and sheep moved through the region's major markets on any trading day.

Meanwhile, more than nine out of 10 retail and wholesale employees were distributing, not assembling, and they were handling food and manufactured goods, not farm commodities. The wholesalers distributed goods from large, primary industries to smaller fabricators, and from industries to retail stores. Wholesale warehouses and retail stores alike were clustered at the region's transportation nodes, from the primary railroad center at the Twin Cities to the smallest crossroads hamlet. They were all central places in the circulation network. They formed a system of trade centers. Rank in the system depended for the most part on accessibility. In wholesale distribution, virtually all the warehouses and jobs were located at the major railroad centers, thus also at the largest cities. Key retail locations

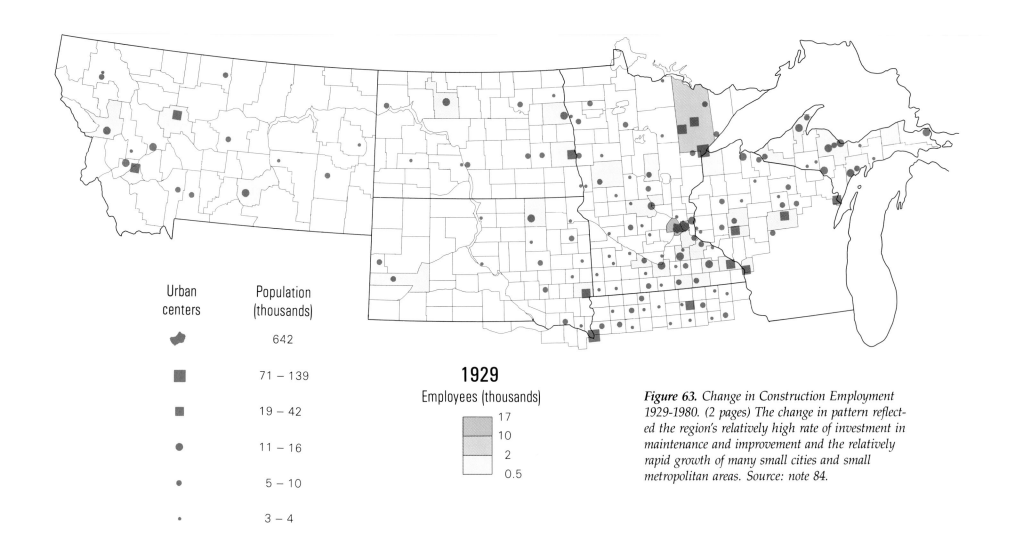

**Urban
centers**

**Population
(thousands)**

642

71 – 139

19 – 42

11 – 16

5 – 10

3 – 4

1929

Employees (thousands)

17
10
2
0.5

Figure 63. Change in Construction Employment
1929-1980. (2 pages) The change in pattern reflected the region's relatively high rate of investment in
maintenance and improvement and the relatively
rapid growth of many small cities and small
metropolitan areas. Source: note 84.

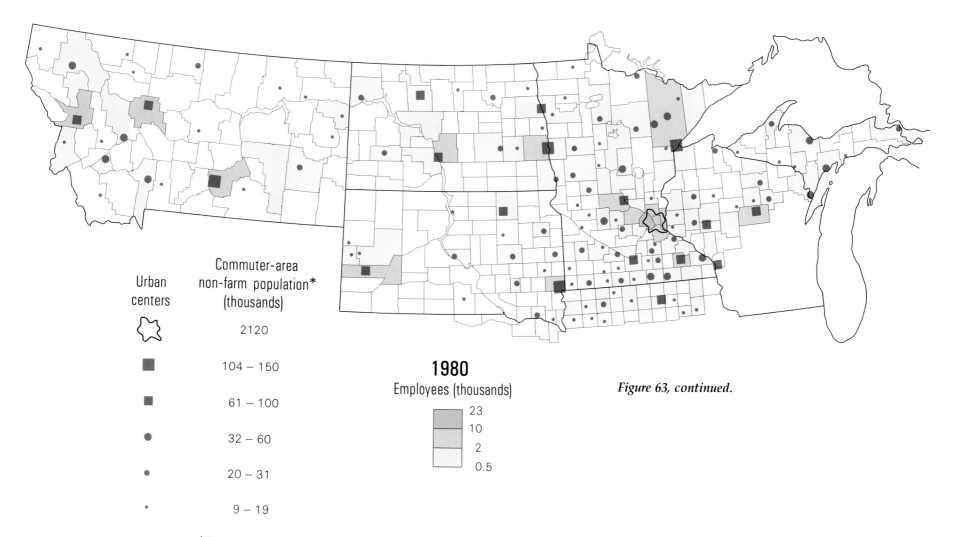

Urban centers

Commuter-area non-farm population* (thousands)

2120

104 – 150

61 – 100

32 – 60

20 – 31

9 – 19

* See note with Figure 1.

1980

Employees (thousands)

23
10
2
0.5

Figure 63, continued.

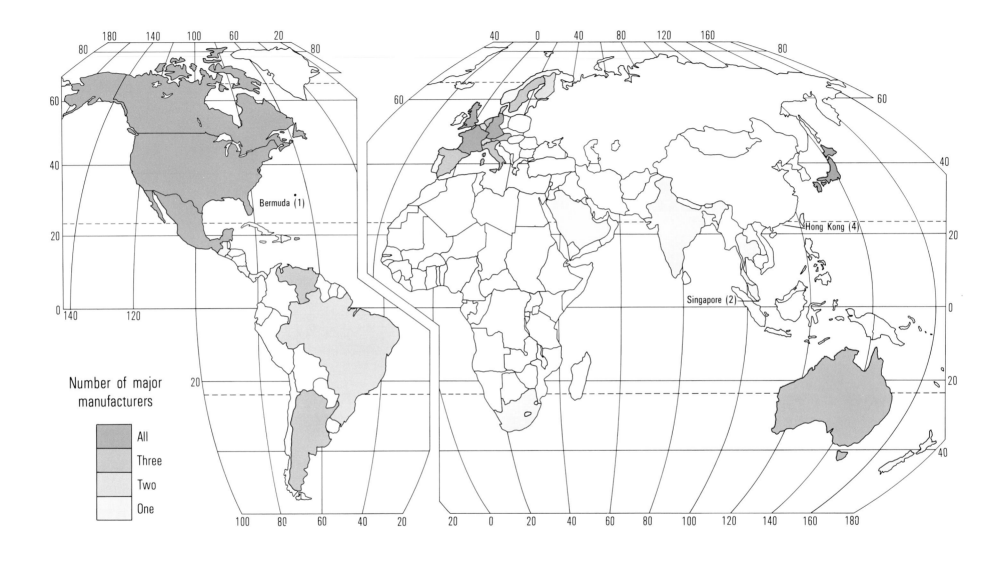

Figure 64. *Worldwide Locations of Major Upper Midwest Manufacturers, 1984. Corporations included 3M, Honeywell, General Mills, and Pillsbury. Source:* Moody's Industrial Manual *(New York: Moody's Investment Services, 1984).*

were at central places in consumer travel patterns. The bigger the market was, the busier the central place, the more numerous and bigger the stores, and the more diverse the goods offered. The greater the diversity of goods was, the larger the number of specialties, and the wider the drawing area.

Geographical expression of the system was a hierarchy of trade centers. The Twin Cities were at the top. A half-dozen primary wholesale-retail centers were next, followed by eight secondary wholesale-retail centers, more than 100 large, medium-sized, and small shopping centers, more than 500 convenience centers, and about 2,000 hamlets, all arrayed in descending order.[91]

The hamlets typically had no more than a dozen businesses—most commonly one or two grain elevators, a creamery, a general store, and a café. Today's ubiquitous business establishments—the bar and the gas station—were not so common in the 1920s. Storefront gas pumps and filling stations had just begun to proliferate. And bars were temporarily out of sight because of the national prohibition law that bore the name of congressman Volstead from Minnesota. The typical hamlet trade area encompassed little or no more than the surrounding township. In contrast, the convenience centers provided grocery, drugstores, hardware and variety stores, a few specialty shops, and banks, as well as eating places and farm services. Each convenience center served the combined trade areas of three or four neighboring hamlets.

Shopping centers were larger urban places—average populations of 5,000 to 10,000. To the array of convenience stores they added department stores and a much wider range of specialty shops, as well as a full range of basic professional services to augment the offerings of the merchants. Thus each shopping center served not only its own convenience trade area but also the convenience trade areas of half a dozen or more neighboring small centers. The shopping centers' trade areas usually spread over parts of two or three counties. Their solid Main Street business facades ran three or four blocks or more. Their high-school sports teams had to travel 30 to 60 miles to find competition from another community as large or larger.

Only 15 urban centers added a substantial layer of wholesale employment on top of the retail base. These centers included the Twin Cities, primary wholesale-retail centers, and secondary wholesale-retail centers. The main wholesale gateway to and from the nation was the Twin Cities. There stood the largest warehouses—massive architectural monuments to proud Yankee family names such as Farwell, Ozmun, Kirk, Janney, Semple, and Hill, or to Chicago's Butler brothers. Miles of smaller warehouses lined the rail corridor through the cities. Their trade territory covered today's primary region of the Upper Midwest and filtered into the Canadian Prairies and the Pacific Northwest. The retail base included several of the Midwest's great downtown department stores. Hundreds of specialty shops did business in the downtowns and in neighborhood shopping districts at major crossings in the streetcar network, and thousands of corner convenience stores opened along the car lines.

Duluth-Superior was the largest of the half-dozen primary wholesale-retail centers. The great Marshall-Wells and Kelly-Howe-Thomson warehouses pressed against the harbor's edge on Minnesota Point, and merchant wholesalers crowded blocks of multistory buildings between downtown Duluth and the waterfront. Their sales territories dominated the western Lake Superior district and reached selectively all across the Upper Midwest and into the Canadian Prairies. The other primary wholesale-retail centers were Fargo-Moorhead, Sioux Falls, and Great Falls in the west, LaCrosse and Eau Claire-Chippewa Falls on the east. The two eastern cities had developed as mercantile centers on the northwest frontier in the nineteenth century. The western centers had developed their own territories across the Dakotas and Montana, especially for high-volume, low-margin goods such as groceries and some lines of hardware, drugs, and sundries. Many of their warehouses were branches or partnerships of Twin Cities and Duluth wholesalers. Secondary wholesale-retail centers distributed more limited lines and carved out smaller, more specialized territories. Wausau merchants filled that niche in the Upper Wisconsin Valley; Mason City, in north-central Iowa. Grand Forks and Minot played the same role at important junctions along the Great Northern High Line through North Dakota; Aberdeen, at a major junction on the Milwaukee Road's transcontinental line across northern South Dakota; Rapid City, for the Black Hills; and Billings, Butte, and Missoula, for southern and western Montana. Beneath the wholesaling superstructure at each primary and secondary center, the retail base included multiple downtown department stores, scores of specialty shops, and hundreds of outlets for convenience goods such as food, hardware, and household supplies.

An umbrella of catalog mail-order retailing spread over the whole region. Minnesotan Richard Sears had started his mail-order watch trade in 1886, when he was a railway station agent near Redwood Falls, in the Minnesota prairies. He had run his fulltime business from Minneapolis through most of the next decade before moving permanently to

Table 5. Wholesale, Retail, and Service Employment in Trade Centers by Size Classes, 1980

Size Class (and Population in Thousands)[a]	Employees (In Thousands)			Percentage of Upper Midwest Total			
	Wholesale	Retail	Service	Wholesale	Retail	Service	Population
Minneapolis–St. Paul (2,120)	59	177	456	38.3	28.7	32.1	25.0
Primary wholesale-retail-service (104–150)							
Duluth-Superior	4	21	46	2.5	3.4	3.2	3.0
Others	26	59	136	16.6	13.0	9.6	7.8
Secondary wholesale-retail-service (61–100)	17	72	165	10.9	11.6	11.6	10.0
Shopping-service centers							
Large (32–60)	8	41	105	4.8	6.6	7.4	7.0
Medium (20–31)	16	74	157	10.1	12.0	11.0	10.4
Small (9–91)	14	57	116	9.0	9.3	8.2	8.9
All other places (<9)	12	116	240	8.0	18.9	16.9	27.4

Sources: See notes 90.

[a] Population includes 1980 population of urban centers over 4,000 plus nonfarm population of surrounding commuter areas.

Chicago to join A. C. Roebuck in their ultimate venture. By the 1920s, the major Minneapolis department stores and the multistory, block-square landmarks of Sears Roebuck and Montgomery Ward carried on the Upper Midwest mail-order tradition from the Twin Cities.

Beneath the mail-order umbrella, most retail stores and many of the warehouses were locally owned. Merchants were positioned at every center throughout the system. Thousands of families eked modest incomes from long hours of work in drugstores, grocery and hardware stores, or crossroads general stores. In the multicounty shopping centers, 100 or so families earned comfortable livelihoods from their local department stores and occupied solid Victorian homes nearby on the elm-shaded sections of the main streets. Merchant families and companies rose to dominant positions in the major cities. Meanwhile, mainly out of Scandinavian traditions, an exceptionally large number of locally controlled marketing and consumer cooperatives arose out of the rural areas to challenge and limit the dominance of the corporate traders.

As the region developed, the merchants had met the challenge to create an orderly, far-reaching trading system. But the system depended on railroad trains. And in the 1920s, it was showing signs of disintegration under the fast-growing influence of auto-era changes. The existing system had to be modified to handle the vastly increased quantity and diversity of goods. And it had to be adjusted to highways, trucks, and telecommunications.

THE CHANGES OF THE AUTO ERA

The hierarchy of trade centers inherited from the railroad era was still evident in 1980 (Table 5). The bigger cities commanded the market. The wholesale-retail centers and the shopping centers had large shares of the region's trade employment compared with their shares of population, while the smaller population centers had even smaller shares of the wholesale and retail payrolls. At the same time, Upper Midwest merchants made major adjustments to the new pattern of accessibility. The local share of the region's trade employment grew faster than the local share of population in some classes of trade centers, slower in others (Table 6).

In the wholesale assembly and forwarding of farm commodities, the smaller trade centers clung to their role. But there were dramatic changes. Many of the old, smaller grain elevators became auxiliary buying and storage stations for newer and fewer steel and concrete compounds with capacities of 300,000 to a half-million bushels. Trucks handled most of the shipments both in and out of the smaller elevators. Long strings of covered hopper cars with capacities of 100 tons replaced the stubby 20- to 40-ton boxcars of an earlier era. The new hoppers served the big elevators. Many were made up into unit trains that moved directly not only to the Twin Cities and Twin Ports but also to major overseas terminals at New Orleans, Houston, Portland, or the Puget Sound. Trucks replaced railway cattle cars almost entirely in the movement of livestock to wholesale markets. As a result, decentralized auction yards—joined by telephone or teletype networks for price and marketing information—operated on the outskirts of scores of county-seat trade centers. Truckers brought the livestock from area farms and ranches and hauled the animals away to feeders and new, decentralized packing plants.

The efficiency and range of trucking transportation had further concentrated wholesale distribution of food and factory products at the larger centers (Figure 65). By 1980 more than two-thirds of all wholesaling employment and three-fourths of sales were located in the Twin Cities and in the primary and secondary wholesale-retail centers. But the auto era brought some changes within that family of top-level trade centers (*See* Table 6). There was limited decentralization from Twin Cities locations to smaller places. While Twin Cities wholesale employment grew dramatically, their share of the region's total wholesale jobs grew somewhat slower than their share of population. In Duluth-Superior, the number of wholesale jobs was stable, but the share of regional total fell catastrophically. Economically troubled Butte dropped out of the wholesale-retail class. Chief beneficiaries of those shifts were the other wholesale-retail centers. Fargo-Moorhead had passed Duluth-Superior in sales and jobs. Billings had surged into the primary ranks and passed Great Falls. Bismarck-Mandan, St. Cloud, Mankato, and Rochester had joined the secondary ranks. Additional beneficiaries were a few smaller places in the Twin Cities Satellite Ring, the neighboring Southern Minnesota urban cluster, and eastern South Dakota. They accounted for most of the surge of wholesale employment in the medium-size shopping centers shown in table 6. Their new warehouses were served partly by rail, mainly by truck. Their trade territories continued to center on the Minnesota metropolitan core while extending not only across the Upper Midwest but also into much of Iowa, Wisconsin, Nebraska, and Wyoming.[92]

Auto-era growth of retail employment concentrated at the Twin Cities, at the seventeen primary and secondary wholesale-retail centers, and at fewer than 50 large and medium-sized shopping centers (Figure 66). Cities in those size classes generally increased their shares of retail sales and employment, but the shares at smaller places declined (*See* Table 6). People could travel farther to shop, and they went to the larger, more widely spaced centers. Increased trade at those places meant more and bigger stores. They attracted the major chains and, eventually, the developers of enclosed malls.

The Twin Cities market by 1980 was organized around eight major malls, built near the belt freeways, with average floor space about one million square feet. Meanwhile, enclosed skyway networks had transformed the rebuilt downtowns into sprawling supermalls. Emerging once more as a unique rendezvous for the region was the linked array of department stores, myriad specialty shops, and classy boutiques in a setting of office skyscrapers and hospitality and entertainment places. There were also enclosed shopping malls at every primary and secondary wholesale-retail center, and the average size of each mall was nearly half a million square feet. The malls brought the shopping amenities of the smaller metropolitan areas practically on a par with all but the most affluent of the Twin Cities suburbs. By 1980 enclosed malls had also been developed at about half of the large and medium-sized shopping centers. Those averaged about 200,000 square feet, with a minimum trade area population of about 50,000.

Changes in business organization of trade accompanied the geographic shifts. To be sure, thousands of individual stores and hundreds of small wholesale firms remained in family hands. But in many cases, a family now owned and operated two, three, or more stores in the same city or in neighboring rural convenience centers. Good roads, phone links, on-line electronic bookkeeping, ample rural bank credit, and cooperative purchasing had enlarged the family store as auto-era innovations had enlarged the family farm. National chains invaded the domain of the family-owned local department stores in the multicounty shopping centers and the metropolitan areas. But they were countered by regional and local organizations. For example, regional chains were developed by entrepreneurs based in Wausau, St. Cloud, Jamestown, North Dakota, Great Falls, and the small Dutch and East Friesian settlement at Clara City, on the western Minnesota prairie. The leading downtown Minneapolis department store built the nation's first enclosed suburban mall, branched to several of the new, smaller metropolitan areas in the Upper

Table 6. Change in Percentage of Upper Midwest Wholesale, Retail, and Service Employment and Population In Trade Centers by Size Classes, 1940–1980

Size Class (and Population in Thousands)[a]	Wholesale Employment	Retail Employment	Service Employment	Population
Minneapolis–St. Paul (2,120)	+5.3%	+2.8%	+8.5%	+10.3%
Primary wholesale-retail-service (104–150)				
Duluth-Superior	−3.3	+0.9	−2.1	+0.0
Others	+7.3	+1.8	+2.9	+3.4
Secondary wholesale-retail-service (61–100)	+3.7	+2.6	+3.0	+5.0
Shopping-service centers				
Large (32–60)	−0.1	−0.5	+0.6	+1.7
Medium (20–31)	+0.6	−0.4	−0.7	+2.7
Small (9–91)	−0.6	−2.5	−3.1	+1.8
All other places (<9)	−12.6	−2.0	−8.8	−24.7

Sources: See note 90.

[a] Population includes 1980 population of urban centers over 4,000 plus nonfarm population of surrounding commuter areas.

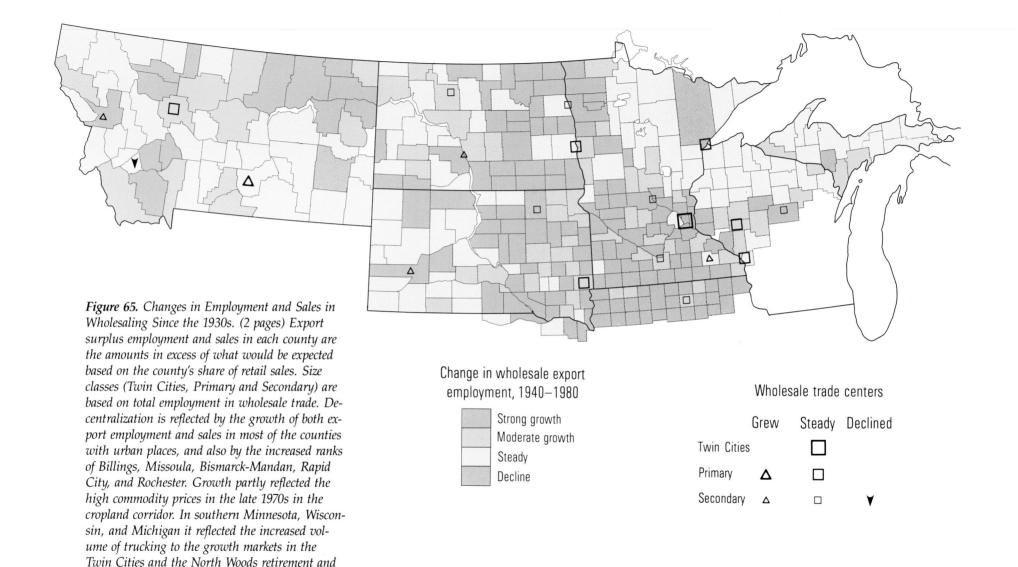

Figure 65. *Changes in Employment and Sales in Wholesaling Since the 1930s. (2 pages) Export surplus employment and sales in each county are the amounts in excess of what would be expected based on the county's share of retail sales. Size classes (Twin Cities, Primary and Secondary) are based on total employment in wholesale trade. Decentralization is reflected by the growth of both export employment and sales in most of the counties with urban places, and also by the increased ranks of Billings, Missoula, Bismarck-Mandan, Rapid City, and Rochester. Growth partly reflected the high commodity prices in the late 1970s in the cropland corridor. In southern Minnesota, Wisconsin, and Michigan it reflected the increased volume of trucking to the growth markets in the Twin Cities and the North Woods retirement and recreation areas. Source: note 90.*

Change in wholesale export employment, 1940–1980

Strong growth
Moderate growth
Steady
Decline

Wholesale trade centers

	Grew	Steady	Declined
Twin Cities	□		
Primary	△	□	
Secondary	△	□	▼

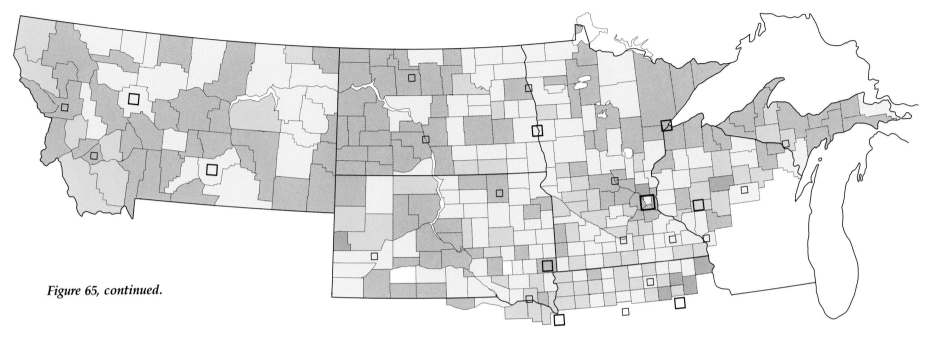

Figure 65, continued.

Change in wholesale export
sales, 1929–1977

Very high growth
High growth
Moderate growth
Decline

Wholesale sales, 1977
(millions of dollars)

21,000

630–1,600

140–450

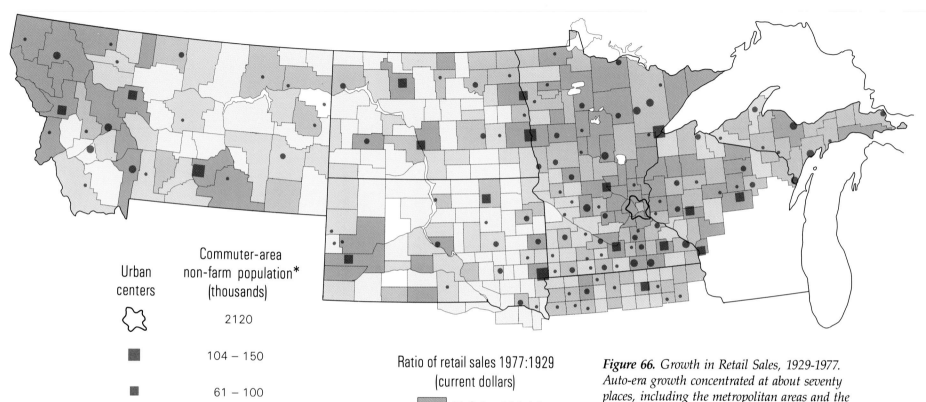

Urban
centers

Commuter-area
non-farm population*
(thousands)

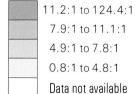 2120

104 – 150

61 – 100

32 – 60

20 – 31

9 – 19

* See note with Figure 1.

Ratio of retail sales 1977:1929
(current dollars)

11.2:1 to 124.4:1

7.9:1 to 11.1:1

4.9:1 to 7.8:1

0.8:1 to 4.8:1

Data not available

Figure 66. Growth in Retail Sales, 1929-1977.
Auto-era growth concentrated at about seventy
places, including the metropolitan areas and the
large and medium-size shopping-service centers.
Source: note 90.

Midwest, then expanded to become one of the nation's half-dozen largest retail corporations (Figure 67). Twin Cities firms emerged among the nation's major grocery and hardware wholesalers (Figure 68). Twin Cities entrepreneurs developed national and international franchising operations in food and general merchandise, as well as leading organizations in direct-mail and catalog retailing and merchandise premiums. Three of the farm cooperatives became retail giants, with outlets across most of the Midwest and Great Plains. One of the grain-trading firms became the world's largest merchant of agricultural commodities. Headquarters of those firms accounted for thousands of retail and wholesale jobs. Meanwhile, general merchandise wholesalers to the old country stores either specialized or drifted into oblivion. Ownership of major store buildings passed from individual merchants on Main Street to local syndicates or regional and national shopping-center developers.[93]

The region's merchants had shifted from rail-era organization to auto-era reorganization and adaptation. Wholesaling patterns had changed to accommodate unit trains, trucks, and mass merchandising. Retailing changes had resulted in cost reductions with increased selection and amenities for enlarged shopping trade areas. At the major shopping centers, the concentrations of stores and customers meant that a greater value and diversity of goods were handled per employee, with lower prices and more outlay per square foot for displays and furnishings. Yet there was also sustained convenience and availability of goods in rural areas despite greatly reduced farm population density. The smaller towns moved a lower volume of goods per retail employee. For most lines of merchandise, their stores were smaller, purchases were smaller, or there were fewer sales. They tended to provide convenience at somewhat higher prices or lower returns for a more dispersed, but more affluent, rural population. Thus many new arrangements emerged; but consistent themes were growth, innovation, efficiency, and practicality.

Service Employment

Nearly one million service jobs were created in the Upper Midwest between 1929 and 1980—double the number of farm jobs that disappeared during the same period. Explosive growth of leisure, and of the production system that made it possible, was accompanied by explosive growth of service employment. When Upper Midwest native Thorstein Veblen published his famous *Theory of the Leisure Class*, leisure time was still a scarce, precious commodity for the great preponderance of Americans. That was in the middle of the steel rail era, just before 1900. The national circulation system was still being completed. Still under construction was the basic framework for the productive system that would pour out far more goods with far less labor and that would multiply the capacity for exchange and interaction. But in 1980, the system had been built for more than half a century and already had been completely transformed once. By the standards of the 1890s nearly everyone in the country was now a member of some kind of leisure class. In both the Upper Midwest and the country as a whole, nearly half of the employed population worked to serve the needs of that ubiquitous class of Americans.[94]

By the 1980s, everyone encountered service employees at every turn in life. That broad job classification included the nurses in the maternity ward at birth; the teachers from kindergarten through high school, technical institute, and college; the camp directors, bus drivers, and custodians. Then service workers appeared as employment agents, counselors, librarians, bartenders, TV artists, and disc jockeys. Service employees ran skating rinks, bowling alleys, ballrooms, and provided the music to dance and romance. For those who were forming families and entering the housing market, they included ministers, real estate brokers, architects, bankers, lawyers, garbage collectors, and plumbers. On business and pleasure trips they appeared as convention managers, hotel staff, ski instructors, horse trainers, sauna employees, and game wardens. In times of misfortune, service employees included the police officer, judge, insurance adjuster, ambulance driver, and social worker. They made the travel arrangements for a return to family roots in Smaaland, Schwabia, or the Hardanger Fjord, or a pilgrimmage to Nashville, Las Vegas, or Waikiki. They included the computer programmer for Medicare, the cemetery lot salesperson, the nursing home attendants, and the mortician.

Some services belong more distinctly to the Upper Midwest. For example, many service employees were paid staff for voluntary organizations. Organized volunteers stretched services still wider and pushed them deeper into the community. Just as the region has been a secure center for organized religions and politics, so it has been an exceptional stronghold of voluntary organizations—cooperatives, neighborhood associations, lodges, health care groups, charities, international exchanges. When a central Minnesota parish priest blessed the snowmobiles before a weekend dash across winter drifts to quaint taverns, that was another example of Upper

Alaska

Dayton Hudson stores

200   100   20

0   100   200 Mi.
0   200   400 Km.

Figure 67. National Expansion of the Upper Midwest's Largest Retailer, 1950s-1984. *The system grew from one store in the early 1950s to this pattern in 1984. Source: note 93.*

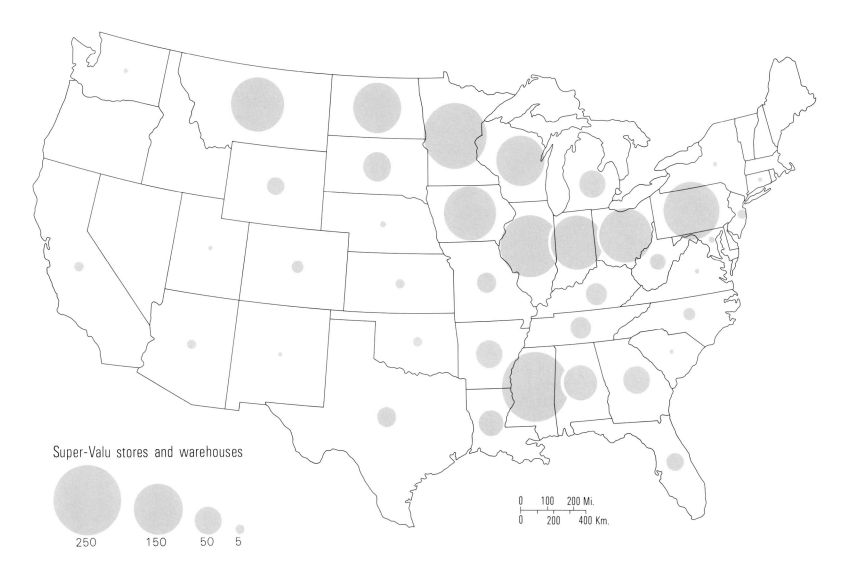

Super-Valu stores and warehouses

250   150   50   5

0   100   200 Mi.

0   200   400 Km.

Figure 68. *Expansion of the Largest Upper Mid-west Grocery Wholesaler, 1940s-1982. The system grew from a single distribution center in the 1940s. Source:* St. Paul Pioneer Press-Dispatch, *March 8, 1982, B-9.*

Midwest service employment. When a line crew came in predawn darkness on Christmas morning and worked in −70° windchill to repair a snapped electrical wire that was flashing eerily where its hot tip writhed in two feet of wildly blowing snow, that was also service— perhaps the most Upper Midwestern of all.

In fact, the service jobs are different from other jobs. Others produce goods and commodities and move them through the productive system. But service jobs are connected with maintenance and with leisure. They are concerned with maintaining knowledge, personal relations, personal health, buildings, equipment, natural resources. They are also concerned with the conservation and use of leisure time. For example, they furnish credit accounts, loans, banking, insurance, or brokerage to conserve time in the management of most people's complex personal business. They furnish reading, study, parks, arts, casinos, and hospitality for the use of leisure. In both positive and perverse ways, service jobs are essential to community organization and continuity.

Service employment in the 1980s was strongly concentrated at the Twin Cities and at the primary and secondary wholesale-retail centers, and the concentration at those places had increased since World War II (Figure 69). Growth was especially strong at the Twin Cities. Service employment there had outpaced retailing and wholesaling as a symbol of regional centrality. A large part of the growth came from innovation, stimulated by the chances for interaction among many minds in a great variety of settings. National and international contacts provided additional stimulus and opportunity. The result was exceptional development in such service fields as health, advertising, marketing, and management.

Colleges and universities accounted for substantial additions to service employment at eighteen of the twenty primary and secondary wholesale-retail centers. A nineteenth—Rochester, Minnesota—was the home of the Mayo Clinic. Only Great Falls lacked one of those major service employers. Other relatively large concentrations of service employment were in smaller, more specialized university towns such as Vermillion, South Dakota; in the major lake resort areas; and on the Indian reservations, where government administration and teaching provided much of the paid employment.

Upper Midwest people in 1980 spent a share of their income on services roughly equal to the national average. But they spent an estimated 5 percent to 10 percent of the total outside the region—mainly in Florida, California, Nevada, and Hawaii. However, they exported services to other parts of the country and the world to pay for their excursions to the Sun Belt, and many other expenditures. Some of the nation's largest bank credit-card operations were operated from Sioux Falls; motel chains from Aberdeen and St. Cloud; franchise campgrounds from Billings; insurance from Wausau, Owatonna, Sioux Falls, Bismarck, and the Twin Cities. Twin Cities offices administered nationwide financial services, international car rental and container-leasing services, advertising accounts, more than a billion dollars a year in national sales of business travel incentive arrangements and hairstyling shops, and hundreds of millions of dollars in convention and resort trade (Figures 70–71). Services were also exported in the arts. There were national broadcasts, tours, and recordings of stage and musical groups. Several thousand people in Minneapolis produced an important share of the country's television commericals. University-based re-

search earned more than $100 million in national support.[95]

Business headquarters play an especially important role in the export of services through the management of national and international enterprises. In the early 1980s the 200 largest Upper Midwest corporations had created $50 billion in assets and nearly one million jobs worldwide. Well over 90 percent of the region's large and medium-size employers and virtually all the corporations headquartered in the region were homegrown. Recall that the story of manufacturing, trade, and services expansion in the automobile era was replete with cases of local innovation and creative development. The unusual concentration of entrepreneurship was evident in the 1970s. The Upper Midwest was one of three high spots on the national map of number of Dun and Bradstreet listed firms per 10,000 population (Figure 72). It also had a high concentration of headquarters of the top 1000, or high-order American business firms (Figure 73). Thus there appeared to be both a large seedbed and a high rate of success.[96]

Regional business entrepreneurship has a long history. The Twin Cities has been a major center of railroad headquarters in the railroad era, a major center of airline headquarters in the air age, a major center of computer industry headquarters in the computer age (Figure 74). A 1974 study showed that for a century— except for wartimes—there was a fairly steady emergence of companies destined to become major forces in the economy.[97]

In the early 1980s the same tendency was still in evidence. A major business magazine made its annual national survey of most promising medium-size corporations, and the Upper Midwest was consistently, strongly overrepresented, for its population (Figure 75). In fact, the Twin Cities had by far the

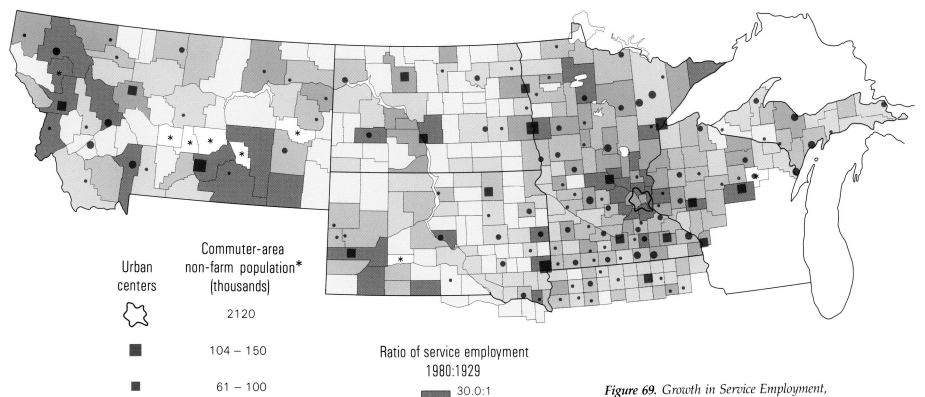

Urban
centers

Commuter-area
non-farm population*
(thousands)

2120

104 – 150

61 – 100

32 – 60

20 – 31

9 – 19

* See note with Figure 1.

Ratio of service employment
1980:1929

30.0:1
4.0:1
2.8:1
2.0:1
1.5:1
0.5:1
*   Data not available

Figure 69. *Growth in Service Employment,
1929-1980. On the map emerges the location pattern of nearly one million service jobs created between 1929 and 1980. Source: notes 78, 90.*

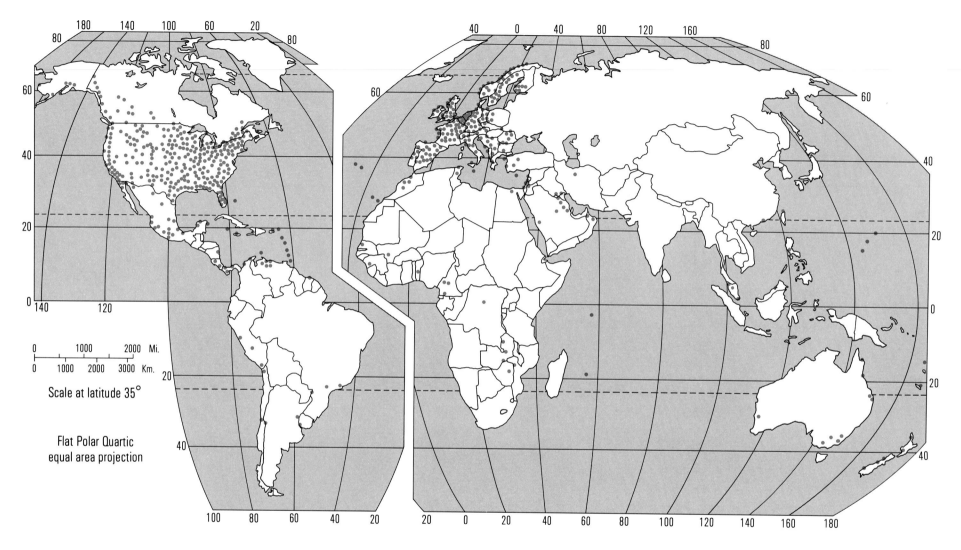

Figure 70. *The Upper Midwest's Leading Car Rental Organization, 1983. The pattern represents expansion from one agency in Minneapolis in the* 1950s. *Source:* World-Wide Directory, National Car Rental, *Sept.-Oct. 1983.*

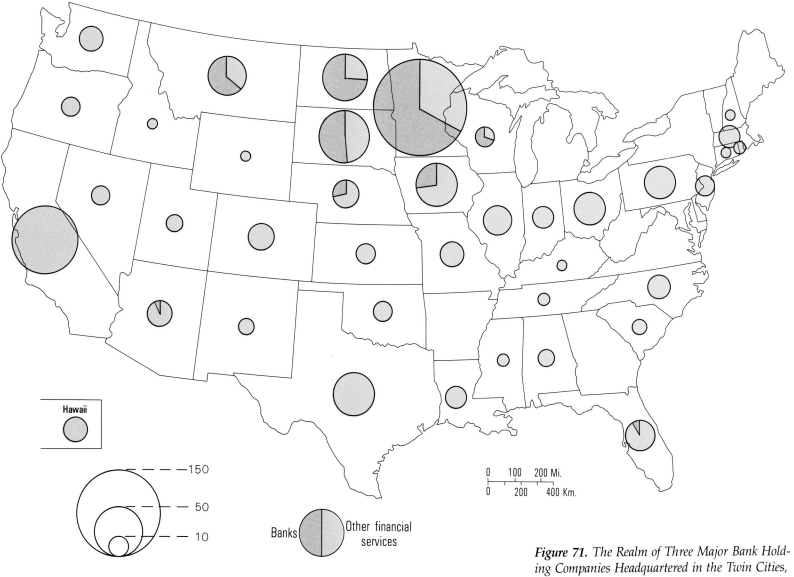

Banks | **Other financial services**

Hawaii

— 150
— 50
— 10

0 100 200 Mi.
0 200 400 Km.

Figure 71. *The Realm of Three Major Bank Holding Companies Headquartered in the Twin Cities, 1984. Sources: Lloyd Brandt, First Bank System, personal communication, January, 1985; Norwest Corporation,* Annual Report, *(Minneapolis, 1984); map of bank locations of Bremer Financial Corporation, St. Paul Pioneer Press-Dispatch, May 14, 1984, B-1 ff.*

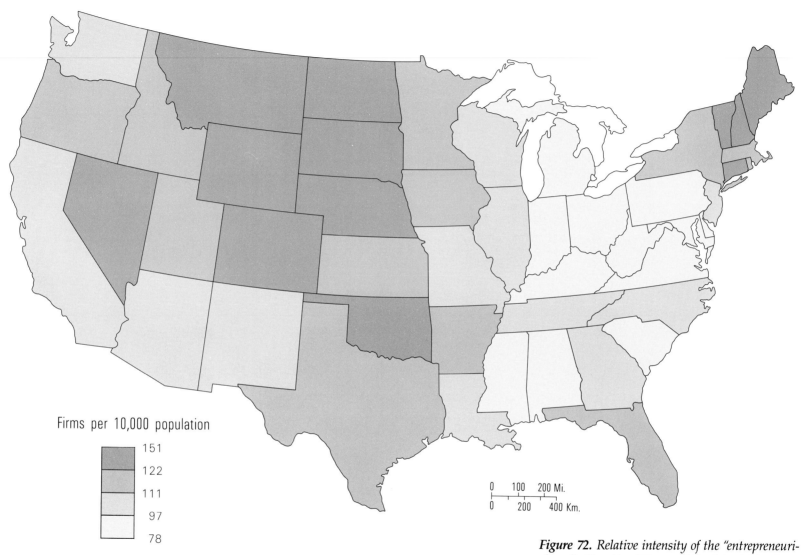

Firms per 10,000 population

151
122
111
97
78

0   100   200 Mi.
0   200   400 Km.

Figure 72. *Relative intensity of the "entrepreneurial seedbed": ratio of Dun and Bradstreet Listed Firms to total population, 1978. Sources:* Dun and Bradstreet Directory, *1978; U.S. Bureau of Census,* Statistical Abstract of the United States 1978.

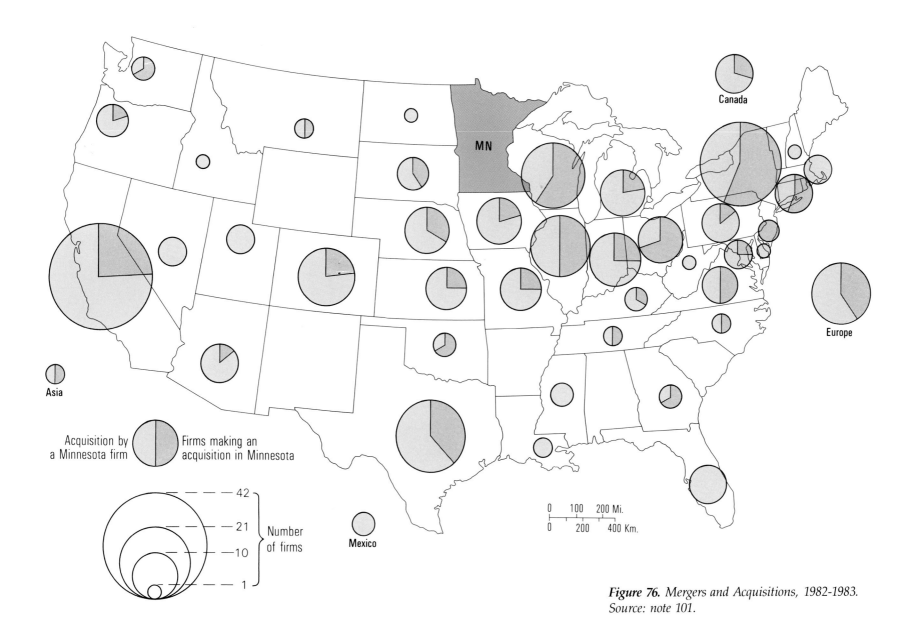

Figure 76. *Mergers and Acquisitions, 1982-1983.*
Source: note 101.

Canada

MN

Europe

Asia

Acquisition by
a Minnesota firm

Firms making an
acquisition in Minnesota

Mexico

42
21
10
1

Number
of firms

0   100   200 Mi.
0   200   400 Km.

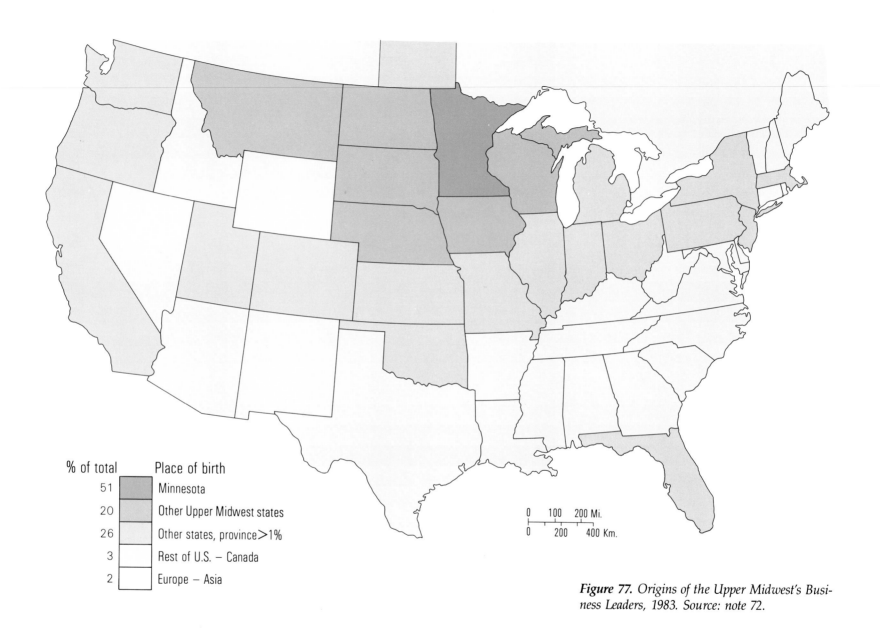

% of total	Place of birth
51	Minnesota
20	Other Upper Midwest states
26	Other states, province >1%
3	Rest of U.S. – Canada
2	Europe – Asia

0   100   200 Mi.
0   200   400 Km.

Figure 77. Origins of the Upper Midwest's Business Leaders, 1983. Source: note 72.

and a place where families and employers could not be isolated from the challenge of new technologies and unorthodox information. (7) A regional transportation and communication network generated constant interplay—often creative tension—between the metropolis and its countryside.

Except for the sixth, none of those elements was unique or even unusual. But the combination of them in one region in one time was unique.

Of course, just how those elements of the region's chemistry really mingled and interacted, in all of their details, is the subject of countless biographies, local histories, diaries, and memories. The details are not synthesized. The collection of elements and events cannot be reproduced. There can be no recreation of the region as it used to be. Perhaps the elements can be abstracted and institutionalized. That is what some people have suggested, but others have been skeptical. In any case, there is a great legacy on which to build.

If the causes of regional entrepreneurship were a mystery, the consequences in the 1980s were clear. A regional service and employment base existed that was highly responsive to shifts of fortune, markets, and technologies worldwide. A cosmopolitan system of linkages joined the world, the metropolis, the small town, and the farm. That system provided avenues of access to the national and international community for local Upper Midwest talent and an avenue into the region for talent from the rest of the world (Figure 77). And a flowing wellspring of investment and philanthropy accompanied a concern about the welfare of people and places in the region.

Government as Employer

Rapid growth of government employment accompanied the auto-era shift from rail to highway transportation and the explosive growth of services. The public had put itself in the business of building roads and airports. And the public was already well established in service enterprises—notably schools; sewer and water utilities; police and fire protection; hospitals; recreation; pension and insurance programs; and direct provision of money, food, shelter, and clothing to the most needy. Thus, while governments continued to perform their roles in the maintenance of order and justice, around 10 percent of the growth in government employment in the auto era reflected the growth of welfare, and 75 percent to 80 percent reflected the growth of transportation and other services. The questions were what services to socialize and how deeply to be involved. Those turned out to be persistent questions with no persistent answers.[104]

All the services the public operates through its government agencies arguably could be—and have been—provided privately. There are—or have been—private schools, hospitals, turnpikes, water systems, police and fire protection, insurance, and charities. Public entry into those fields has been an extension of the idea of basic rights and of the quest for individual and collective security. The logic of the right to a decent education or a decent road can be extended to decent water and sewer and even to minimum levels of diet, shelter, and clothing. Like other rights, the guarantee of those services and goods hopefully serves government's basic purpose of justice and order in the long run.

With unregulated private supply in many fields, not everyone was served, and costly duplication was common. Two services often competed for one customer, while both bypassed another customer who could not afford to pay enough.

Three responses evolved over the years. One was outright public operation. Direct welfare was an outright public operation from the start. There are many other local and state examples: municipal liquor stores, municipal electric utilities, and, of course, highways. Another solution was public granting of an exclusive private franchise—for example, to an electric, gas, or telephone company—to avoid costly duplication, accompanied by rate regulation to try to ensure affordability. However, exclusive public operation or franchising created a monopoly within each governmental jurisdiction, with the risk of resistance to change or of selfish control by a specialized, politically powerful interest group. Thus a third approach was to retain the public monopoly but contract the operations to private firms on periodically reopened, competitive bids.[105]

In the 1980s, one or another of those principles had come to be applied in virtually all linear public services, from highways to power lines to school bus routes to police beats. Whichever approach was taken, rates and costs were averaged so that income from areas that were larger, wealthier, or more densely populated could help to provide service to areas that were smaller, poorer, or less densely populated. There was an implied assumption in those policies: the service area of the school, hospital, highway, or utility system is a geographical community of interest; there is a common benefit from raising the level of health and safety and the ability to communicate and carry on commerce. To be sure, the logic has sometimes been strained. The public monopolies have led to widespread benefits, bursts of vigilance, review, reform, reduction, and expansion, with constantly changing blends of ideals, images, and immediate issues. And their long-term evolution has scarcely begun.

Nevertheless, all the activity has required both employees and workplaces. Hence the number of government jobs in the Upper Midwest—between 75,000 and 100,000 at the beginning of the auto era in 1920—had grown to more than 250,000 by 1946 and nearly 600,000 by 1980. The regional growth matched national trends, with adjustment for the slower growth of Upper Midwest population compared with national population as a whole. The picture varied for the three different levels of government in 1980.

The federal government employed 99,000 people in the region—73,000 civilians and 26,000 military. Compared with other regions of the country, defense employment was weak, and so was employment in most of the civilian agencies. Only the Veterans Administration and Agriculture Department were comparatively strong employers. Federal jobs were geographically widely distributed. Forest Service and National Park employees were located mainly in the western mountains and North Woods, Fish and Wildlife Service employees in the glaciated wetlands areas. Veterans hospitals as well as the state and district offices of the various transportation and human services agencies were located at the state capitals and other principal cities. Department of Agriculture agents were dispersed most widely. They worked at every county seat and at the land grant universities.[106]

Several hundred employees of the Bureau of Reclamation and Army Corps of Engineers operated billions of dollars worth of public works at key points on the major rivers. Employment sites included the big dams on the Kootenai and Flathead in the Montana Rock-ies, and on the Missouri from Fort Peck, Montana, to Gavins Point, above Yankton, South Dakota. The Missouri's dams mark the historic riverboat route through the Great Plains. Visitors to the mammoth hydroelectric stations stand on meticulously landscaped grounds near the spots where the stockades of Forts Sully, Thompson, and Randall stood in 1870. Indians from the nearby reservation communities were employed at some of the dams in the 1980s. Army Corps of Engineers employees also operated the navigational locks and dams on the Mississippi from St. Anthony Falls southward toward St. Louis, opened in the 1930s; the small, turn-of-the-century dams that control lake levels in the Mississippi headwaters; the deep harbors on Lake Superior; and the locks at Sault Ste. Marie.[107]

But most of the 30,000 military employees—both active duty and civilian—were not in the Corps of Engineers (Figure 78). They worked at the six Upper Midwest air and missile bases. The number of military had grown from only a few hundred before World War II, and it was 10 times the total troop strength in the lonely stockades commanded from St. Paul in 1870. The military had returned to the region in some force after a lapse of nearly a century, but the orientation and scale had changed in keeping with the times. The bases in the 1870s had been aligned along the eastern and western frontiers of a 900-mile-wide swath of Indian-occupied shortgrass prairie. The bases in the 1980s—each about 500 to 1,000 times as extensive as its typical pioneer predecessor—were lined up on a northern frontier facing the heartland of the USSR across 5,000 miles of Canadian and Soviet boreal forest, tundra, and polar ice cap. And each was presumably a target for the warriors at similar bases in Siberia.[108]

Several thousand Agriculture Depart-ment employees played a particularly important role. They administered the direct payments to farmers under federal programs for production control and price support. Those payments accounted for 12 percent of the region's gross farm income in 1980, and Upper Midwest payments accounted for 18 percent of the national total. Whereas those payments were aimed at controlling production, additional indirect subsidies were paid to hold products off the market in times of low prices and to move marketed products into the channels of international trade. The combined effects of all federal agricultural subsidies equaled perhaps 4 percent of the total Upper Midwest economy. Thus, through the support of farm income, these subsidies were the underpinning for perhaps as much as one job in every 25.

State employment within the region totaled about 160,000 in 1980. Roughly one-fifth of the jobs were located in the state capitals; the bulk of the others at state universities, hospitals, prisons, and highway district offices and garages. Aside from the big air bases, the states were the major factor in geographical concentration of public employment. In the entire region, there were only 15 counties with unusually large concentrations of nonmilitary government employees. Four of those counties included state capitals, and the other 11 had state university campuses.

Local governments accounted for another 350,000 jobs. Employers included not only counties, cities, and rural townships, but also school districts and special districts with purposes ranging from airports and sewer operations to irrigation, drainage, and mosquito control. Employees in the greatest numbers ran the elementary, secondary, and vocational schools. County seats were especially important local government employment centers.

Minot

Grand Forks

Marquette

Great
Falls

Duluth

Rapid City

Twin
Cities

— 5,000

— 1,000

— 10

Figure 78. Armed Forces Employment in the Upper Midwest, 1980. Most of the 29,000 military
employees — both active duty and civilian —
worked at the six largest air and missile bases.
Source: note 60.

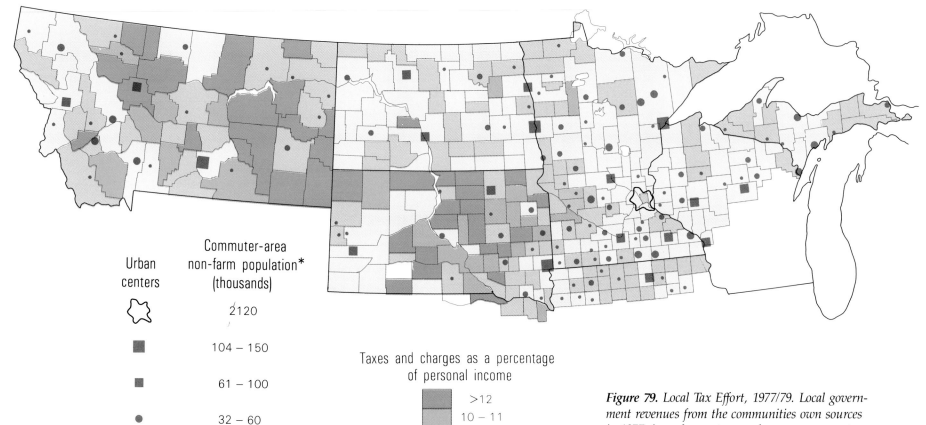

Urban
centers

Commuter-area
non-farm population*
(thousands)

⬖ 2120

◼ 104 – 150

◾ 61 – 100

● 32 – 60

• 20 – 31

· 9 – 19

Taxes and charges as a percentage
of personal income

>12
10 – 11
7 – 9
<7
Data not available

* See note with Figure 1.

*Figure 79. Local Tax Effort, 1977/79. Local govern-
ment revenues from the communities own sources
in 1977, in each county, are shown as a percentage
of personal income of residents of the same county
in 1979. Local effort was generally higher where
state aid payments to local governments were lower. Sources: 1977 U.S. Census of Governments,
vol. 4, table 36; 1957 Census of Governments,
vol. IV, table 36; income data, see note 115.*

Financial support for local government jobs came from three sources: federal aids, state aids, and local taxes (Table 7).

Table 7. Revenue Sources for State and Local Governments in Upper Midwest States, 1977 (In Percentages)

State	U.S. Grants and Aids	State Taxes and Charges	Local Taxes and Charges[a]
Iowa	20%	44%	36%(40%)
Minnesota	21	49	30 (48)
Montana	29	37	34 (29)
North Dakota	26	49	25 (42)
South Dakota	27	37	37 (19)
Wisconsin	20	50	30 (48)

Source: U.S. Bureau of the Census, *Statistical Abstract of the United States*, 1979.

[a] The numbers in parentheses indicate the percentages of local revenues from state aids.

Both state and local governments received payments from the federal government to meet part of their expenses. Some of the revenue raised by the states was passed along to local governments to augment their own revenues. The percentage of local revenue derived from state aids varied widely in the region.

In the late 1970s, state aids made up the highest proportion of local revenues, on the average, in Wisconsin, Minnesota, and North Dakota (Figure 79). Both Wisconsin and Minnesota established important precedents for state aids to local governments during the Great Depression. An avalanche of tax-forfeiture of submarginal, cutover land had left many North Woods counties at the edge of bankruptcy. Destitute small farmers could not leave quickly. They had no money to pay taxes, yet roads and other services had to be continued. Also, both states had comparatively wealthy, nationally oriented metropolitan areas from which to tax and redistribute income. Minnesota, in the earlier years, and North Dakota, in recent years, have had nationally based mineral income which could be taxed and redistributed. In contrast, local taxes made up a larger share of local revenues in Michigan, Iowa, and South Dakota. Federal aid payments were highest in South Dakota, North Dakota, and Montana. They reflected the impact of air bases on several local communities and the importance of payments to Indian populations in the reservation areas.[109]

While local governments in the region's states differed in the way they raised money, they were very much alike in the proportion of their citizens they employed. For local governments fulltime equivalent employment ranged between 3.1 percent and 3.5 percent of state populations. All the states were slightly below the national average. Minnesota, with high state aids and high expenditures, employed virtually the same percentage of its population in local government as did South Dakota, with low aids and low expenditures. The percentages of state populations employed in education alone were also quite similar, but those percentages were all substantially above the national average. On the other hand, the states differed greatly in the amount they paid public employees. Per capita expenditures of tax money from all sources for local governments in North Dakota and South Dakota were 33 percent to 40 percent lower than they were in Minnesota and Wisconsin. The differences reflected a combination of state aid policies, general local wage scales, and the political power of public employee organizations.

Aside from the effects of state policies and traditions, there were some notable variations among different localities. Most variations reflected chance differences in the local history and timing of major public improvements and bond issues. The most systematic differences between places depended on size and commercial activity. The bigger and busier a place was, the more people it employed in its local government. Very little difference showed up across state lines. The amount of work to be done, and the number of people engaged to do it, seemed to be little affected by tax and expenditure policies—or vice versa.

Predominantly agricultural areas that were less urbanized had two distinctive characteristics. First, they generally showed a rather high tax effort—percentage of personal income paid for local government taxes—regardless of the state. That was because average farm incomes reported to the Census Bureau were low, and real estate taxes, on large farms especially, were a big item. The lower income was probably partly the result of different methods of calculating farm and urban personal income for census reporting. But it is impossible to adjust the data to make the counties more nearly comparable. Farm counties had not only higher average tax effort but also more variation in tax effort from year to year. That simply reflects the fact that income varies drastically from year to year according to the whims of climate and markets, while many of the costs of local government cannot be changed very much on short notice. The saying that nothing is so sure as death and taxes applied especially to the farming areas, and most particularly in the semiarid country. After we had once watched an unusually vigorous discussion of a proposed bond issue at a rural town meeting, a small-town lawyer commented, "Whatever happens, these people will pay their taxes."

Compared with the rest of the country, Upper Midwest government had some distinctive characteristics in the early 1980s. Its people made an exceptionally high tax effort

Table 8. Major Expenditures of State and Local Governments in Upper Midwest States, 1981 (In Percentages)

Area	Highways	Natural Resources	Education	Per Capita (U.S. = 100)	Per Dollar of Personal Income (U.S. = 100)
Iowa	15%	2%	42%	96%	98%
Minnesota	11	2	38	115	117
Montana	18	3	41	97	120
North Dakota	18	4	38	102	106
South Dakota	17	3	38	85	111
Wisconsin	10	1	41	106	111
United States[a]	8	1	38	100	100

Sources: U.S. Bureau of the Census, *Statistical Abstract of the United States*, 1984, tables 465, 750.

[a] Information about average U.S. state and local government expenditures offers a point of comparison for each Upper Midwest state.

per dollar of personal income for highways, protection and management of natural resources, and education (Table 8). Even South Dakota appeared to be well above the average in expenditures per dollar of personal income, its low per capita outlay notwithstanding. Public expenditures for health care (not included in the accompanying table) appeared to be low except for Minnesota. But those numbers did not reflect actual performance—partly because the region's traditions in religion and voluntary organizations gave it an especially large dependence on private hospitals and nursing homes, and partly because of the multistate geographical focus on specialized facilities at Rochester's Mayo Clinic and the Twin Cities. In the Twin Cities–Rochester concentration, the Upper Midwest supported a regional medical service center that ranked in the top half-dozen in the nation. Higher ratios of physicians to population occurred only in the giant centers of New York and California and amid the almost immoral affluence of the national capital and its suburbs. Furthermore, the Upper Midwest ratio was growing at a rate comparable to the growth of New York City and Chicago and ahead of other areas except

for metropolitan Washington, D.C. The outlying areas of the region supported health care at a level comparable to other parts of the United States with similar degrees of urbanization. But the Upper Midwest growth in number of physicians per capita exceeded that of any other area of the country—again with the exception of the national capital.[110]

In their sum, these characteristics reflected low population density, high standards, willingness to do what was necessary and practical to meet high standards at low density, and considerable diversity of approaches to the problem. E. A. Willson's pioneer study of social conditions in western North Dakota, in the raw, hard years of the early 1920s, would remind any reader that many regional characteristics of the 1980s still reflected the spirit of the early settlers of the northern Great Plains.[111]

Meanwhile, the growing role of government enterprise had helped to reduce somewhat the coherence of the region. To be sure, the regional business services and financial network was virtually unchanged in pattern and intensity. But wholesaling became more dispersed in the auto era; the migration stream

lost some of its regional focus; and the growth of a second national metropolis in California to rival New York had divided some of the region's national business contacts between East and West. The main stream still went through the Twin Cities to New York. But another stream went to California through either the Twin Cities or Denver.

In addition to those changes in the private sector, the booming state and federal share of the economy focused on the individual state capitals rather than on centers of private business. Hierarchical lines joined the capitals with a different set of places outside the region. Contacts with the federal regional centers most likely led to Denver or Chicago, perhaps to Omaha or Kansas City. The channel to national headquarters passed through the Twin Cities but on to Washington, D.C., instead of New York.

Growing public efforts promoted economic development through agencies of state and local government. The efforts focused on retaining, attracting, and helping to incubate businesses within the state or city boundaries. First, the promotion tried to ensure employment opportunities for state or local people entering the labor force, or to ensure continued employment for people who already lived and worked there. Second, the promotion sought to ensure growth, or no decline, for the tax base to support the local public enterprise. The governments used several types of subsidy to private firms in these promotions. Funds came from their own taxes and borrowing power, sometimes in conjunction with federal grants. Subsidies were used to cover credit risks that could not justify private loans, to reduce interest rates below market level on development loans, or to reduce costs of constructing and leasing buildings. All those programs were still further extensions—some said distortions—of the role of governments as agents and organizers of communities in search of both individual and collective security. It seemed highly unlikely that those efforts could significantly reorganize or balkanize along state lines the nation's resources or its markets for labor, commodities, or factory goods. But in the 1970s and early 1980s, the programs did have a localizing effect within the Upper Midwest and other regions as well. Shifts of businesses into South Dakota were the principal Upper Midwest example.

Thus, while Upper Midwest government employment more than doubled in the auto era, the increase was symptomatic of important factors that had somewhat diluted the economic coherence of the region. But that was only a small side effect of the region's adaptation to the new global and national environment of the auto era.

A New Round of Adaptation

In the 1970s and 1980s, the region appeared to be headed into a second round of adaptation and transformation.[112] An intercontinental land-air-electronic network was in place. There was a rapidly intensifying world exchange of factory products, commodities, knowledge, and capital; a world market was emerging in industrial labor, engineering, management, and professions. Important technological changes in agriculture, medicine, and waste recycling seemed likely, if not imminent. Major changes in the organization of health care, banking, transportation, and agriculture appeared to be under way. Upper Midwest markets were more open than they had ever been to world-wide producers of services and goods. Even more than before, Upper Midwest firms had to reach out to the nation and world to expand or keep abreast of national growth rates. Then there was the enigma of significant climatic change due to the increasing carbon dioxide content of the earth's atmosphere.[113] Some scientists saw such a climatic change as a possibility; to others, it was a virtual certainty. The effect in the Upper Midwest would be more variable rainfall, slightly milder winters and warmer summers, though the climate still would be the most extreme in the country. Even the more certain trend toward higher average age of the American-born population left abundant room for speculation about its effects.

In the early 1980s, demographic projections put the region's population at 9.1 million by the year 2000—a gain of about 1.1 million from the 1980 census (Table 9 and Figure 80). At that rate, the region would continue to grow more slowly than the nation as a whole. Its share of national population would continue to decline slightly because of continued net emigration to the West and South, and despite continued immigration from the East.[114]

The Twin Cities area would account for more than 40 percent of the region's growth. But density would continue to decrease in the Central Counties and build up in the Commuter Ring. Strong growth would continue in the Twin Cities Satellite Ring, in the lake regions of north-central Minnesota and northern Wisconsin, in the zone of spreading urbanization and industry in the eastern Dakotas, in the new metropolitan areas of the Great Plains, and in the Western Montana Valleys. Net growth would continue to be slow in the rural parts of the Corn Belt, and near zero in much of the Great Plains and North Woods. Urbanization would continue at a slowed pace in the smaller cities and towns of the Corn Belt and Great Plains. Farm population would decline further, from 620,000 to about 370,000, and make up only 4 percent of the regional total in the year 2000.

The projected changes were not dramatic in either numbers or geographic pattern. But a great deal of turbulence churned beneath the rather smooth surface. Past performance indicated that in the average Upper Midwest county, in any given decade, the actual nonfarm population change would be nearly 50 percent more or less than the long-term projection. And the turbulence of the demographic stream would continue. With a net growth of 1.1 million for the two decades from 1980 to 2000, a total of 7.7 million would be born, move into or out of the respective states or die. To those measures of population turnover and short-term variability of growth rate, add the effects of the region's changing position within the uncertainties of the world circulation system and climatic trends.

Yet all those sources of change and uncertainty would also be sources of opportunity for new enterprises and organizations created by people who live in the region. Adaptation and innovation, community and continuity would be still more important in the half-century following the 1970s than they were in the half-century preceding.

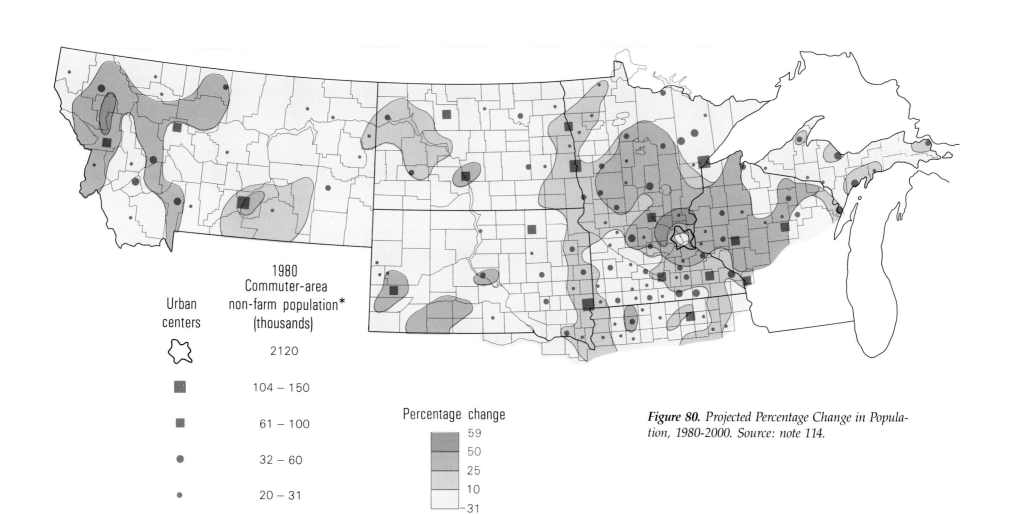

Urban
centers

1980
Commuter-area
non-farm population*
(thousands)

2120

104 – 150

61 – 100

32 – 60

20 – 31

9 – 19

* See note with Figure 1.

Percentage change

59
50
25
10
–31

Figure 80. Projected Percentage Change in Population, 1980-2000. Source: note 114.

Table 9. Projected Population in the Upper Midwest, 1980–2000 (In Thousands)

Area	1980 (Observed)		2000 (Projected)	
	Number	% of Total	Number	% of Total
Nonfarm Urban Clusters				
Minnesota Core	2,682	33.9	3,218	35.4
Central Counties	1,400	17.7	1,365	15.1
Commuter Ring	805	10.2	1,247	13.6
Satellite Ring	477	6.0	606	6.7
Minnesota Lakes	261	3.3	348	3.8
Southern Minnesota	283	3.6	309	3.4
Chippewa Valley–LaCrosse	287	3.6	352	3.9
Upper Wisconsin Valley	212	2.6	282	3.1
Fargo-Moorhead	130	1.6	160	1.8
Grand Forks Area	112	1.4	126	1.4
Sioux Valley	152	1.9	184	2.0
Bismarck-Mandan	75	0.9	109	1.2
Minot	55	0.7	64	0.7
Billings	105	1.3	158	1.7
Black Hills	98	1.2	127	1.4
Homestake[a]	17	0.2	19	0.2
Western Montana Valleys	342	4.3	455	5.0
Butte-Anaconda[a]	51	0.6	41	0.5
Lake Superior Mineral Districts				
Mesabi-Duluth	278	3.5	308	3.4
Gogebic-Menominee	65	0.8	65	0.7
Marquette	74	0.9	87	1.0
Copper Range	39	0.5	44	0.5
Outlying Areas				
Corn Belt	866	11.0	966	10.6
Great Plains	707	8.9	896	9.9
Northern Forest	342	4.3	360	4.0
Montana Rockies	55	0.7	65	0.7
Farm	620	7.8	370	4.1
Total[b]	7,908	99.5	9,113	100.4

Sources: See note 114.

[a] Mining district populations are separated from the remainder of Black Hills and Western Montana Valleys.

[b] Percentage totals contain minor discrepancies due to rounding.

CHAPTER 8

Income, Wealth, and Quality of Life

Auto-era changes created an Upper Midwest that was not only physically transformed but also more prosperous. In the 1920s, the region, compared with the national average, had less than three-fourths the per capita income, less than one-eighth the per capita value of physical improvements, and only about half the per capita monetary savings. By 1980, per capita income and monetary savings were virtually equal to the national average, and per capita value of physical improvements exceeded the national level. An underbuilt, capital-poor, developing region had become a well-built, prosperous, middle class neighborhood of America.[115]

Income and wealth had not grown equally everywhere. On the eve of the 1980s, the income map showed notable contrasts within the region (Figure 81). One set of income differences mirrored the urban trade and service hierarchy. The Twin Cities area, together with the medical and computer center at Rochester, not only led the region but also ranked among the highest-income metropolitan areas in the United States. Average income was progressively less down the urban size order to the small towns, hamlets, and rural areas.

High average income in urban areas reflected their centrality in the circulation system. They were the busiest centers of exchange and the largest concentrations of professions, management, and innovation. Average income was also less on the least productive farmland. In the marginal farming areas and the Indian reservations, 50 of the region's 342 counties ranked among the poorest one-third of all counties in the country. The Upper Midwest is one of the more egalitarian parts of the United States; nevertheless, communities of fine homes and luxury apartments contrasted with communities of sagging frame houses, used trailers, and remodeled boxcars. Where job opportunity, wages, and investment were low, so were the local tax bases and government revenues.

The geographically uneven income distribution led to transfers from wealthier communities to poorer. Transfers through the public economy took the form of higher state aids in the poorer counties, or higher local property taxes in upper income neighborhoods to help pay for improvements in poorer neighborhoods. In the private economy, income transfers took the form of philanthropy and were

encouraged by tax concessions. The transfers were an attempt to meet minimum needs; they equaled only a small fraction of the income differentials between either individual families or county averages. Nevertheless, the system of income transfers reflected the combination of drive for efficiency and sense of community that has appeared at many points in the story of the region's development.[116]

The difference between the lower and higher income counties was reduced from the time of the earliest census of income in 1950 to the most recent in 1980 (Figure 82). That reduction was partly the result of a relative decline in the Twin Cities Central Counties with the growing concentration of low-income population in the inner areas of St. Paul and Minneapolis. But it was mainly the result of strong income growth in the cities in the wholesale-retail and shopping center classes, in the recreational lake districts, and in the major areas of commercial farming. Economic growth outside the metropolitan core was stimulated by several decentralizing factors: highway transportation and telecommunication; growth of government employment; and increased transfer payments through state

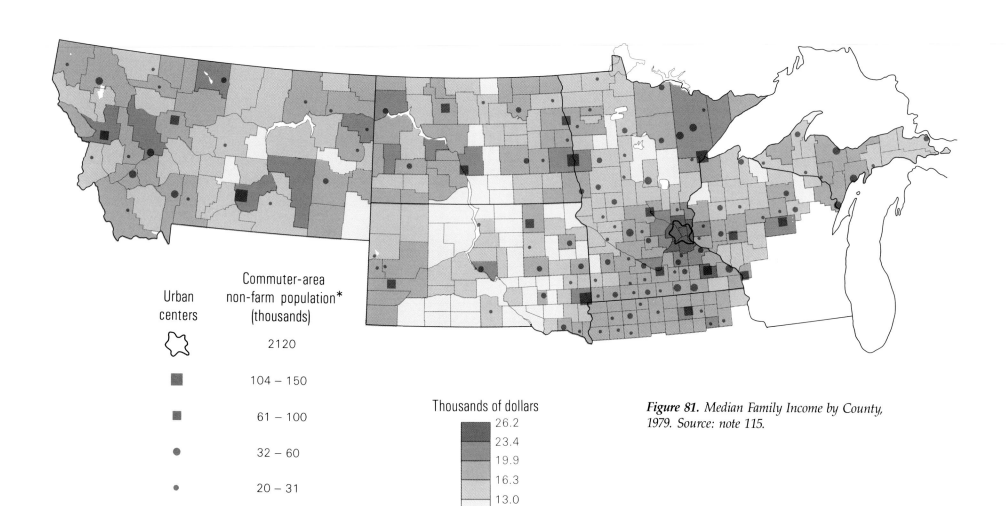

Urban
centers

Commuter-area
non-farm population*
(thousands)

2120

104 – 150

61 – 100

32 – 60

20 – 31

9 – 19

* See note with Figure 1.

Thousands of dollars

26.2
23.4
19.9
16.3
13.0
9.5

Figure 81. Median Family Income by County,
1979. Source: note 115.

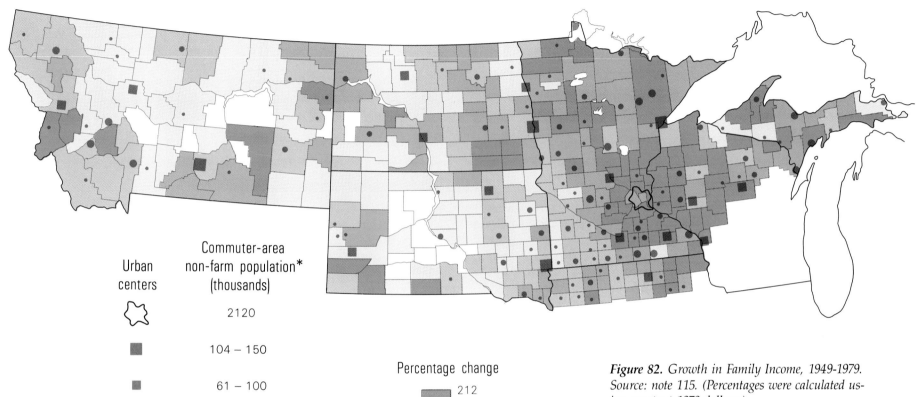

Urban
centers

Commuter-area
non-farm population*
(thousands)

2120

104 – 150

61 – 100

32 – 60

20 – 31

9 – 19

Percentage change

212
109
85
69
9
Data not available

Figure 82. *Growth in Family Income, 1949-1979.*
Source: note 115. (Percentages were calculated us-
ing constant 1979 dollars.)

* See note with Figure 1.

aids, private and public pensions, and welfare. Rural economic growth also reflected the higher income per farm that accompanied the increase in farm size and productivity. While decentralized growth was facilitated by technological changes, it was also attracted by relatively underemployed rural labor, lower wages, and lower taxes. The effects of transfer payments were most obvious on the map and of greatest relative importance in the counties with large rural Indian populations. A century after the conquest, average Indians remained impoverished and segregated.

The pattern of income change in the Great Plains highlights the climatic risk to farming in that part of the region. There was a mixture of very high and very low income gains among randomly distributed groups of farm counties. Nineteen seventy-nine was a bad crop year in parts of South Dakota and in some areas along the High Line, but a good year in other parts of North Dakota. The result was an erratic pattern of farm income change in 1979 compared with 1949.

Whether net income grew or not, there was a very large increase in the amount of money flowing through the major farming areas. Recall the threefold increase in value of farm products that were sold per square mile in the major farming areas, in constant dollars, between the 1920s and the 1970s. The growth was also evident from the geography of bank accounts. Of 169 counties with per capita bank deposits above the regional median, all but nine were in the cropland corridor from southeastern Minnesota to northern Montana. Fifty-eight of those counties were well below the regional median family income. The anomaly of big bank accounts and low income probably reflected in part the different definitions and assumptions in reporting farm personal income, compared with urban income, to the

Census Bureau. But the major fact was that the farmers were running a very large, highly capitalized enterprise on very narrow and variable margins.

As a result of post–World War II changes in the income pattern, the differences between the larger and smaller cities were narrowed, but the differences between many smaller cities and their rural hinterlands were sharpened. Thus there was less apparent need for income transfers between urban areas. At the same time there was a larger, more dispersed urban base for income transfers to the residual low-income rural areas. That change was well illustrated by a 1983 South Dakota advertisement for industrial development. It devoted full pages to the industrial gains and opportunities in Sioux Falls, Rapid City, Aberdeen, and Huron while it also pointed out that the state government had doubled aids to local schools and vocational training centers in the preceding four years. South Dakota took pride in holding down state expenditures. But as the state's urban income base grew, state aids could also grow—and the need was there.

Several measures of assets suggested the magnitude of savings and capital accumulation in the region by the early 1980s. Bank and savings-and-loan deposits had reached $60 billion in 1981, and bank assets were in the neighborhood of $80 bilion—3.1 percent of the country's total. Two hundred corporations, including 11 cooperatives, with annual sales greater than $25 million, had combined assets of about $200 billion. That was 3 percent of the assets of all United States corporations in that size class. Because of the concentration of finance and corporate headquarters in New York, the rest of the country's share of banking and corporate assets has always been less than its share of population. But the primary region centered on the Twin Cities was one of the few

such regions in the country where the reverse was true: the share of major business assets surpassed the share of population.

Within the region, bank and savings-and-loan deposits were spread rather evenly. The share of deposits was at most only one or two percentage points above or below the share of population in the wholesale-retail centers, shopping centers, and rural areas alike. Even the Twin Cities share of deposits exceeded their share of population by less than four percentage points. But the concentration of bank assets at the Twin Cities was substantially larger than the share of deposits. Assets were enlarged by a central pool that the major Minneapolis and St. Paul banks provided for management of short-term surplus funds from many smaller institutions throughout the region. In total the region's wealth was surprisingly large, and it was relatively dispersed throughout both the population and the area. The pattern reflected long-standing traditions of a high savings rate, decentralized control, and regional cooperation. All three traditions reflected a distinctive historical mixture of creative tensions and practical necessities.

Of course, there is an ultimate, practical question about the growth of income and wealth: Did it enhance the quality of living? After a century of earning, saving, building, and rebuilding, what kind of a place to live had people created in the Upper Midwest?

In the early 1980s, *Places Rated Almanac* was the most widely read, general compilation that attempted to "rank places according to the factors that most affect quality of life." That image-making reference book ranked 277 metropolitan areas in the United States. Thirty of the 277 areas make up all or most of each of the nation's thirty high order metropolitan areas. Population of each of those 30 areas was over one million. Ten of the 277 areas were specialized suburbs of the "big thirty" and could therefore not be compared with others in their size classes. One hundred twenty-nine ranked were outside the 30 high order urban areas, under one million population, but with at least 250,000 population. The remaining 108 were small metropolitan areas, with populations less than 250,000. Ten Upper Midwest urban areas were included in the small metropolitan class, and the Twin Cities were in the high-order group.[117]

Using the almanac's rating system, we find that the "best" places had modest housing costs, low heating and air-conditioning costs, abundant health care, little violent crime, easy internal circulation, frequent regional and national air connections, abundant school capacity with ample staff and equipment, abundant and varied recreational facilities, abundant and well-patronized libraries and arts, professional sports, ample available jobs, good pay, low taxes, and mild climate. Those broad classes of descriptive attributes certainly were relevant in the 1980s. Curbstone observation of American behavior left little or no doubt that they reflected modal standards and aspirations. They also described very well the most likely residential environment of the modal household on the American socio-economic scale at that time: the middle-income suburbs of a metropolitan area.

According to those criteria, the Twin Cities ranked fifteenth among the 30 high-order metropolitan areas. Among the smaller centers, six of the 10 Upper Midwest cities ranked in the top one-quarter, and all except Great Falls ranked above the median.

But those ratings included the climate factor. It was surprising to see any Upper Midwest places—with the country's most intemperate climate—ranked above the cellar. If the climate factor had been neutralized, the re-

maining score would have depended on what a community had built, the services it provided, how effectively its people had adapted to economic change, and how well it managed its public affairs.

With only those community factors considered—climate neutral—the Twin Cities ranked second after Dallas-Fort Worth, not only among the high-order centers but also among all the metropolitan areas in the United States. Among the 108 small metropolitan areas under 250,000 population, Duluth-Superior ranked first, LaCrosse second. The addition of Sioux Falls, Rochester, St. Cloud, and Fargo-Moorhead put six of the nation's nine highest-rated places in the Upper Midwest. Billings, Grand Forks, and Eau Claire-Chippewa Falls brought the Upper Midwest total to nine of the top 27. Nine-tenths of the region's small metropolitan areas ranked in the top one-quarter in their size class nationwide. All 10 were above the national median. While other studies and surveys had also placed the Twin Cities at or near the top among the nation's large centers, smaller Upper Midwest cities had not been included in earlier national comparisons.

On the face of it, the ratings seemed to indicate that the growth of income and wealth had indeed enhanced the Upper Midwest quality of life and did so at a rate well above the national average. To be sure, the precise numbers and ranks were probably impossible to defend rigorously and hardly worth debating. They would no doubt fluctuate within a fairly wide range in future editions of the almanac. Yet the notion that these cities are very desirable living places with an extreme climate problably matched very closely the feelings of virtually everyone who had ever put down roots in the region. The ratings would have projected the same image to any stranger who took the

trouble to separate the climate factor from the others. So perhaps the ratings were reasonable, by the standards of social evaluation and artistic criticism.

But the ratings do not reveal what the people in these places had to do to make them rank high as communities in which to live. Clearly one necessity was to reconcile conflicting criteria for desirability. The most notable conflict matched the criteria of high-quality health care, education, recreational facilities, and streets and utilities against low taxes. The optimal solution surely depended on a continuing search for efficiency, innovation, good government, and a spirit of community. People in these Upper Midwest communities also had to reconcile some criteria for quality with a disadvantageous location. For example, jobs at competitive wages and salaries had to be reconciled with a location distant from the center of gravity of the national markets. That reconciliation depended on innovation, entrepreneurship, organization, and management. National air connections that were frequent and direct had to be provided for a region with a comparatively small, thinly spread population and a remote location. The solution depended not only on entrepreneurship in the transportation business but also on concentration and focus of the regional market at a relatively small hierarchy of major centers. Those conditions necessary for a high rating appeared often in the story of the auto-era transformation of the Upper Midwest: innovation, entrepreneurship, management, good government, urban hierarchy.

In order to rate highly, a place clearly had to have a high proportion of the physical and socio-economic characteristics of a middle-class or upper middle-class suburb. In terms of some important descriptive statistics, the region's cities have had certain suburban socio-economic characteristics almost from the start. That seems strange at first, because commercial farming had been and still was in the 1980s a larger part of the economic base here than in other regions, and because few places are far from the countryside. Because so much of the basic industrial economy has always been on farms and in small towns, the cities have had exceptionally high concentrations of the region's white-collar population: merchants, professionals, clerical workers. Functional classifications of the nation's cities showed almost every one in the Upper Midwest specialized in services rather than manufacturing. Travelogues characterized the places as "clean." Among the million-size metropolitan areas in the almanac's rating, the Twin Cities have embodied the same characteristics as the smaller cities. The region's agriculture has always accounted for an exceptionally high proportion of the Twin Cities economic base. The metropolis has been the culminating concentration of offices, professionals, and business services in the region. It has been more a service center than an industrial center. Even the Minneapolis–St. Paul manufacturing growth in the auto era strongly reflected the service and professional base.

A very large heavy industrial economic base of Upper Midwest cities has been in the fields and farmyards. Production lines have been the furrows, feeding troughs, milking parlors, silos, pens, elevators, country roads. The blue collar parishes, clubs, bars, and halls—so popular among students of city industrial neighborhoods—have been at the small towns and country crossroads. The vast rural part of what had become truly an urban system could not appear fully in the city statistics used in ratings. The smells, sweat, sprawling storage and assembly yards, the capital-intensive plants with declining labor require-

ments—features that added to the size, but not to the ratings, of many industrial cities—have been mostly between these Upper Midwest cities, not within them. To a significant degree; the cities rated were, like some large suburbs, a selected statistical section of their larger working communities. But there the similarity to suburbs ended abruptly.

On closer inspection, a great many of the production workers turned out to be business men and women. Farm households commonly managed a half-million-dollar or larger physical plant and inventory. For about half of them, animals made up a major part of the production equipment. Each creature had its own idiosyncrasies and had to be treated with care or lost to the productive enterprise. Thousands of independent, small-town shopkeepers were skilled at custom welding, custom shaping and machining of metal, improvising replacement parts, and adapting mass-produced machines to unique soil and drainage problems. Thousands of independent truckers and small transportation firms knew the territory and knew how to keep track of what needed to be moved, where, when, and why. The roster went on and on.

The cities were selected parts of an interactive network that tied the countryside to the world's cultures and commerce. Despite apparent isolation and small size, the cities afforded a pragmatic, rather distinctly sophisticated view of the world. Farm trade centers had elements of suburban life style. Farmers were urban. They were heavy industrial laborers but also owners, managers, and entrepreneurs. The biggest banks and trading firms were as rural as they were metropolitan, yet also national and international. The risks of climate and world markets were everyday experiences. Many medium-size as well as large industrial and service firms were national and

international; as were the church denominations. The industries depended on innovation and efficiency. The churches were committed to tradition and humanitarianism. Many of the same local people were involved in both, worldwide. Ninety percent of the highway mileage was subsidized by the other 10 percent; and the economy could not function without the entire system. The whole regional structure had been built from wilderness within four generations. In such a community it was unusually difficult to dispute rapid change or deny the importance of humanitarianism, entrepreneurship, subsidies, tradition, the inevitability of risk, or the drive for security. Under those circumstances, tolerance, truth, and, above all, pragmatism had an above-average chance to prosper. The community ratings in a way reflected the role of both the rated places and the others in this regional environment. But the numerical rating criteria could not catch the spirit or the history.

Now consider the additional role of climate in the regional culture. No matter how highly those places rated on the community scale in the early 1980s, people still had to deal with the climate. Coping with the climate added to the unusual character of the places, though surely not to their ratings—at least not directly.

Many steps were taken to neutralize the temperature extremes. Shelter for every purpose was designed, built, or upgraded for efficient heating—not only homes and commercial buildings but also specialized structures including the Twin Cities skyways and domed stadium. Winter clothing was designed for light weight, convenience, and warmth. Transportation equipment was maintained and routes were designed for operation in severe low temperatures, wind, ice, and snow. Indoor social, recreational, and cultural winter activities were rich and varied. The ratings in recreation and arts partly reflected that effort. Midsummer hot spells were partly neutralized by the way in which buildings were designed for winter. Ample insulation not only reduced winter heat loss; but also made summer air-conditioning cheaper and more efficient. At the same time, nature provided most of the antidote for summer heat—frequent mild, dry, breezy, sunny days and several thousand large recreational lakes.

For those who spent virtually all their time in intellectual activity, conditions were ideal for simply ignoring the temperature extremes. To be able to concentrate, those people needed to be warm but not hot, cool but not cold. They could remain indoors any time of year and enjoy those conditions. And since heating is more efficient than air conditioning, they could enjoy optimal indoor climates in the Upper Midwest more cheaply than they could in the warmest parts of the Sun Belt.

Rather than neutralize the extreme climate—or ignore it—many people used it and enjoyed it. With an ample supply of ice and snow certain for several months of every year, they could justify investing in specialized equipment with full knowledge that they would use it. Vilhjalmur Stefansson, the famous Arctic explorer and author who was reared on the Dakota pioneer fringe in the 1880s and 1890s, wrote many years later, "With Southerners it is a miracle to walk on water. To Northerners the most commonplace use of water is to walk on it."[118] Thus ice-fishing houses, skates, hockey equipment, skis, snowshoes, snowmobiles, snow tires, four-wheel drives, lightweight warm-up suits, parkas, thermal underwear, moon boots, mittens, and earmuffs were commonplace. They were as necessary as the bats, balls, golf clubs, outboard motors, tennis rack-

ets, three-wheelers, 10-speeds, fishing rods, and snorkeling equipment with which they shared vast amounts of household storage space.

But the winter gear was more than a set of exercising tools. It offered more than a chance to test survival skills, grist for conversation over hot coffee, or even the means to get from one warm spa to another—although those were important. It opened the unique natural environment of northern winter. People could experience the thrill of seeing the remarkable amount of life and activity in nature in the "dead" of winter—the fish beneath the ice, the green watercress in an icy spring-fed creek between deep snowbanks, the great variety of tracks and burrows in the snow, the green grass and forbs beneath the snow's protective blanket, the variety of birds in the freezing air and the sheltering evergreens. The winter season began with the near certainty of a frosty Thanksgiving and a white Christmas, ended with the suddenness of the spring breakup. In three weeks, a trillion gallons of meltwater trickled through the leaves and needles on the floor of the North Woods, gathered in rocky streams, and poured into Lake Superior and the headwaters of the Mississippi and the Red. Thirty-foot drifts—packed and grotesque—began to soften, gush water from their undersides, pull away from Montana's mountain walls, and quickly fill the reservoirs in the headwaters of the Missouri. Muddy streams ripped the walls of the Badlands and the breaks of the Great Plains. Ridges of dark soils and stubble appeared above the melting snow in the grain fields; meltwater seeped into the ground to be stored and used by the crops of the coming summer.

Winter activities were a part of intense year-round outdoor recreation. That feature of Upper Midwest living was reflected in the

high rate of public expenditures for conservation and natural resources, the high ownership of recreational homes, and the high "recreation" scores on the metropolitan ratings.

Those who neutralized, ignored, used, or enjoyed the climate were also those who accounted for the high Upper Midwest ratings on community factors. They provided the current of continuity in the turbulent demographic stream: built the communities, maintained them, and kept them anchored in their places on the land. Those people came from many backgrounds. Many were Upper Midwest natives—more than 70 percent in 1980. Many others immigrated to a place in the region, and their commitment and affection grew. Many eventually moved on, in the nation's mobile society. But for a time each adapted, adopted, and contributed. Community building and climatic adaptation characterized the region's distinctive quality of life, and it rated highly.

Yet the region continued to be segregated in much of the national image by the perception of isolation and uninhabitable climate. *Places Rated Almanac* indirectly quoted the masses who pictured the "howling wilderness of the Northern Plains." Newcomers and visitors were sometimes baffled by the regional culture.

In the early 1980s, a widely read business author prescribed a new form of social-political organization to cure some of the nation's ills.[119] The prescription was based on his experience in analysis of corporate management patterns. In fact, at least one of his business prototypes was the Upper Midwest's largest industrial corporation. He emphasized a combination of autonomy with interdependence, "loosely structured networks of interaction to facilitate familiarity and idea-sharing." Almost predictably, he came to the regional metropolis of the Upper Midwest and discovered his prescribed form of organization in action in an entire community. People who collectively developed the region's circulation network and built a system of interacting settlements on the network appeared somehow to have invented an optimal system. It needed only to be identified by an outside observer as a generic type, and named.

A group of graduate students from prestigious private business schools, working as summer interns at corporate offices in Minneapolis, summarized their impressions for a business magazine in 1983. One of them, who had been working previously in New York City, said, "The life style is about as different as I can imagine. . . . it provides the basis for a location decision." She and others were pondering the combined expressions all around them of a unique regional history and a unique location. They were in a metropolis in the countryside, yet they were working for local multinational corporations. Several were students at Harvard and Stanford, the most richly, privately endowed universities in the world. Yet here in the Upper Midwest, the local state university that year ranked third, after these two, in private support—highest in private support among American public institutions. Local symphony and chamber orchestras, choirs, and theaters had earned international acclaim. A doctor, a state legislator, and a parish priest led three of the remarkable array of old-time polka bands on the recording and regional ballroom circuit. Fine arts programs brought national recognition to small cities such as Devils Lake, North Dakota. Farm couples made annual theater trips to New York.[120]

The interns were also near the northern frontier of world settlement. The great circle flight from London takes more than six daylight hours over the subpolar North Atlantic, the Greenland ice cap, the subarctic tundra, and the nearly empty boreal forest of eastern Canada and northeastern Minnesota before the Twin Ports come suddenly into view—and the Twin Cities northern suburbs follow after only a few more minutes over forests, lakes, and scattered farms. In this region, the northern wilderness presses farthest south in North America. Aside from cold waves, nature provides other occasional headline-catching reminders. A wayward black bear once entered a downtown Duluth cocktail lounge. A six-point buck recently wandered into a suburban Twin Cities supermarket on a busy afternoon.

One of the interns said the Twin Cities seemed ideal for young marrieds but wondered "what it's like when you run out of things to do." People who know might say that you get involved in building and maintaining the community, experiment with the climate, and get acquainted with the neighbors and places. Go out to the Bear Paws, over to the Porcupines, up to the Rainy, down to the Skunk!

NOTES

Notes

Chapter 1. One-Tenth of America's Land

1. The early regional research project was the Upper Midwest Economic Study. Summary publications included James M. Henderson and Anne O. Kreuger, *National Growth and Economic Change in the Upper Midwest* (Minneapolis: University of Minnesota Press, 1965); John R. Borchert and Russell B. Adams, *Projected Urban Growth in the Upper Midwest* (Minneapolis: Upper Midwest Economic Study, 1964).

2. Douglas W. Johnson, Paul R. Picard, and Bernard Quinn, *Churches and Church Membership in the United States, 1971* (Washington, D.C.: Glenmary Research Center, 1974); Gove Hambidge, ed., *Climate and Man: Yearbook of Agriculture* (Washington, D.C.: U.S. Department of Agriculture, 1941).

3. John R. Borchert and Russell B. Adams, *Trade Centers and Trade Areas of the Upper Midwest* (Minneapolis: Upper Midwest Economic Study, 1963), 25; Clay Kaufman, Manager, WCCO Radio, personal communication on Twins and Vikings networks, Minneapolis, 1983; Fred M. Shelley and Kevin F. Cartin, "The Geography of Baseball Fan Support," *North American Culture* 1 (1984), 77–95.

4. *FAA Statistical Handbook of Aviation* (Washington, D.C.: U.S. Dept. of Transportation, Federal Aviation Administration, 1981), tables 4.9–4.11, "Total Air Departures Performed, 12 months ended December 31, 1980"; John R. Borchert, "America's Changing Metropolitan Regions," in John Fraser Hart, ed., *Regions of the United States* (New York: Harper and Row, 1972), 352–73.

5. Clarence W. Nelson, *Reflections from History: First Half-Century, Minneapolis Federal Reserve Bank* (Minneapolis: Federal Reserve Bank of Minneapolis, 1964); Harry P. Willis, *The Federal Reserve System: Legislation, Organization, and Operation* (New York: Ronald Press, 1923), vol. 2, ch. 23.

6. Torsten B. Hagerstrand, "The Domain of Human Geography," in Richard J. Chorley, ed., *Directions in Geography* (London: Methuen, 1973), 68–87, is a concise discussion of the problem of linking millions of individual, self-centered geographies and lifetimes to the regions and epochs which are abstracted and aggregated from individual experiences.

7. Hambidge, *Climate and Man*, 701–47. Data on annual range of temperature are synthesized from map of average January temperature (705) and average July temperature (704); Alfred Glueck, *Minnesota and the Manifest Destiny of the Canadian Northwest* (Toronto: University of Toronto Press, 1965).

8. Richard Boyer and David Savageau, *Places Rated Retirement Guide* (Chicago: Rand McNally, 1984). Map of "Where not to retire" is based on distances from 107 places selected for analysis in the guide because they "reflect the expressed preference of many mobile retirees." (Quotation is from an advertisement for the guide in *Parade* magazine, *St. Paul Sunday Pioneer Press*, June 4, 1984). The map, "National Image – College Students," is synthesized from maps in Peter R. Gould and Rodney White, *Mental Maps* (Baltimore: Penguin Books, 1974), 95, 99, 101.

9. Upper Midwest environmental regions are synthesized from maps in Arch C. Gerlach ed., *National Atlas of the United States*, U.S. Department of the Interior, Geological Survey, 19 (Washington, D.C.), 55–128; and from the map by Erwin Raisz, *Landforms of the United States* (Cambridge, Mass., 1957).

10. John R. Borchert, "The Climate of the Central North American Grassland," *Annals of the Association of American Geographers* 40 (March, 1950), 1–49; and Borchert, "Regional Differences in World Atmospheric Circulation," *Annals of the Association of American Geographers* 43 (March 1953), 14–26; F. Kenneth Hare and Morley K. Thomas, *Climate Canada* (Toronto: Wiley Publishers of Canada, 1974), 70, 75.

11. Clifford L. Lord and Elizabeth H. Lord, *Historical Atlas of the United States* (New York: Henry Holt, 1953). Pages 104–23 present a concise summary of the advance of the frontier and the patterns of foreign-born population in the period of development of the Upper Midwest.

12. John R. Borchert, "American Metropolitan Evolution," *Geographical Review* 57 (July 1967), 301–32.

Chapter 2. Dissolving the Wilderness

13. Background for the interpretation of maps in this section came from the following works and atlases: Theodore C. Blegen, *Minnesota: A History of the State* (Minneapolis: University of Minnesota Press, 1963); Lord and Lord, *Historical Atlas of the United States*; William F. Laney, *Wisconsin: A Story of Progress* (New York: Prentice Hall, 1940); Michael P. Malone and Richard B. Roeder, *Montana: A History of Two Centuries* (Seattle: University of Washington Press, 1976); John R. Milton, *South Dakota: A History* (New York: Norton, 1975); Edward Van Dyke Robinson, *Early Economic Conditions and the Development of Agriculture in Minnesota* (Minneapolis: University of Minnesota Studies in the Social Sciences, No. 3, 1915); Elwyn W. Robinson, *History of North Dakota* (Lincoln: University of Nebraska Press, 1961); Herbert S. Schell, *History of*

South Dakota (Lincoln: University of Nebraska Press, 1961); David J. Wishart, "The Changing Position of the Frontier Settlements on the Eastern Margin of the Great Plains, 1854–1890," *Professional Geographer* 21 (May 1968), 153–57; Writer's Project of the Federal Works Progress Administration, *Iowa: A Guide to the Hawkeye State* (New York: The Viking Press, 1938); W.P.A., *Michigan: A Guide to the Wolverine State* (New York: Oxford University Press, 1941); W.P.A., *Minnesota: A State Guide* (New York: Viking Press, 1938); W.P.A., *North Dakota: A Guide to the Northern Prairie State* (1938; reprint, New York: Oxford University Press, 1950); W.P.A., *South Dakota: A Guide to the State* (1938; revision, New York: Hastings House, 1952); W.P.A., *Wisconsin: A Guide to the Badger State* (New York: Duell, Sloan, and Pierce, 1941); John R. Borchert and Neil C. Gustafson, *Atlas of Minnesota Resources and Settlement* (Minneapolis: University of Minnesota Center for Urban and Regional Affairs and Minnesota State Planning Agency, 1980); Charles W. Collins, *Atlas of Iowa* (Madison, Wis.: American Publishing, 1974); Collins, *Atlas of Wisconsin* (Madison, Wis.: American Publishing, 1972); Lowell R. Goodman, *The Atlas of North Dakota* (Fargo: North Dakota Center for Regional Studies, 1976); Edward P. Hogan, *Atlas of South Dakota* (Dubuque, Iowa: Kendall-Hunt Publishing, 1970); Arthur H. Robinson, *Atlas of Wisconsin* (Madison: University of Wisconsin Press, 1974); Lawrence M. Sommers, ed., *Atlas of Michigan* (East Lansing: Michigan State University Press, 1977); Robert L. Taylor, J. Edie, and Charles F. Gritzner, *Montana in Maps* (Bozeman: Montana State University, 1974).

14. Joel F. Overholser, *World's Innermost Port! Fort Benton* (Ft. Benton, Mont.: River Press Publishing Co., 1980), is a rich collection of historical photos, recollections, and newspaper stories of Ft. Benton's most knowledgeable local historian); Jerome E. Petsche, *The Steamboat Bertrand* (Washington, D.C.: U.S. National Park Service, 1974), is a detailed account of the cargo on a boat that sank in the spring of 1865 en route from St. Louis to Ft. Benton, and that was entombed in silt on the floodplain and excavated in 1969.

15. Paul D. McDermott and Ronald E. Grim, "Maps of the Mullan Road," Washington, D.C., U.S. National Archives, 1974 (typescript).

16. Richard S. Prosser, *Rails to the North Star* (Minneapolis: Dillon Press, 1966).

17. Clarence A. Glassrud, *Roy Johnson's Red River Valley* (Fargo, No. Dak.: Red River Valley Historical Society, 1982); Betty M. Madsen and Brigham D. Madsen, *North to Montana!* (Salt Lake City: University of Utah Press, 1980); Helen M. White, *Ho! For the Gold Fields: Northern Overland Wagon Trains of the 1860s* (St. Paul: Minnesota Historical Society, 1966); State Highway Commission of Wisconsin, *A History of Wisconsin Highway Development, 1835–1945* (Madison, 1945).

18. Data are from *Compendium of the U.S. Census 1870* (Washington, D.C.: U.S. Government Printing Office, 1872).

19. David A. Walker, *Iron Frontier* (St. Paul: Minnesota Historical Society Press, 1979); Arnold R. Alanen, "The Planning of Company Communities in the Lake Superior Mining Region," *Journal of the American Planning Association* 45 (1979), 256–78.

20. Frank Eliel, Eirne and Lambert Eliel, *Beaverhead Revisited* (Dillon, Mont.: Authors and Finefrock Publishing, no date); John N. DeHaas, *Historic Buildings in Bannack and Dillon* (Dillon, Mont.: Ghost Town Preservation Society, 1976).

21. Edwin T. Denig, *Five Indian Tribes of the Upper Missouri* (Norman: University of Oklahoma Press, 1961), is the memoirs of an educated, careful observer of natural environment and Indian life, a factor at Ft. Union between 1833 and 1855 who also raised and educated four children by two Assiniboine wives; Lucille M. Kane, ed. and trans., *Military Life in Dakota: the Journal of Phillipe Regis de Trobriand* (St. Paul: Alvord Memorial Commission and Minnesota Historical Society, 1951); U.S. Senate, *Reports of Exploration and Surveys to Determine the Most Practicable and Economical Route for a Railroad from the Mississippi River to the Pacific Ocean*, vol. 1, 33rd Congress, 2d Session (Washington, D.C.: Beverly Tucker, Printer, 1855); U.S. Department of Dakota, *Roster of Troops, Department of Dakota*, (Washington, D.C.: U.S. Government Printing Office, 1871); Horace E. Stevens, "A Trip from Jamestown to Bismarck in 1872," personal communication from files of Elizabeth Oakes Clarke, Scandia, Minnesota, 1983; Fred Sturnegk (draughtsman and quartermaster, Department of Dakota), *Rice's Sectional Map of Dakota* (St. Paul: St. Paul Lithography and Engineering, 1872); *Table of Distances in the Department of Dakota*, compiled by the chief quartermaster, Department of Dakota, (n.p., 1875); Raphael P. Thain, *Notes Illustrating the Military Geography of the United States, 1813–1880* (Washington, D.C.: U.S. Government Printing Office, 1881; reprint, Austin: University of Texas Press, 1979); Jos. S. Wilson and Theodore Franks, *Map of the United States and Territories* (Washington, D.C.: U.S. Department of the Interior, General Land Office, 1866).

22. Jeanne Kay, "John Lowe, Green Bay Trader," *Wisconsin Magazine of History* 64 (Autumn 1980), 3–27; Roger L. Nichols, "The Black Hawk War in Retrospect," *Wisconsin Magazine of History* 65 (Summer 1982), 239–46; Anthony F. C. Wallace, "Prelude to Disaster: The Course of Indian-White Relations Which Led to the Black Hawk War of 1832," *Wisconsin Magazine of History* 65 (Summer 1982), 247–88.

23. Walter J. Harris, *Chequamegon Country* (Fayetteville, Ark.: Walter J. Harris, 1976); William Gray Purcell, *St. Croix Trail Country* (Minneapolis: University of Minnesota Press, 1967).

24. Borchert, "American Metropolitan Evolution," *Geographical Review* 57 (July 1967), 301–32.

25. Net migration was estimated using state population changes together with birth and death rates from U.S. Bureau of the Census, *Historical Statistics of the United States, Colonial Times to 1970*, (Washington, D.C., 1975). Gross migration, as well as domestic and foreign components, was estimated from tables showing state of residence at time of census by state of birth. Figures for Upper Midwest parts of Iowa, Michigan, and Wisconsin were interpolated from state totals.

26. *Rand McNally World Atlas* (Chicago: Rand McNally, [ca. 1895]); *Rand McNally Family Atlas of the World* (Chicago: Rand McNally, [ca. 1891]).

27. *Pioneer Atlas of the American West* (Chicago: Rand McNally, 1956), 10–11.

28. Patrick Donn, *The Soo Line* (Seattle: Superior Publishing, 1979); W. Kaye Lamb, *History of the Canadian Pacific Railway* (New York: Macmillan, 1977); Albro Martin, *James J. Hill and the Opening of the Northwest* (New York: Oxford University Press, 1976); Lloyd J. Mercer, *Railroads and Land Grant Policy* (New York: Academic Press, 1982); Gustavus Myers, *History of the Great American Fortunes* (New York: Modern Library, 1936). The latter three works provide insight into Hill's organizational talent and energy, the remarkable accomplishment of building his transcontinental system without a federal land grant, and the controversies stirred by his actions.

29. Vernon S. Holst, *A Study of the 1876 Bismarck to Deadwood Trail* (Sturgis, So. Dak.: Butte County Historical Society, 1983); Lee Silliman, "The Carroll Trail: Utopian Enterprise," *Montana: The Magazine of Western History* 24 (April 1974), 2–17.

30. Agnes M. Larson, *History of the White Pine Industry in Minnesota* (Minneapolis: University of Minnesota Press, 1949).

31. Schell, *History of South Dakota*, ch. 9–10; U.S. Department of Interior, National Park Service, *Big Hole Battlefield* (Washington, D.C.), is an undated folder of maps of battle locations and route of Nez Perce effort to reach Canada from eastern Oregon and their surrender in

the Bear Paws in 1877; Richard H. Weil, "Loss and Recon-struction of Sioux Tribal Lands in South Dakota," paper read at meetings of the Association of American Geographers, 1983; *Voices from Wounded Knee* (Rooseveltown, N.Y.: Mohawk Nation, 1973), is a chronology of historic events and later symbolic importance of the place.

32. LeRoy Bennett, "The Buffalo Bone Commerce of the Northern Plains," *North Dakota History* 39 (Winter 1972) 23–42; M. I. McCreight, *Buffalo Bone Days* (Sykes-ville, Pa.: M. I. McCreight, 1939).

Chapter 3. Mature Settlement System

33. R. Newell Searle, *History of the Boundary Waters Wilderness Area* (St. Paul: Minnesota Historical Society, 1984); Susan L. Flader, ed., *The Great Lakes Forest: an Environmental and Social History* (Minneapolis: University of Minnesota Press, 1983).

34. John C. Hudson, *Plains Country Towns* (Minneapolis: University of Minnesota Press, 1985).

35. U.S. Census, *Historical Statistics* Series Q 12–22, 707; Q 331–45, 732–33; Q 530–41, 762–63; Q 251–63, 722.

36. U.S. Census, *Historical Statistics*, Series A 195–209, 24–36; C 15–24, 89–92; *Canada Today/Aujourd'hui* 16 (December 1985), 6.

37. Harold B. Allen, *The Linguistic Atlas of the Upper Midwest* (Minneapolis: University of Minnesota Press), vol. 1, 1973; vol. 2, 1975; vol. 3, 1976 (maps reflect regional patterns of ethnic immigration); Isaiah Bowman, "Jordan Country," *Geographical Review* 21 (1931), 22–55; Robert M. Finley, "A Budgeting Approach to the Question of Homestead Size on the Plains," *Agricultural History* 42 (1968), 109–14; June D. Holmquist, ed., *They Chose Minnesota* (St. Paul: Minnesota Historical Society, 1981); John C. Hudson, "Migration to an American Frontier," *Annals of the Association of American Geographers* 66 (1976), 242–65; Hudson, "Two Dakota Homestead Frontiers," *Annals of the Association of American Geographers* 63 1973), 442–62; Hildegard B. Johnson, "King Wheat in Southeastern Minnesota: A Case Study of Pioneer Agriculture," *Annals of the Association of American Geographers* 47 (1957), 350–62; Grace Lee Nute, *Rainy River Country* (St. Paul: Minnesota Historical Society, 1950); James P. Shannon, *Catholic Colonization on the Western Frontier* (New Haven: Yale University Press, 1957); William C. Sherman, *Prairie Mosaic: An Ethnic Atlas of Rural North Dakota* (Fargo: North Dakota Institute for Regional Studies, 1983); Douglas Marshall, "Minnesota: The U.N. in Miniature," a map reprinted from the *Minneapolis Star and Tribune*, Aug. 28, 1949, Territorial Centennial Section, 1.

38. Hiram Drache, *The Day of the Bonanza* (Fargo: North Dakota Institute for Regional Studies, 1964).

39. Mildred L. Hartsough, *The Twin Cities as a Metropolitan Market* (Minneapolis: University of Minnesota Series in the Social Sciences, No. 18, 1925); Lucille M. Kane, *The Waterfall that Built a City* (St. Paul: Minnesota Historical Society, 1966).

40. *Schedules of Mail Trains, No. 357*, St. Paul: 10th Division, U.S. Post Office Department, June 20, 1927; *No. 465*, Chicago: 6th Division, November 1, 1924; *No. 101*, Seattle: 13th Division, April 1, 1924 (courtesy of Dr. Frank Scheer, Railway Mail Service Library, 18 East Rosemont Ave., Alexandria, Virginia).

41. Helen Clapesattle, *The Doctors Mayo* (Minneapolis: University of Minnesota Press, 1941).

42. Sinclair Lewis, *Main Street* (New York: Harcourt Brace, 1921); Vilhelm Moberg, *The Emigrants* (New York: Popular Library, 1951); O. E. Rolvag, *Giants in the Earth* (New York: Harper, 1931).

43. American Automobile Association, *Official Road Map of Michigan, Northern Peninsula* (Washington, D.C., 1926); official state highway maps, prepared and published by the State Highway Commissions of Iowa (Des Moines, 1928), Minnesota (St. Paul, 1925), South Dakota (Pierre, 1926), North Dakota (Bismarck, 1925), Wisconsin (Madison, 1925); *Rand McNally Junior Auto Trails Map of Montana* (Chicago: Rand McNally, 1925).

44. Borchert, "American Metropolitan Evolution," *Geographical Review* 57 (July 1967), 301–32.

Chapter 4. Turbulence and Continuity

45. National data on numbers of vehicles by type are from U.S. Census, *Historical Statistics* and *Statistical Abstract* for years subsequent to 1970.

46. See n. 43 for official highway maps of individual Upper Midwest states, 1924–1928.

47. National data on ton-miles of freight and passenger miles by type of carrier are from U.S. Census, *Historical Statistics*, and for years subsequent to 1970 are from *Statistical Abstract*. Locations of transmission lines and generating station are from U.S. Federal Power Commission, *Electric Power Facilities* (maps), 1978. Pipeline locations come from U.S. Geological Survey, *Pipeline Transportation Systems* (map), 1974; *Oil and Gas Journal*, 1978; "Map of Natural Gas Pipelines of the U.S. and Canada," *Oil and Gas Journal*, 1974; and U.S. Department of Energy, *Major Natural Gas Pipelines, March 31, 1980* (map).

48. Data on intercity airline flights are from *Official Airline Guide* (North American edition), vol. 10, no. 5; and

Official Airline Guide (Worldwide edition), vol. 8, no. 10 (Oak Brook, Ill.: Official Airline Guides, December 1983). Only one-stop and nonstop, one-plane intercity connections were counted. Commuter airline flights were included where paired metropolitan areas are less than 250 miles apart; numbers of commuter flights were multiplied by 0.2 to allow for difference in plane size, based on personal communication with Dr. Robert Britton, Republic Airlines, Minneapolis.

49. Data on volumes of telephone messages and first-class mail come from U.S. Census, *Historical Statistics* and *Statistical Abstract* for years subsequent to 1970. Data on electric power produced by each type of prime mover, power delivered, amount of coal used, and amount of power produced by coal, come from U.S. Census, *Statistical Abstract* and *Historical Statistics*. Coal equivalent of power delivered was calculated from those data.

50. Borchert and Adams, *Trade Centers*; Minneapolis Citizens League, *The Twin Cities Economy*, 1977, 40–41; U.S. Post Office Department, Office of Materials Handling, *National Parcel Post Density Summary* (Washington, D.C., 1965).

51. Based on the share of long-distance phone traffic to and from the Twin Cities which originated or terminated outside the Upper Midwest.

52. The amount of $1.7 billion (45% of aggregate Minneapolis–St. Paul metro personal income) equaled approximately 10% of the aggregate personal income of the rest of the banking region. If "export" employment accounted for 40% of the personal income in the average community (a "nonbasic" employment ratio of 1.5), then 30% of the basic income in the remainder of the region would have been earned from transactions with the rest of the world, other than the Twin Cities.

53. Robert C. Ostergren, "Land and Family in Rural Immigrant Communities," *Annals of the Association of American Geographers* 71 (1981), 400–411. Data on national origin of foreign-born by county are from *U.S. Census of Population*, 1910 and 1980. Indian population numbers are available for 1890 in volume 10 of the *Eleventh Census of the United States: 1890*.

54. League of Women Voters of Minnesota, *Indians of Minnesota* (St. Paul, 1974); Minnesota State Planning Agency, "Demographic Overview of Minnesota's Indian Population, 1980," *Population Notes* (St. Paul, 1983).

55. Data on population numbers, decennial change, births, deaths, and migration come from U.S. Census, *Statistical Abstract* and from Russell B. Adams, *Population Mobility in the Upper Midwest* (Minneapolis: Upper Midwest Economic Study, 1964).

56. See n. 55.

57. Minnesota Department of Energy, Planning, and Development, "Minnesotans Come from Northeast and North Central Area, Move to South and West," *Population Notes* (St. Paul, 1983). Migration data for 1975–1980 are from *U.S. Census of Population 1980*, cross-tabulations of 1980 and 1975 states of residence.

58. Neil C. Gustafson and Mark S. Cohan, *Population Mobility in the Upper Midwest: Trends and Prospects* (Minneapolis: Upper Midwest Council, 1974).

59. Chaucy D. Harris, "Agricultural Production in the United States: The Last Fifty Years and the Next," *Geographical Review* 47 (1957), 175–93, is a concise, comprehensive description of the changes in the first half of the twentieth century. Case studies include: John A. Alvin, "Jordan Country: A Golden Anniversary Look," *Annals of the Association of American Geographers* 71 (1981), 479–98; Darrell H. Davis, "The Return of the Forest in Northeastern Minnesota," *Economic Geography* 16 (1940), 171–87; Walter M. Kollmorgen and George Jenks, "Suitcase Farming in Sully County, South Dakota," *Annals of the Association of American Geographers* 49 (1958), 27–40; Kollmorgen and Jenks, "Suitcase Farming in Toole County, Montana," *Annuals of the Association of American Geographers* 49 (1958), 209–31; R. W. Murchie and C. R. Wasson, *Beltrami Island Resettlement Project* (St. Paul: University of Minnesota Agricultural Experiment Station Bulletin 334, 1937).

60. John R. Borchert, "America's Changing Metropolitan Regions," in Hart, *Regions of the United States.*

Chapter 5. Concentration of Nonfarm Growth

61. Nonfarm population by county is derived from data on total population and farm population in the *U.S. Census of Population* for each decade 1940 through 1980. Data on numbers of seasonal homes are from *U.S. Census of Housing, 1980*. Value of land and buildings, and value of products sold, by county, are from the *U.S. Census of Agriculture* for 1920, 1974, and 1978. For years preceding 1940, total farm population was estimated by multiplying the number of farms from the *U.S. Census of Agriculture* by average household size from U.S. Census, *Historical Statistics*. Declines in farm population are due in part to changes in census definition of a farm, but that component does not affect the inferences or conclusions from the data.

62. John R. Borchert, George Orning, William Craig, and Leslie Maki, *Minnesota's Lakeshore* (Minneapolis: University of Minnesota Center for Urban and Regional Affairs, 1970) part 1; Phillipe Cohen and Joseph Stinchfield, Minnesota Department of Natural Resources, *Shoreland Development Trends* (St. Paul, 1984); Roland Nichols, "Lakeshore Leisure Homes in Northwestern Wisconsin: A Geographical Analysis of the Twin Cities Ownership Pattern," Ph.D diss., University of Minnesota, 1968.

63. Glenn V. Fuguitt, Daniel Lichter, and Calvin Beale, *Population Deconcentration in Metropolitan and Non-Metropolitan Areas of the United States, 1950–1975*, University of Wisconsin College of Agriculture and Life Sciences, Population Series 70-15 (Madison, 1981); John Fraser Hart, "Population Change in the Upper Lake States," *Annals of the Association of American Geographers* 74 (1984), 221–43.

64. John R. Borchert, "Instability in American Metropolitan Growth," *Geographical Review* 73 (1983), 127–49.

Chapter 6. Reorganizing the Cities

65. John R. Borchert, David Gebhard, David Lanegran, and Judith Martin, *Legacy of Minneapolis: Preservation amid Change* (Minneapolis: Voyager Press, 1983), part 5; Michael Gleeson, "Estimating Housing Mortality," *Journal of the American Planning Association* 47 (1981), 185–94.

66. Descriptions, interpretations, and the accompanying maps of Fairmont, Fargo-Moorhead, Sioux Falls, Bismarck-Mandan, Billings, Duluth-Superior, and the Copper Range are based on both early and recent topographic maps of those areas published by the U.S. Geological Survey; field observations and interviews; historical photographs reviewed in the respective state historical society archives; Insurance Maps published in New York by the Sanborn Map Company for Fairmont (1917), Fargo (1922), Bismarck (1919), Duluth (1909), Superior (1914), Sioux Falls (1924), and Billings (1923); and information from the Federal Writers' Program Guides (see n. 45).

67. Warren Upham, *Minnesota Geographic Names* (1920; reprint, St. Paul: Minnesota Historical Society, 1969).

68. Arnold R. Alanen, "The Rise and Demise of A Company Town," *Professional Geographer* 24 (1977), 32–39; C. Langdon White and George Primmer, "The Iron and Steel Industry of Duluth," *Geographical Review* 27 (1937), 82–91; Lee Egerstrom, "As Ag Exporter Goes, So Goes the Railroad," *St. Paul Pioneer Press*, Dec. 26, 1983, B–3. Data from interview with Burlington Northern Railroad official, coupled with U.S. Department of Agriculture data on grain production in Burlington Northern's territory, indicate that about 44% of the region's grain moved to domestic markets and about 56% moved to foreign export in 1983. About three-fourths of the domestic flow moved eastward, mainly through Duluth-Superior; about 70% of the export trade moved to West Coast ports, and the remainder was divided about equally between Duluth-Superior and Gulf ports.

69. Ronald Abler, John S. Adams, and John R. Borchert, *St. Paul and Minneapolis: The Twin Cities* (Cambridge, Mass.: Ballinger Publishing Co., 1976); John R. Borchert, "The Twin Cities Urbanized Area: Past, Present, Future," *Geographical Review* 51 (1961), 47–70; Carol Brink, *The Twin Cities* (New York: Macmillan, 1961); Richard Hartshorne, "The Twin Cities District: A Unique Form of Urban Landscape," *Geographical Review* 22 (1932), 431–42; Judith Martin and David Lanegran, *Where We Live: the Residential Districts of Minneapolis and St. Paul* (Minneapolis: University of Minnesota Press, 1983); Lindsay Schumacher et al., *Orientation Study: Minneapolis–St. Paul Area* (Bloomington, Minn.: K. Bordner Consultants, 1981); Twin Cities Metropolitan Council, *The Structure of the Twin Cities Economy: An Input-Output Perspective* (St. Paul, 1976); Citizens League Committee, *Report of the Citizens League Committee on the Twin Cities Economy* (Minneapolis, 1977).

70. Thomas Baerwald, "The Emergence of a New Downtown," *Geographical Review* 68 (1978), 308–18.

71. Edward L. Knudson, *Regional Politics in the Twin Cities: A Report on the Politics and Planning of Regional Growth Policy* (St. Paul: Twin Cities Metropolitan Council, 1976).

72. Corporate Report Magazine, *Corporate Report Fact Book, 1983* (Minneapolis, 1983).

73. David Carr, "Public Pays Price of Development," *Citybusiness*, Sept. 26–Oct. 9, 1984, 30; Twin Cities Metropolitan Council, *Regional Fiscal Profile* (St. Paul, 1979).

74. Borchert, Gebhard, Lanegran, and Martin, *Legacy of Minneapolis*, ch. 5; and Gleeson, "Estimating Housing Mortality," *Journal of Amer. Planning Assoc.*

75. John R. Borchert, Earl E. Stewart, and Sherman Hasbrouck, *Urban Renewal: Needs and Opportunities in the Upper Midwest*, Upper Midwest Economic Study, Urban Rept. No. 5 (Minneapolis, 1963); John R. Borchert, Thomas L. Anding, Donald V. Klein, Ellis Waldron, and C. Lee Gilbert, *The Why and How of Community Planning*, Upper Midwest Economic Study, Urban Rept. No. 4 (Minneapolis, 1963); John R. Borchert, Thomas L. Anding, and Morris Gildemeister, *Urban Dispersal in the Upper Midwest*, Upper Midwest Economic Study, Urban Rept. No. 7 (Minneapolis, 1964). Those studies summarized the problems

perceived and the policies emerging in urban communities of all sizes outside the Twin Cities metropolitan area in the aftermath of the post–World War II boom. One of the most interesting and effective programs was the North Dakota Community Development Program, whose actions are recorded for many years between 1960 and 1981 in the North Dakota Economic Development Commission County Data Files, State Archives, State Historical Society of North Dakota, Bismarck.

Chapter 7. Reorganizing the Region's Work

76. Data on incorporations and Dun and Bradstreet listed firms come from *Statistical Abstract*, editions of 1971 through 1984, and from U.S. Census, *Historical Statistics.*

77. Data on change in total employed population and increases in persons employed by private firms, by public agencies, self-employed, and unemployed, 1960–1980, are from U.S. Census, *Statistical Abstract*, 1962 and 1984.

78. Data on all employed persons come from the *U.S. Census Bureau of Population, Social and Economic Characteristics, 1930*, and from 1980 U.S. Census tapes provided by the University of Minnesota Center for Urban and Regional Affairs, the Minnesota Analysis and Planning System, and the Minnesota Land Management Information Center.

79. Estimates of dependence on agriculture were made by comparing state shares of the national totals of population and employment in agriculture, mining, transportation, and manufacturing. Results were compared with information in the office of Dr. Wilbur Maki, Minnesota State Economist, in personal communication, May 24, 1985. Data on part-time farming and characteristics of farm operators are from *1982 U.S. Census of Agriculture*, Geographic Area Series, vol. 1 (Washington, D.C., 1984), ch. 1, table 46, and ch. 2, table 5; also from U.S. Census, *Statistical Abstract*, 1959 edition, tables 829 and 830, and 1984 edition, tables 1162 and 1163.

80. Data on employment in transportation, communication, and utilities by county of residence of employees are from *U.S. Census of Population, Social and Economic Characteristics, 1940*, and from U.S. Census tapes for 1980 (see n. 78).

81. Mining employment data come from *U.S. Census of Mineral Industries* (Washington, D.C., 1979).

82. Clyde F. Kohn and Raymond E. Specht, "The Mining of Taconite, Lake Superior Iron Mining District," *Geographical Review* 48 (1958), 528–39; Sanford Rose, "The Sponge Iron in Steel's Future," *Fortune* 95 (1977), 106–13; D. J. Tice, "The Thing of the Hill," *Corporate Report*, June

1983, 91–99, offer careful analysis of the evolution of the taconite industry's problems in the 1980s of excess capacity and possible replacements for lost jobs. North Dakota Economic Development Commission, *Resources and North Dakota* (Bismarck, 1982); Donald R. Nelson, "A Fuel and Its Money," *Corporate Report*, June 1983, provide data on the Great Plains coal gasification plant and analysis of its "ten-year survival of political, legal, and financial battles that have killed similar projects elsewhere."

83. Russell L. Olson, *The Electric Railways of Minnesota* (Minneapolis: Minnesota Transportation Museum, 1976).

84. Data on manufacturing and construction employees by county of residence are from *U.S. Census of Population, Social and Economic Characteristics, 1940*, and 1980 Census tapes (see n. 34). Data on production and nonproduction employees and on wages of production workers are from *U.S. Census of Manufacturing* for 1954 and 1977.

85. James Gray, *Business without Boundary: The Story of General Mills* (Minneapolis: University of Minnesota Press, 1954); Virginia Houck, *The Brand of Tartan: The 3M Story* (New York: Appleton-Century-Crafts, 1955); C. W. Nessell, *Honeywell: The Early Years* (Minneapolis: Minneapolis-Honeywell Regulator Company, 1960).

86. John S. Adams et al., *The Minnesota Economy* (Minneapolis: Bureau of Business and Economic Research, University of Minnesota School of Management, 1981); Wilbur Maki, Peter Stenberg, and Mason Chen, *Economic Importance of Export-Producing Industry in Minnesota* (St. Paul: University of Minnesota Department of Agricultural and Applied Economics, 1981); Susan Van Mosch, *Manufacturing Changes in the Twin Cities Economy* (St. Paul: Twin Cities Metropolitan Council, 1983); Minnesota Department of Economic Development, *Minnesota Directory of Manufacturers* (St. Paul, 1981) and earlier editions; North Dakota Business and Industrial Development Department, *Directory of North Dakota Manufacturing* (Bismarck, 1981); Department of Administration, Division of Research and Information Services, *Montana Directory of Manufacturers, 1980–81* (Helena: 1981); Department of Economic Development and Tourism, *South Dakota Manufacturers and Processors Directory* (Pierre, 1982).

87. "FMC Picks South Dakota Plant Site Over Minnesota," *St. Paul Pioneer Press*, Sept. 20, 1984, D–9, describes one of perhaps a dozen cases; data on comparative wage and local tax levels left virtually no doubt about the decisive role of differentials in state subsidies, taxes, and mandated labor benefits; James A. Papke and Leslie E. Papke, *Investment Tax Incentives as State Industrial Policy* (West Lafayette, Ind.: Purdue University Center for Tax

Policy Studies, 1984), discusses "realities of the competitive environment" at that time in U.S. economic and political history, importance of tax incentives "to encourage economic development," and the public cost of those incentives in "reduced levels of public services or increased taxes on individuals and nonbenefitted businesses." This was a widely argued issue in the Upper Midwest.

88. "Firm Moves Offices to Duluth," *St. Paul Pioneer Press*, April 19, 1984, C–4.

89. See n. 65.

90. Data on wholesale and retail trade employment by county of residence are from *U.S. Census of Population, Social and Economic Characteristics, 1940*, and from Census tapes (see n. 78). Data on retail and wholesale sales by county, and detailed breakdowns by type of establishment are from *U.S. Census of Business* for 1929, 1958, and 1977.

91. John R. Borchert and Russell B. Adams, *Trade Centers and Trade Areas of the Upper Midwest*, Upper Midwest Economic Study, Urban Rept. No. 3 (Minneapolis, 1963); Neil C. Gustafson et al., *Recent Trends/Future Prospects: A Look at Upper Midwest Population Changes* (Minneapolis: Upper Midwest Council, 1973); Joan Finch, *Upper Midwest Retail Trade Centers: The Structure of the Region* (Minneapolis: Upper Midwest Council, 1977). The trade center classifications in these three studies are similar to one another but not identical. The classes used in the maps in this book were synthesized from those developed by Finch, Gustafson, and Borchert and Adams.

92. Robert H. Brown, *Political-Areal-Functional Organization, with Special Reference to St. Cloud, Minnesota*, University of Chicago Department of Geography Research Paper No. 51 (Chicago, 1957); James R. Smith, *The Geographic Range of Various Goods and Services Provided at Sioux Falls, South Dakota, 1965*, Augustana College Press Monograph Series No. 2 (Sioux Falls, 1970); David Dahl, *Preliminary Banking Markets* (Minneapolis: Federal Reserve Bank, 1982), is a map that delineates areas within which a branch bank is "officially" within the same market area as its parent bank, for regulatory purposes, in the Ninth Federal Reserve District; Douglas Chittick, *Growth and Decline of South Dakota Trade Centers, 1901–1951*, South Dakota State Agricultural Experiment Station Bulletin No. 448 (Brookings, 1955); John R. Borchert, *Upper Midwest Urban Change in the 1960s* (Minneapolis: Upper Midwest Council, 1968). These studies document both the persistence of shopping and wholesale trade area boundaries and the profound changes in sizes and functions of the individual centers within each area during the auto era.

93. J. Dennis Lord, "Shifts in the Wholesale Trade

Status of U.S. Metropolitan Areas," *Professional Geographer* 36 (1984), 51–63 (for years 1948–1977); Larry Carlson, Dayton Hudson Corporation, Office of Area Planning and Development, personal communication, Minneapolis, 1984.

94. Joseph Dorfman, *Thorstein Veblen and His America* (New York: Viking Press, 1945). Data on service employees by county of residence are from *U.S. Census of Population, Social and Economic Characteristics, 1940* and from 1980 Census tapes (see n. 78).

95. Corporate Report Magazine, *Corporate Report Fact Book*, of which the annual editions 1968 to present provide fiscal, historical, locations, employment, and management personnel data on Upper Midwest business corporations, both publicly and privately held; Moody's Investment Service, *Moody's Industrial Manual* (New York), published annually, is a source of data on national locations of foreign operations of General Mills, Pillsbury, 3M, and Honeywell; John Merwin, "Let's Make a Deal," *Forbes*, (Nov. 21, 1983, 84–92, provides data on Citibank operations in Sioux Falls, after South Dakota's "stagnant population" had struggled for years with "a punishing climate, erratic rainfall, and ungenerous geography." Also David Shaffer, "Minneapolis Seeing Stars on Horizon," *St. Paul Pioneer Press*, Dec. 26, 1984, C–1 ff., has data on local production of movies, TV commercials, special productions, videos, and industrial films; Dale Jester, "Travelling Trophies," *Corporate Report*, June 1984, 71–75, gives data on products and sales of business incentive travel agencies based in Twin Cities.

96. John R. Borchert, "Major Control Points in American Economic Geography," *Annals of the Association of American Geographers* 68 (1978), 214–32.

97. John R. Borchert, *Entrepreneurship and Future Employment in Minnesota* (St. Paul: Minnesota State Planning Agency for the Commission on Minnesota's Future, 1975).

98. "Where Entrepreneurs Grow," *Forbes*, Feb. 28, 1983, 52–53; also "The Up-and-Comers," *Forbes*, is an annual listing of several hundred medium-size corporations with the strongest statistical chance to attain ranking in the top one thousand corporations within a decade (listings for 1980–1983).

99. "The Other Favorite Fifty," *Forbes*, Feb. 28, 1983, 132–33.

100. Corporate Report Magazine, *Corporate Report Fact Book*, 1968–present.

101. Jay Novak, Jean Goble, and Nina Shepherd, "Additions to the Corporate Payroll," *Corporate Report*, Feb. 1985, 37–49, and previous annual reports of acquisitions and mergers involving Upper Midwest firms, 1979 through 1983.

102. Paul H. Banner and Francis D. Brosnan, Jr., "Labor Productivity in Rail Transport," *Rail Freight*, Transportation Research Record Series, No. 917 (Washington, D.C.: National Academy of Sciences/Transportation Research Board, 1983) 29–34.

103. Don W. Larson, *Land of the Giants: A History of Minnesota Business* (Minneapolis: Dorn Books, 1979); Carol Pine and Susan Mundale, *Self-Made* (Minneapolis: Dorn Books, 1982); Carol Pine, "Old Wealth and New Wealth," *Corporate Report*, July 1978, 41–44ff.

104. Data on government employees by county of residence come from 1980 Census tapes (see n. 78); federal, state, and local government revenue and employment data, and data on physicians, hospital beds, and nursing home beds per capita are drawn from U.S. Census, *Statistical Abstract of the United States, 1981* and *U.S. Census of Governments, 1977*.

105. John R. Borchert, *Taxes and the Minnesota Community* (Minneapolis: University of Minnesota Center for Urban and Regional Affairs, 1979); Ted Kolderie, *Many Providers, Many Producers: A New View of the Public Service Industry* (Minneapolis: University of Minnesota Hubert H. Humphrey Institute of Public Affairs, 1982).

106. Advisory Commission on Intergovernmental Relations, *Regional Growth: Historical Perspective* (Washington, D.C., 1980); Jerry Gerlach, "A Spatial View of Military Spending in the United States, 1980" (paper delivered at the annual meetings of the Association of American Geographers, 1983, text provided by personal communication); Thomas B. Connery, "Guns and Butter," *Corporate Report*, Sept. 1983, 19–20; Jay Novak, "The Land of Milk and Money," *Corporate Report*, Feb. 1983, 58–64; Wayne Nelson, "Farm Supports: Congress Struggles with a Runaway Budget," *Citybusiness*, Aug. 3, 1983, 19–20; Lee Egerstrom, "U.S. Role in Farm Lending Reexamined," *St. Paul Pioneer Press/Dispatch*, Oct. 17, 1983, B–1ff. The first three studies deal with federal defense expenditures in the region; the last three with agricultural subsidies.

107. Raymond H. Merritt, *Creativity, Conflict, and Controversy: A History of the St. Paul District, U.S. Army Corps of Engineers* (Washington, D.C.: U.S. Government Printing Office, 1979).

108. Data on military employees and personnel by county of residence are from Census tapes for 1980 (see n. 78).

109. See n. 103.

110. Paul Berman and Sara Peterson, "The Cost of Public Education," in *An Assessment of Minnesota K–12 Education* (Berkely, Calif.: Berman, Weiler Associates, 1984), part R-105, offers extensive interstate comparisons; Clarke A. Chambers, "Welfare on Minnesota's Iron Range," *Upper Midwest History* 3 (1983), 1–40, is an analysis of 1900–1920 development of tax-welfare relationships which profoundly affected Minnesota state and local government expenditure patterns.

111. Edwin A. Willson, *Rural Changes in Western North Dakota*, North Dakota Agricultural Experiment in Station Bulletin No. 214 (Fargo, 1928).

112. John R. Borchert, "Instability in American Metropolitan Growth," *Geographical Review* 73 (1983), 127–49; Cargill Incorporated, *World Grain Trade in Focus* (Minneapolis, 1983).

113. Karl W. Butzer, "Adaptation to Global Environmental Change," *Professional Geographer* 32 (1980), 269–78.

114. Each county population was projected by assuming that the county's share of the U.S. population change would be the same over the decades of the 1980s and 1990s as it was during the decade of the 1970s. The U.S. Bureau of the Census Series B projection for the United States as a whole was used as the source of U.S. projected national population change. The result was almost identical with official state agency projections for the year 2000 for almost all counties in the region. In a few counties, with relatively small populations, my projections were above the official projections. In a few metropolitan counties, official projections were higher. In both cases, I accepted the higher of the two projections. Sources of official county population projections for each state: Iowa: Iowa Census Data Center, *Bulletin Board* (Des Moines, July 5, 1984), Michigan: not available at time of writing, March 1984; Minnesota: State Demography Unit, Minnesota Department of Energy, Planning, and Development, *Minnesota Population Projections, 1980–2010* (St. Paul, May 1983); Montana: *Revised Population Projections* (Helena, 1983); North Dakota: Richard W. Rathge and F. Larry Leistritz, *Population Projections for Age and Gender, 1980–2000*, Series 1 (Fargo: North Dakota Agricultural Experiment Station, 1982); South Dakota State Planning Bureau, *Projections of South Dakota Population, 1980–200*, Series 2 (Pierre: 1980); Wisconsin: Wisconsin Department of Administration, *Population Projections, 1980–2010* (Madison, 1983).

Chapter 8. Income, Wealth, and Quality of Life

115. Personal income data are from *U.S. Census of Population, Social and Economic Characteristics*, for 1950 and

1980. Incomes for 1949 were multiplied by 3.28 to convert them to 1979 dollars; the conversion factor was derived from GNP price deflator published annually in the U.S. Census, *Statistical Abstract*, and published for each year, 1970 and earlier, in *Historical Statistics of the United States, Colonial Times to 1970*. Data on total bank deposits and savings and loan deposits by county are from U.S. Census *County and City Data Book 1982* (Washington, D.C., 1983); Mathew Shane, *The Flow of Funds through the Commercial Banking System, Minnesota and North Dakota* (St. Paul: University of Minnesota Department of Agricultural and Applied Economics, 1971).

116. Borchert, *Taxes and the Minnesota Community*.

117. Richard Boyer and David Savageau, *Places Rated Almanac* (Chicago: Rand McNally, 1981), provides explanations and definitions of criteria and evaluation scales, 1–371; scores and overall ranks of 277 metropolitan areas, 372–78; quotation from 296; *The AMBA Executive* 6 (June 1977), 1–32.

118. Vilhjalmur Stefansson, "The Colonization of the Northern Lands," in *Climate and Man, Yearbook of Agriculture* (Washington, D.C.: U.S. Department of Agriculture, 1941), 205–16, quotation from 208.

119. William G. Ouchi, *The M-Form Society: How American Teamwork Can Capture the Competitive Edge* (Reading, Mass.: Addison-Wesley Publishing, 1984).

120. Interviews in *Corporate Report*, November 1983, 23–26; "U Ranks Third in Private Support," University of Minnesota *Report* 11 (June 1980), 8.

INDEX

Index

John R. Borchert has been Regents' Professor of Geography at the University of Minnesota since 1981 and a University of Minnesota faculty member for nearly forty years. As a consultant, Borchert has worked with the Upper Midwest Council as well as many state and federal agencies on regional land development and geographic education. He has contributed to the *Annals of the Association of American Geographers* and other geography journals, and was elected in 1976 to both the National Academy of Sciences and the American Academy of Arts and Sciences.